The
Co-Parenting
Method

The Co-Parenting Method

Six steps to raise happy kids after separation and divorce

MARCIE SHAOUL

Vermilion
LONDON

Vermilion

UK | USA | Canada | Ireland | Australia
India | New Zealand | South Africa

Vermilion is part of the Penguin Random House group of companies
whose addresses can be found at global.penguinrandomhouse.com

Penguin Random House UK
One Embassy Gardens, 8 Viaduct Gardens, London SW11 7BW

penguin.co.uk
global.penguinrandomhouse.com

First published by Vermilion in 2025

1

Typeset in 10.25/15.38pt Birka LT Pro by Jouve (UK), Milton Keynes.
Printed and bound in Great Britain by Clays Ltd, Elcograf S.p.A.

The authorised representative in the EEA is Penguin Random House Ireland,
Morrison Chambers, 32 Nassau Street, Dublin D02 YH68

A CIP catalogue record for this book is available from the British Library

ISBN 9781785045509

Penguin Random House is committed to a
sustainable future for our business, our readers
and our planet. This book is made from Forest
Stewardship Council® certified paper.

For my children.
And for the children of separated parents everywhere.
This book is for you.

CONTENTS

Foreword   ix

Introduction   1

Step One: Moving to a Long-Term Mindset   23

Step Two: Managing Strong Emotions   55

Step Three: Setting Boundaries and Recognising Your Co-Parent's
Perspective   83

Step Four: Communicating without Conflict   119

Step Five: Making Good Co-Parenting Decisions   167

Step Six: Beyond Surviving to Thriving   211

Conclusion   243

Resources   255

Acknowledgements   261

Notes   265

Index   267

FOREWORD

You can get there from here.

The idea behind this inspirational book is to reach as many parents as possible to give them a new way of co-parenting by moving through, and then away from, the conflict that so often follows the breakdown of an adult relationship. It is written using an effective combination of learning, practical tools, coaching language and memory techniques, so that parents may learn something and immediately know how to put it into practice.

Marcie Shaoul's firm belief is that parents have a responsibility to continue to raise their children together (where it is safe to do so), even if they are no longer together in a relationship. Based on years of experience in developing and then providing the online resource of 'The Co-Parent Way', the book provides a strong and clear framework for parents to follow in order to give themselves the key tools for maintaining a co-parenting relationship despite all of the hurt, anger, sadness and many other emotions that they, as adults, may be dealing with after separation.

The book, which at every turn is illustrated with first-hand accounts from parents who have already walked 'The Co-Parent Way', is based on a six-step methodology.

The six steps are:

- Step One: Moving to a Long-Term Mindset
- Step Two: Managing Strong Emotions

- Step Three: Setting Boundaries and Recognising your Co-Parent's Perspective
- Step Four: Communicating without Conflict
- Step Five: Making Good Co-Parenting Decisions
- Step Six: Beyond Surviving to Thriving

Co-parenting means acting together as parents and sharing responsibility for a child, even when they, as adults, cannot maintain any other positive feelings towards each other. This is by no means easy, but, as one who has seen children in the midst of parental conflict in the court system over the past four decades, I cannot stress how important a successful co-parenting relationship will be for the child at the centre of it all, if that can be achieved. As Marcie says: 'Co-parenting may be the hardest thing you ever do, but it's probably also the most important'.

One of the principal innovations brought in by the Children Act 1989 was the concept of 'parental responsibility'. Normally, both parents will each have parental responsibility for their child, which they share with the other parent. If a case comes to court, all that the court will do, if necessary, is to dictate how parental responsibility will be shared in any particular case. *The Co-Parenting Method* aims to encourage and allow parents to negotiate and then operate their own arrangements post-separation, without any need to involve a court. The court is a time-consuming, costly (in both emotional and financial terms) and blunt instrument for resolving a parental dispute. It will be much, much, better for a child and for their parents if they can develop a workable parenting relationship together, rather than have a third party (the judge or magistrate) telling them what to do. Without, I hope, pushing things too far, I would suggest that part of the 'responsibility' that comes with parental responsibility, is to find a way of respecting the position of the other parent and sharing responsibility with them for the care of their child. *The Co-Parenting Method* shows how this can be done, and does so in a most accessible and practical manner.

Foreword

I have no hesitation in endorsing this book. It is inspirational. I am not aware that anything like it has been written before. Marcie knows that her method works. Her energy and enthusiasm spring off every page.

Many of you who have taken up a copy of this book will have done so at a sad, bewildering and most difficult time of your lives. I hope that you will have the confidence and courage to trust in the method and see it through, even though the idea of getting to a state of a 'thriving' co-parental relationship by the end of step six may seem, at the moment, an impossible goal. There is an American expression for such situations: 'you *can* get there from here'; I am confident that the advice in these pages will give you a very good chance of doing so.

The Rt Hon Sir Andrew McFarlane
President of the Family Division and Head of Family Justice
January 2025

INTRODUCTION

Welcome to *The Co-Parenting Method*. It's important that you're here. I understand that the circumstances that made you pick up this book might be really difficult to live through at the moment. But you can breathe now. By choosing this book you've taken that important first step towards helping yourself become an effective co-parent.

There could be many reasons why you're here. It might be that you're at the early stages of separation and you're feeling overwhelmed with how much life may change and all that needs to happen. You might have found yourself suddenly and unexpectedly separated from your partner, having to deal with the range of big emotions that arrive with the realisation that you are not only now single but a co-parent too. Perhaps you're further along on your journey and have been co-parenting for a while, but something has happened to cause your co-parent relationship to break down. Maybe you're not in conflict but are just looking for some tips to make your co-parenting even better, or perhaps you're only thinking about separating and want to understand what co-parenting well looks like. However you've arrived, you're here, and you're going to take six steps that will give you really practical ways to approach and improve your co-parenting. You might be reading this book alongside your co-parent or you may be reading it without them – either of those approaches is fine and at every step of the way we'll help you understand how to apply the method alone or together.

Co-parenting is when two parents, who aren't in a relationship, choose to communicate constructively with each other as parents to bring up their children. (We'll go into this in much more detail later.) For some, co-parenting is when they have chosen to have children together outside of a relationship. If that's you, you'll find the tools in the book really helpful, but this method is primarily about learning how to co-parent after separation.

As parents, we want happy and resilient children who are equipped to deal with life's ups and downs. Because, let's face it, life throws us curve balls and there are always challenges alongside the good stuff. It's how we deal with those challenges that is important. When we initially become a parent, we're awash with feelings of wanting to do the best we can for our child, no matter what gets in our way. We become used to those feelings over time – we don't forget them, but they're sometimes no longer at the forefront of our mind.

This can be especially true during the turbulent storms we pass through in life, such as separation from our partner. Separation can be one of life's toughest challenges. Untangling the spaghetti of a joint life can be complicated, messy, emotional, and raw. When we separate with children, trying to navigate how to bring them up together becomes much harder. The separation process may become confrontational; and when children watch their parents fight, or if they become pawns in that fight, the safe parental bubble they have lived in up to that point bursts and it becomes harder for our children to be happy and resilient. This is why we need to think about how we parent with our ex after separation. It's important that kids have a stable and happy childhood. This means they can grow up into resilient adults who are well equipped to deal with tough times. The responsibility of that starts as soon as your child is born and it doesn't end because you're separating from their other parent. You see, we are always going to be parents, and our job is to find a way through the mess of separation, however bad we are feeling right now, in order to parent as well as we can. The Co-Parenting Method will give you the tools to do that in just six steps.

Being a co-parent is the single biggest security blanket that we can offer our kids during and after separation. Your choice to become a co-parent, to keep both parents parenting together whether they like each other or not, is such an important one. Becoming a co-parent is not something that many of us plan for and because of that it can feel as though you're groping around in the dark trying to find the right direction to go in. It's an unknown. I'll guide you through this period, and the tools and techniques that you'll learn on the way will be transformative. I've used them with my face-to-face clients for many years, including with couples who haven't spoken for a long time, and watched them form effective co-parent relationships that put the interests of their children first.

You might be reading all this thinking, 'It's too hard', or, 'I've already done it wrong', or, 'My kids have already been damaged by the process so should I even bother trying?' Don't panic. It's all OK. It's always fine to start from now, where you are today, and move forward positively from that place. When you take on board the learning and implement the actions in this book, then you will feel confident to co-parent. By following the six-step method and trusting in the process, you will minimise the conflict and enable your kids to thrive and be their best selves. Your children don't need you to be perfect co-parents. They just need your co-parenting to be good enough. If your co-parenting can be kind, respectful and neutral, then your children will reap the benefits. All you need to do to make that happen is take responsibility for your piece of the puzzle. (More on that later!)

If you're emerging from a relationship where it's not safe to co-parent, either for you or for your child, then please do find appropriate support to help with that. You're welcome to use all the steps of the method to help you, but if it's not safe for you to have any sort of continuing relationship with your ex-partner, then co-parenting probably isn't for you.

Divorcing and separating with children

Maria was one of my earlier clients. I clearly remember the story she told me of the moment when she realised that she was going to be a co-parent:

'It was a Wednesday morning and I was eating my breakfast. Weirdly I can remember exactly what it was. Porridge with banana on top. My husband was sitting opposite me, looking uncomfortable. Then, out of the blue, he announced that he had met someone else and had been in another relationship for three years. He was leaving. We weren't going to be together anymore. Our daughter, who was very small, was going to have divorced parents. The shock was huge. My heart was racing. I sat at the breakfast table in our house feeling really sick. My relationship was over. But the realisation that I was going to have to share my child, that I wouldn't be with her all the time, came a few hours later. This is when the grief and anger kicked in. I smashed up all the plates and then I sat on the floor in the middle of all the broken crockery and I sobbed.'

This book isn't a guide through separation and divorce, but they will be the context that brought many of you here, so it's important that we talk about that for a moment. Separating from your partner when you have kids is one of the hardest, most life-defining moments you may have. Whether you have decided to end the relationship or the decision was taken by your partner, the process is often shocking, complex and emotionally traumatic. Coming to terms with the idea of not being with your partner anymore can be very hard and it can take a long time to accept. In separations when the decision isn't mutual, then one person can be way ahead of the other in terms of how they're coping. It's often these different starting points that heavily contribute to conflict during separation.

Regardless of whether you have been the instigator of the separation or not, you'll both still go through a period of coming to terms with things known as the loss cycle. You may have heard it called the five stages of grief.[1] It's a term that is used to refer to a five-step process that happens to us after a bereavement or a separation. You don't necessarily experience the steps in order; it's not as neat as that. They're big feelings and big feelings are often complicated and rarely happen as a linear process. Often you'll be experiencing more than one at a time, or they might cross over as you move from one stage into another. The five stages are: denial, anger, bargaining, depression or sadness, and then finally acceptance. Denial can be the numb or shock-like feeling you have when a break-up initially happens. Anger, a completely natural emotion, is strong partly because your world has changed, maybe the split was out of your control, or because your plans for the future have now been upended. We enter the bargaining stage because it can be hard to accept something and you want it to go back to how it was, or you say you'll change so things can go back to normal. Depression is the sadness you feel at the loss or the change, and acceptance is the stage where you can live your life again in your new reality.

When you're both going through this cycle, everything starts to change. You're moving from being in a couple, to not being in a couple anymore. You have to shift your mindset to being single and then you have to shift it again to parent together with the person you're no longer in a relationship with. When you're feeling the big emotions of these five stages it can make it really hard to think about co-parenting. You might really not want to co-parent with someone who you are angry with, or sad about not being with. It might feel completely overwhelming for you right now. Please keep reading. I've been there, and so have many of my clients. All I want you to do is take one small step at a time. It's important that you step into co-parenting as soon as you can, regardless of where you are in this cycle, so your kids have the continued support of both of their parents. This book will give you the tools to do that.

I want to acknowledge you if you're here and you're in a place of emotion. You did exactly the right thing choosing to learn how to co-parent with your ex. You may not be able to stand your ex at the moment, you may be traumatised and upset, but just focus on your children. Your kids aren't choosing to separate from their parent, and so we each have a responsibility to make parenting together work, even if it's just through basic communication to start with. Some of the tools in step two will help you manage the strong emotions that you're feeling. I know it can be hard.

> **EXTRA HELP**
>
> If you're reading this and wondering where you can find extra support in the UK, if you turn to page 255 you'll find a resources section which will signpost you to helpful organisations.

It's daunting to go from bringing up a child in a relationship to becoming a co-parent. Following a separation, you might be finding it hard to think straight, people from all corners of your life might be offering you their opinions and the road you now have to travel is unpredictable and unclear. It might feel like the future is a huge and unwanted challenge. Like Maria, there may have been a fundamental breakdown in trust, and if you don't trust someone, how can you co-parent with them? Whatever path you took to arrive here, whether your parenting journey up to now has been conflict-free or not, this book is written for you. Every day in my co-parent coaching practice I work with parents who are starting out on this journey, who have been doing it for years, or who are at one of the many stages in between.

Becoming a co-parent is unexpected and, for many of us, a shock to the system. You might be dealing with a lot of different issues and emotions in the run-up to and during your break-up, but often a big part of the turbulence comes from just how unexpected the situation is. Imagine you are looking forward to a holiday in Italy and when the plane touches down you find to your shock you are in Peru: it's not what you were expecting. You've not planned for Peru, and you haven't packed the right things in your suitcase. You feel worried about being somewhere unexpected. But after the initial shock you find that Peru can be an enjoyable destination, too. It's different to Italy, but your worries on arrival were unwarranted. You learn some different phrases, sort yourself out with some different clothes and things feel more in control again. *The Co-Parenting Method* is just your guidebook, if you like, to something you weren't expecting.

Co-parenting may be the hardest thing you ever do, but it's probably also the most important.

My story

I started my co-parent journey in 2009 when my husband and I separated. At the time our son was one. It was such a strange time. It was emotional, angry and fearful. None of my peers were separating and there was little support available for co-parents like me. I largely had to find my own way. At the beginning, people around me were telling me that I should be the primary carer. At that time it was still usual for children of divorced parents to spend the majority of time with their mum, although this was starting to change. People who cared about me were upset for me and just wanted to have an easy solution for me. But in that noise, there was a lone voice who sat me down one evening in a busy bar and told me that my son needed his dad too. And that cut through the noise of the bar and the well-meaning opinions of the people in my life. It was true, and sometimes truth has a chime to it that just cannot be ignored. And whatever the circumstances of my separation (and they were really tough), in that moment, on that Thursday night in the ICA bar on The Mall in London, a new path had been set.

Then came the hard bit. Learning to co-parent in a world that had been turned upside down. And learning to put our son first. We definitely didn't always get it right. In fact, sometimes we both got it spectacularly wrong. But what we both did realise was that we had a small child and we needed to protect him and make him feel safe and stable whatever was going on for us as adults. Parenting came before whatever was going on in our separation. It had to, and now I look at our child and how he thrives and I'm completely sure that it was the only way to move forward.

Remaining parents is the most important thing you can do.

A few years later I left my job in the diplomatic sector. I'd been working for over a decade running communications departments and helping governments and NGOs communicate and listen well to each other in order to bring about issues-based change. Governments and NGOs communicate in really different ways. Governments would be really formal, use long words and phrases to say something simple, and NGOs would use provocative language to elicit an emotional response to bring about change more rapidly. Sometimes there would be disagreements that escalated really quickly because of the way that each of them was trying to get their message across. When we actually unpacked the discussion, often there were lots of things that they were agreeing on, but the language they were each using was being heard by the other as inflammatory. So rows escalated where actually none were necessary. What I learned there was the language that we use is critical to help keep things from escalating and when people listen well to each other everybody can move forward more easily.

As I trained to become a coach and moved into executive coaching, I realised that many of the coaching tools I was using and developing with my business clients could also help separated parents with their co-parenting. In other words, I started to see that while these coaching tools were designed to help professionals with their careers and decision-making, they could also be very helpful for people wanting to become better co-parents. Tools around how to manage fear and how to make decisions, how to build positive relationships, how to set goals and reach them and so many more.

This, plus my communications experience and the fact that I was co-parenting, led me to start The Co-Parent Way, a coaching methodology enabling separating parents to work together to bring up their kids. Until now, the methodology has only been available through working with me directly, or through my award-winning online programme which you can find on www.thecoparentway.com. Through both of those methods we've reached thousands of parents. The knowledge and experience of that work has been refined and honed to become *The Co-Parenting Method*, the book that you're reading today. I created this method because I fundamentally believe that where it's safe to do so, children have a right to be raised by both parents. The evidence shows they also have a need for both their parents to work together and communicate effectively about them, even though they're no longer in a relationship. Our children are our priority, and this book acts as a reminder of that priority.

What Is Co-Parenting?

Co-parenting means 'co-operative parenting'. If we boil it down, it simply means that two parents who are no longer in a relationship (or who never were) want to co-operate sufficiently to bring up their children jointly. There is no single definition of co-parenting, although most of the definitions have similarities. My definition, which I think best describes the essence of co-parenting, is:

'Co-parenting means both parents put their children front and centre and communicate effectively about them. It means children can grow up secure in the knowledge that their parents will work together, even though they're no longer in a relationship.'

That's a bit of a mouthful, so let's break it down.

Putting your children front and centre means that both you and your co-parent think about your children's needs before your own. It means being conscious of the impact that your behaviour and your decision-making will have on your children.

Communicating effectively means you need to be able to talk to each other respectfully and share sufficient information about the children between houses to make good decisions about their needs. Co-parents each have to control their own emotions adequately to have conversations about their children with their ex, without it escalating into an argument. Easy to write, hard to do, but I will show you exactly how to achieve this as we move through the book.

Your children can grow up secure in the knowledge that their parents will work together, even though they are no longer in a relationship means that your children feel confident that, using effective communication, you as parents will speak often enough about the kids' needs to ensure these needs are being met in both houses. Kids need this knowledge and this surety in order to feel secure. I go into this in more detail later. But needless to say, if you feel far away from that at the moment, don't worry, I will take you through each step so you can get to a place where you can make good decisions about your children with your co-parent.

It's important to differentiate co-parenting from other forms of parenting after a separation. You may have heard the terms parallel parenting and shared parenting. These are different from co-parenting. When it's not possible to co-parent, parents may choose to parallel parent, which means that they don't communicate very much at all; in fact, parents usually disengage with each other to reduce conflict and emotional strain. Shared parenting is a slightly different term that is sometimes incorrectly used instead of co-parenting. However, shared parenting means children spend an equal or close to equal division of time with each parent. In shared parenting, parents may or may not communicate depending on their situation. Co-parenting isn't focused on children spending equal time with each parent, it's focused on how well those parents can work together to raise them.

Why Choose Co-Parenting?

Becoming a co-parent isn't something we often set out to do unless we've made a choice to have a child outside of a relationship, yet it happens to tens of thousands of us each year, often in the context of a difficult separation. Having a framework to get through it is not only helpful for us, but essential for our children, who need extra stability at this tricky time in their lives.

A good co-parenting relationship can really make a difference to your child. It means your child will still have two parents who can work together as parents, which is essential for their stability and wellbeing. It might be hard for you to imagine that right now, especially if your separation has been a shock, but hold on to it, because I've seen plenty of co-parents go from that same place to one where they fully support their child together.

It goes without saying that we want to minimise damage to our children following the breakdown of our adult relationship. The psychological and emotional impact on children who experience divorce and parental separation is well known. Whether it's emotional distress, low self-esteem, children acting up at school or at home, as well as social or academic challenges, all of these, if they're not properly managed, build up over time and can have a longer-lasting impact on your child.

In a research interview for this book, psychotherapist Adele Ballantyne[2] says:

'Research tells us that it is parental conflict, and not necessarily the separation itself, that is harmful to the emotional and, in the long term, physical wellbeing of children. Finding help at the very beginning of parental separation is key. Looking for emotional and practical information and support can positively affect the outcome on children. Continuing couple hostility may lead to the erosion of potential positive parenting, and it can be hard for adults negotiating their relationship breakdown to understand what their children might need from them as their newly shaped family is forming and roles are being redefined.

'Children of separated parents who remain in conflict can suffer the impact of the separation into adulthood. They may struggle with trust, communication and intimacy. And no parent wants that for their child.'

Ballantyne goes on to say: 'As children develop, much is learned from caregivers, including how we learn about trust, intimacy and how we communicate. The long-term consequences of formulating healthy relationships, allowing vulnerability and forming deep connection with partners is limited if the parental separation is laden with conflict and poor co-parenting.'

The good news is, that if we can learn to put the needs of our children front and centre, then we can limit the negative effects on them. And even if that feels really far away right now, following the six steps in this book will give you a framework to help support you to do just that.

The Family Justice Young People's Board, a collection of young people who experienced their parents' divorce, have a list of 25 reasons why it's important to listen to your child when you're separating. One of the most fundamental things they say is, 'Remember it is OK for me to love and have a relationship with my other parent.'[3] And that's why co-parenting is important to your children. In the heat of a separation, it can be so hard to remember that it's crucial for your children to have positive relationships with both their parents. It's not easy to do, but this book will get you there.

Managing to do this from the early stages of separation or conflict is important. We know that positive and early interventions to stop conflict between parents are highly effective at protecting children's mental health. By working earlier on to help children in the relationship breakdown you are limiting the amount of conflict that they are potentially exposed to.

In 2021 the UK government issued guidance called 'Reducing Parental Conflict: the impact on children'.[4] This guidance states that:

Frequent, intense and poorly resolved conflict between parents can place children at risk of mental health issues, and behavioural, social and academic problems. It can also have a significant effect on a child's long-term outcomes. There is a strong body of evidence to show how damaging inter-parental conflict can:

- harm children's outcomes, even when parents manage to sustain positive parent–child relationships
- put children at more risk of:
  - having problems with school and learning
  - negative peer relationships
  - physical health problems
  - smoking and substance misuse
  - mental health and wellbeing challenges

The earlier we can intervene and work together as parents to reduce our conflict, the better the outcomes for our children. Ballantyne says: 'the improvement to the quality of children's lives, relationships and social abilities, their mental health and more that comes from reducing parental conflict cannot be underestimated.'

Remembering that it's crucial for your children to have positive relationships with both of their parents is essential.

Co-parenting encourages us as parents to put the needs of our children front and centre. It requires us to manage our own powerful emotions about our ex-partner so we can improve essential communications with them and avoid significant parental conflict. This is what our children want and need – when children have co-parents who can communicate respectfully with each other, kids feel safer and more secure, meaning they can grow up emotionally resilient in a supportive psychological space. Better communication also means you as parents can take better decisions about your children.

Reducing conflict and being able to co-parent is what the method is designed to do and it will benefit not only your children, but you too. Living in high conflict with your other parent is exhausting. Implementing the tools of the book to bring about good co-parenting will also create a positive spiral that means you will reduce conflict with your ex. This will benefit you; it will benefit your mental wellbeing and allow you to be able to live your life and thrive. Reducing conflict is better for both us and our kids.

What's in the book?

The Co-Parenting Method, based on the award-winning coaching methodology of The Co-Parent Way, guides co-parents through their parenting journey in a way that allows them to keep their children safe and protected. It helps children remain happy, without the worry and responsibility that they can feel from their parents' separation. It gives co-parents the skills and knowledge they need to keep a safe parental bubble intact for their children, whatever they may feel about each other.

It uses a unique and highly effective formula:

Learning + Coaching + Practical Tools (delivered using proven memory techniques) = Transformed Co-Parenting

Let me explain. The learning is the factual knowledge that accompanies each of the steps. So, at the beginning of each step and before each exercise you'll learn why you're doing what you're doing. It's important to know this so you can understand why it's important to use the practical tools that accompany the steps. You're much more likely to use them when you know why you need to use them.

The coaching is the style that the book is written in. I use open questions and self-reflection throughout, but I'll also challenge you too. These coaching techniques make it easier for your brain to absorb new information, because they work to remove the blocks we sometimes have when trying new things.

The practical tools are easy and effective ways to implement good co-parenting techniques, including how to handle your emotions, how to have more control over how you're acting and how to communicate effectively. I've used each of these tools hundreds of times with separating parents, and when parents put them into practice, they work so well.

Practical tools are really helpful when we are finding something hard. Talking and theory are both fine, but on their own they don't easily bring about results. I have woven practical tools into each step so you can use them to make positive changes in your co-parenting.

The six steps of The Co-Parenting Method will enable you to:

1. Move from short-term pain to long-term gain
2. Manage the strong emotions that come with separation and co-parenting
3. Set boundaries with your co-parent and see things from other perspectives
4. Communicate with your ex in a way that prevents conflict from escalating
5. Make decisions effectively together about your children
6. And finally, not only to survive all the way through but also to thrive by staying in control and managing your stress.

Going through these steps is important if you are to become an effective co-parent. The learning in each step will address really important hurdles to co-parenting and show you exactly how to overcome them.

I've used lots of real-life examples throughout the book. I've done this so you can see where other people have been stuck and how they've moved forward. Using other people's stories can help us to feel as though we aren't the only person to experience something and it's also helpful to see how others have faced problems and overcome them. All my work with clients is confidential – that's really important to me and to them as it enables clients to speak freely and without fear of judgement. So, while the case studies throughout the book represent real issues, all the names and details have been changed and the stories and quotes are amalgams designed to best illustrate the points being made. But they are all authentic reflections of the reality of issues faced daily by co-parents I have worked with.

The memory techniques are one of the things that makes this method so powerful. By using memory techniques to help us remember the approaches and tools we've learned, it becomes easier for us to recall them the moment we need them. In the book I'll give you two ways to remember. At the end of each step, I'll summarise what you've learned. I do this to help embed the learning that you're doing. Repetition is a really effective way of helping your new knowledge stick better in your memory.

Your Body Toolkit

The second technique I use is what I call 'Your Body Toolkit', which is an imaging technique to help you remember the tools you've learned. Let's zoom in on that now so you're ready to go when we get to your first tool.

Highly exaggerated, surprising or unexpected sights, sounds, smells or colours tend to anchor strongly in our memory. So, you're going to create an image or an idea that is highly exaggerated for each tool and link it to a place on your body. For example, you might 'attach' one of your tools to your belly button. Memory tools are great for helping us in moments of high emotion or crisis. When you're upset, it's really hard to remember to be calm, and so by associating each of the tools with a body part, you'll have an immediate way to recall information in the heat of the moment, and I want to give you as many ways to support yourself as possible. If you want to write them down, draw them or find images online to help you remember them, please feel free to do that.

By the end of the book, with each of the tools you've learned 'attached' to your body, you'll be able to easily access them so you can use them when you need to support your co-parenting, even in the heat of a difficult conversation. That way they're always with you and ready to help you move into your long-term thinking, away from your break-up story or conflict and into a forward-focused place where you can thrive.

If you want to you can draw the tools on an outline of a body. If you're going to do that, let's get you prepared now. Get yourself a notebook and pen to start with. I'd like you to draw an outline of a person.

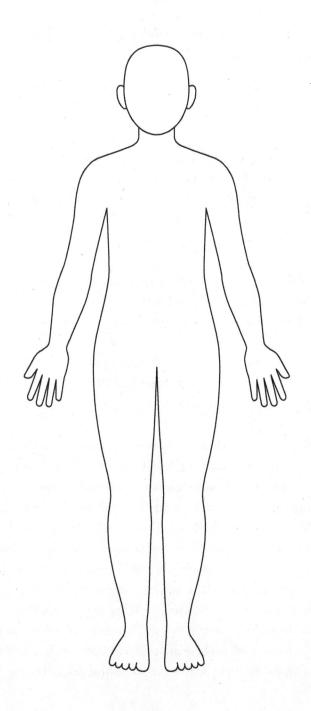

You can copy the one on the previous page if, like me, you're no da Vinci. Make it quite large as you're going to need to hang all your 20 tools on the different parts of the body. If you don't want to draw, that's completely fine, you can just use your imagination.

Is there a best way to read the book?

The six steps are written in order. Each step builds on something you've learned previously and acts as a stepping stone to the next one. But if you're in a crisis and need to quickly reference something, then please feel free to dip into it as you need it.

The six steps of The Co-Parenting Method are:

- Step One: Moving to a Long-Term Mindset
- Step Two: Managing Strong Emotions
- Step Three: Setting Boundaries and Recognising Your Co-Parent's Perspective
- Step Four: Communicating without Conflict
- Step Five: Making Good Co-Parenting Decisions
- Step Six: Beyond Surviving to Thriving

In each of the steps you'll learn really practical tools that will enable you to fully step into your co-parenting. You'll learn how to set boundaries with the Three Worlds tool, how to manage all those big emotions with your own personal avatar, how to keep thriving with your very own Resilience Bucket. These are just a small insight into the 20 practical tools that will transform your co-parenting and enable you to raise resilient kids. I am really excited to share them with you and be on this journey with you.

Have a pen and paper with you or a tablet or computer with a new document to take notes about what you're learning. Throughout the book I'll ask you to write in your notebook, but that could just as easily be your computer or tablet. There are practical exercises in all of the steps and most of them require you to write something down. Having a specific notebook or document on your computer to record information will be really useful. If writing isn't for you, then some people go through the tools and make voice recordings to keep hold of the things they want to remember. Others just write in the book. It's completely up to you. The very act of writing things down or repeating them means that you're more likely to retain information, and that can be helpful when you need to remember something in the heat of the moment.

If you'd like to leave a couple of days between steps to let what you've learned sink in, it can really help to embed the information. But it's completely up to you. At the end of each step there is a summary of what you've learned and you can always revisit the different steps when you need them.

TAKE ACTION!

My biggest tip for reading the book is 'take action!' This is perhaps the most important tip of all. Going through the steps might feel a bit like learning to ride a bike. We need to learn the theory of doing it, practise riding and then remember how to do it until it becomes second nature to us. If we don't keep trying and practicing, we'll never learn to ride the bike, so I want you to keep practicing the tools you learn in the six steps even if it's sometimes hard or uncomfortable. Just like riding a bike, we might get a couple of scrapes along the way, but soon we'll be confident about what we're doing. Sometimes the solution, even when you know it's the right one, can feel harder than staying in the conflict because it means you'll have to make some changes. Keeping your eye on the end goal of having happy, resilient children will help you to embrace the solution and the six steps. Be proactive and realise that you have the choice as to whether you implement what you've learned or not. Choosing to act will mean you bring about change.

Some of you will be reading this book because you know absolutely that you want to co-parent. Others of you will be less convinced at this point.

You may even be here because your ex has thrust this in your hands and told you that you need to read it! You may not be sure that you want to co-parent with someone who has let you down. Well, I'm here for all of you. I don't assume for a moment that this is an easy path for you to take and I want to help make it easier for you. The simple reason I want to do that is so your children can grow up emotionally secure and have strong and long-lasting relationships with you both. Even if you can't bear to be in the same room as your other parent right now, the tools here will enable you to co-parent with them. One life-changing discovery you'll make as you go through the six steps is that you don't need to *like* your ex-partner to be able to parent effectively together. You simply need to be polite and respectful and spend just enough time talking and listening to each other to make good decisions about your children. Nothing more. And remember, I'm with you every step of the way as we learn together how to do that.

You don't need to like your ex to be able to co-parent with them.

This book contains practical co-parenting tools which will transform your approach to co-parenting. As you move into step one, just hold on to the thought that you will have plenty of tools to draw upon to help you to co-parent better.

I'm often asked by one parent how to get their other parent to do The Co-Parenting Method with them. It can be hard, when there is conflict, to get someone to agree to do something with you. The first thing I invite parents to do is to have a conversation with each other about the long-term impact on their children if they don't co-parent. You can find that information in step one. Talking to them neutrally about why it's important that you work together as parents can really help them see the value of that. Going through the six steps yourself and putting into action what you have learned is also a good way to get them to do the work. When you go through the method on your own, the way you interact will change. Explain that you've been through The Co-Parenting Method and ask them to do that too. It's worth noting that even if they won't read the book, by changing your own approach to co-parenting and the way you interrelate with them your co-parenting will be improved by the style of your communication and the way you set boundaries.

MY CO-PARENT IS AWFUL

I want to take a moment to reassure you if you're reading this introduction and thinking that no matter what you do, your co-parent won't change. I can't give you a magic wand to change them but I can assure you that you're not alone in experiencing that. Sometimes it's just not possible to get your co-parent to engage, or to stop them from being toxic. If that's the case for you, use the tools here to focus on building the best and most stable environment for your kids that *you* can. We'll learn throughout the book that putting these tools into practice on your own will teach your kids resilience, make them feel stable and let them see you as an amazing parent who can do hard things.

Protecting your children's mental health and wellbeing and managing how we co-parent in order to enable them to grow up in a stable and loving environment are all at the heart of this book. The learning, the tools and the memory techniques are all supporting that outcome for your children. Keeping this in mind as you go through The Co-Parenting Method will help you want to put what you're learning into practice. Successful co-parenting is essential for children.

If you're ready to begin, I'll see you in step one!

Moving to a Long-Term Mindset

In this first step of *The Co-Parenting Method*, we are going to focus in on how to come out of the immediacy of the situation you are in and get into a longer-term mindset. The key takeaway I want to get across in this step is that if you're in a short-term mindset it's very hard to co-parent effectively. Your behaviour will be informed by the things that are frustrating you today rather than the long-term welfare of your children.

You might be going through a messy financial settlement and the anger you feel may be affecting your co-parenting; you may be locked in a court process which takes your attention away from the decisions you need to make as parents; you might still be in 'the loss cycle' I described in the introduction and find it hard to look beyond your own emotions to what your children need. All of these things, and others like just feeling sad, can make it harder for you to see past where you are now and think about what will help your children in the long term.

Co-parenting isn't a short-term project. Your kids will always be your kids and that means that you'll be a parent and a co-parent for the rest of your lives. Having a structure to support you will help you enormously. Of course, the interaction you have as parents is likely to decrease massively as your children become adults, but there will always be significant events that you will need to show up to with your co-parent; graduations, weddings, big birthday parties, perhaps when you become grandparents. It's really important that – however much we don't want to (and I get that you may *really* not want to) – we get into the right mindset now and that we are in it for the long term. By the end of step one you'll have a way of focusing on the future, accepting the long term and knowing what actions to take now in order to help you get there, so you can get out of the short-term mindset and be able to co-parent effectively.

You'll be a parent and a co-parent for the rest of your lives.

Why Is the Short-Term View Not Helpful?

Fraser recounts his experience of co-parenting with someone who would only focus on the small things and the effect that had on their ability to co-parent.

'Parenting with Gemma was always going to be difficult. When we first separated, Charlie and Lucy were seven and four. Gemma had always done the majority of parenting because I would be away a lot with work for long periods of time. So when I said I wanted to have 50/50 care of the kids, Gemma hit the roof. She said there was no way I could look after them because I didn't know what they needed for school and when, that I didn't know what they liked to eat and what they wouldn't eat. She became obsessed with telling me all the things I didn't know how to do and obsessed with stopping me from having my children half the time. She would find all kinds of reasons for me not to have them, it felt like she was playing a game, which she would only stop when she had "won" by me giving in and saying that she could have the kids full-time. It was exhausting.

'When she said that they couldn't stay with me on Sunday nights because I wasn't capable of getting them to school on time with a clean uniform on Mondays, I lost it. I contacted my lawyer and he wrote Gemma a letter telling her to stop, otherwise we were going to take her to court. I wanted time with my children just as much as Gemma did and I wasn't just going to let her take it away from me. Looking back, I can see that I was also trying to win. All the time this was going on Charlie and Lucy were becoming more and more unsettled. They didn't have a routine – Gemma changed it all the time and there were all sorts of excuses why it needed to change. I'm ashamed to say it now, but Gemma and I got into this awful competitive parenting mode. We would both make a massive fuss of the kids when they were with us, trying to outdo each other and impress the kids so that we became their favourites. It makes me wince now, but this became my focus, and I lost sight of the fact that the kids needed us to work together and not in competition with each other.

'I still don't know why it all came to a head over some stuffed toys, but it did. I was picking the kids up and Gemma said they couldn't take their cuddlies from her house to mine. She completely lost sight of the fact that these were the kids' teddy bears, not hers or mine. And Lucy burst into tears. It was when Charlie put her arms around her to comfort her to say, "Don't worry, everything will be OK and one day everybody won't fight anymore," that Gemma and I had the shock that we needed in order to change. I felt sick. Hearing my seven-year-old say that was just a massive wake-up call to our competitive and short-term thinking.

'We did The Co-Parenting Method and understood really quickly that if we wanted Charlie and Lucy to be happy and robust growing up and have healthy relationships when they were adults, we needed to each modify how we were with each other. I remember Gemma messaging me one evening to say that the only losers of this game we had found ourselves in would be the kids and that she was glad that we were moving away from that and into a healthier longer-term approach.

'It's much better now. We work together. Keeping in mind the endgame of having happy kids is what prevents us from going back to the pettiness. Thank goodness we know that now.'

When we separate, it's really natural to be in the moment. Surviving and just getting through the day may be all you can think about. Things may be heated between you and your ex and you may have engaged family lawyers to help argue your point of view. Where you are on your co-parenting journey may be all about who spends what time with your child and when. You might be focused on money, negotiating over pension pots, house sales and child maintenance. Or maybe there is a new partner on the scene and you're having to navigate introducing them to your ex and your child and it could be there is a lot of animosity around that. Perhaps you simply have really different parenting styles, which are showing up now more than ever before, and you can't get past the time your kids go to bed, or that they don't eat well when they're with their other parent. Maybe your ex suddenly wants to be a hands-on parent for the first time and you feel shortchanged because you've always been the primary parent.

If you're in any sort of disagreement with your ex, then, as with any conflict, you will be trying to get your point of view across. Both of you will want to be right. It might be that all of this means that you can't bring yourself to speak to your ex or you are unable to make decisions with them about the children. Perhaps you're too angry at them to be able to listen to what they're saying. Maybe you're trapped in the 'winning' mindset, more focused on getting your point across and the outcome you want than anything else. Whatever it is that's going on for you, it may be keeping you in a short-term mindset. And when we're in a short-term mindset it can be hard to see that we're having a negative effect on our long-term co-parenting relationship and therefore how our children are experiencing their parents.

Moving away from a winning mindset is crucial. When someone wins, someone else has to lose. When you're in the winning mindset, you may think the loser will be your ex, but we know that the loser is often your children.

LAWYERS AND PROFESSIONALS

You may have instructed lawyers and so might your ex. Who you have decided to work with can have a significant impact on how your separation unfolds. Some lawyers are committed to helping their clients separate with a minimum amount of conflict. They might be members of a body like Resolution, or they may be collaborative lawyers. Whoever you instruct as your legal representation, remember that you are paying, which means you get to tell them how you want to separate. Being clear that you want them to use language in their correspondence that is respectful, supportive and collaborative and not inflammatory is really helpful. Telling them not to send letters that could be upsetting to your ex on a Friday evening just before the weekend is also something to do. We need lawyers for many things, and their support, wisdom and experience can be really invaluable. Making sure they are positively contributing to keeping your children at the centre of your separation and not making conflict worse is really important. I know you may be angry and I know you may be hurting, but take the long-term view. It's cheaper and it's better for your children if you can sort the legalities out quickly and cleanly.

Best Case, Worst Case

We're going to jump straight into your first tool now. It's called Best Case, Worst Case and it will help you to start thinking about how a long-term mindset can positively impact your co-parenting. Grab a pen and paper and a comfortable place to sit and try to be somewhere where you won't be interrupted. In this tool, I'll be asking you to use your imagination. Sometimes in coaching, when we ask people to imagine things, it's to help them understand what's possible and to help the brain remove some of the 'should' and 'can't' thoughts that it often puts in our way. It can be really helpful to do this at the beginning of our journey together as it's a great way of separating out the long-term thinking and actions from the short-term thinking and actions. If you find visualising imagined scenarios difficult, then just answer the questions below to the best of your ability; however you approach the exercise, something valuable will come from it. Ready?

Best-case scenario

I'd like you to take a deep breath in and imagine your co-parenting when it's working well. Remove all the things that have made it difficult. Just for a few moments, really embrace the idea that it's running smoothly. Ask yourself the following questions and write your answers down.

- When it's working well, what would I like my co-parenting to look like?
- What does it feel like for me when everything is running smoothly?
- What's happening for my children when it's like this?
- What is the good interaction like between me and my co-parent?

Worst-case scenario

Now I'd like you to imagine your co-parenting when it's not working at all. This might be easier for you, but I'd like you to really imagine it at its worst. Ask yourself the following questions and take some notes down before continuing.

- When co-parenting is going badly, what's happening?
- How is it feeling for me to be in this situation?
- How might it be feeling for my children?
- What's the bad interaction like between me and my co-parent?

Worst-case scenario – your starring role

The next thing I'd like you to do is read over what you wrote down under your Worst Case. I'd like you to think about what it is *you* would need to do to make the worst-case scenario come true right now. I just want you to think about what *you* would need to do – not your ex, just yourself. So maybe you've written down under worst-case scenario that the co-parenting is really argumentative, that you disagree with each other on everything and every day is filled with awful emails and messages. Your role in making that happen might be, 'I'll wake up in the morning and send an email to my ex with all the things they have done wrong in the last 24 hours.' Or, 'I refuse to be polite to my ex at pick-ups and drop-offs and ignore them.' Or, 'I'm going to roll my eyes whenever I see them.' You see where I'm going with this.

Write down whatever comes to mind and take a deep breath when you're done.

Best-case scenario – your starring role

Now I want you to move back to your best-case scenario and re-read what you wrote down for that.

I'd like you to think about what it is *you* would need to do to make the best-case scenario come true. What actions can you change, what things can *you* do to make those positive scenarios, the best possible outcome, happen? So, if you've written that you work well together with your ex, that you can have a conversation without it turning into an argument and that you're both working together for the sake of your children, what is it that *you're* doing to make that happen? Even if the best-case scenario feels really far away, remember that it's OK to visualise it.

One small step towards co-parenting

Now we are going to focus on the last piece you have just done. Have a read of what you've written. Your best-case scenario and the things you need to do to get there are all about long-term thinking. This is the ideal place that you want your co-parenting to be in. We can't just make that happen though – we have to take small steps to get there. I want you to come up with one action, even if it's really small, that you can start today, to help you move towards your best-case scenario. You might write down that you're going to bite your tongue and not get angry at your co-parent, or maybe you're going to make sure all the school stuff is ready for your kids at handover. Perhaps you're going to ask your children in a happy tone of voice what they did at their other parent's house. Whatever it is, make a note of it and decide how and when you will take the action. If it's feeling scary, just take a little action, but it's important to take an action, even if it's small, so you can feel like you're moving forward. It may only be a small step, but you're taking it, and by taking it you're on your road to better co-parenting. Even if it doesn't change the way your co-parent interacts with you, just keep taking that step. It's important for you and it's important for your kids.

As we go through the six steps, try to remember that, even though you might be feeling really far away from this right now, your best-case scenario is what you want your co-parenting to look like. It will make it easier for you to make changes if you have that long-term goal in mind.

Storing your Best Case, Worst Case tool

Remember in the introduction on page 16 I explained that we would be using a memory technique to help us recall all the tools we are going to be learning throughout the method? Using outrageous imagery is one of the ways we will do that throughout this book and we're going to start that now.

The first thing I'd like you to do is to picture a briefcase. This is your 'best-case scenario briefcase'.

Perhaps it's a briefcase which, when you open it, allows you to step into a magical world full of palm trees and beaches and relaxation, or perhaps your case is made out of glittering diamonds and jewels, or maybe it's full of gorgeous watches. Whatever it is, really imagine your best briefcase next to your worst one, which has got holes in it and cobwebs on it and is covered in something that smells. Imagine yourself choosing to pick up your best-case briefcase in your left hand. Your left hand is where you will store this tool.

In the introduction I also invited you to draw a body outline so you could label each tool on the body. If you want to, I'd like you to label your best-case scenario tool in the left hand of your body outline now.

The Long-Term Impact of Co-Parenting

We know that when we co-parent well we are more likely to have a better relationship with our kids over the course of a lifetime. Our children are adults for longer than they are children and so it's fundamental to put the building blocks in place now to secure a good relationship with them going forward. I want you to hold on to that long-term perspective as you work your way through each of the six steps of The Co-Parenting Method. We're going to be parents for the rest of our lives. This is not a sprint, it's many marathons, and we need to be in a long-term headspace when we think about our parenting responsibilities.

When we co-parent well we are more likely to have a better relationship with our kids over the course of a lifetime.

Let me show you what I mean. Alex and Martina (now adults) shared the story of their parents' break-up with me and what it was like for them growing up. The story is written by Alex.

'I was eleven and Martina was seven when the arguing started. Our dad had found out that Mum had been seeing another man. We were too young to understand fully what that meant, but we started to experience a change in our lives which went from happy and calm to emotionally volatile and unpredictable. We both remember it because it came on so suddenly.

'Mum and Dad started focusing a lot more on their stuff and their arguing and their separation and less on doing the fun stuff we used to do. In fact, for a long while, it felt like they weren't really parenting us at all. Martina started to wet the bed and she would come to me in the night because she didn't want to start the arguing again between Mum and Dad. I'd change her sheets and stuff them in the washing basket hoping no one would notice.

'Dad was so angry, and he would take me aside and tell me that we couldn't trust Mum anymore. That she was a bad person and had broken up our family. Looking back, he must have been hurting so much, but he was intent on making us both hate Mum. And eventually it started to work.

'I don't really remember the process too much, but we ended up going to live mainly with Dad and going to Mum's some weekends. We had both been adamant that we didn't want to live with Mum. They didn't even speak to each other anymore and we would move from one house to the other without any kind of understanding of a routine. It was clear that they didn't speak to each other because they would both pump us for information when we arrived at one house after being at the other. Martina was affected really badly. She barely spoke for a year. She became really timid and school was a real ordeal for her. I just bottled it up, pushed it all down inside. I think I did become more aggressive at school because I was always looking for a fight with the other kids, but I didn't realise at the time it was because I had so many emotions that I wasn't dealing with. It's only been recently, now I'm in my twenties, that I have realised just how much it affected me. It's had a massive impact on my relationships. Well, I don't have relationships. I have short-lived romances that I don't let amount to anything. I'm in therapy now.

'It was Dad badmouthing Mum that made it worse. His constant happiness that we were with him, almost like he had won, was strange. His discrediting of Mum, destroying our vision of our mother, was so damaging and irresponsible that we just can't forgive him for that. We both made up with Mum and we see her a lot. We don't see Dad so much. We find it hard to forgive him for what he did after he found out about Mum's affair.'

Conflict with our other parent, especially where we are seeking short-term gains and victories, can cause lasting damage to our future relationship with our children and their long-term emotional wellbeing. Let's just zoom in on that.

What might have happened if Alex and Martina's parents had chosen to take a co-parenting approach? Of course, Dad would still have been angry at the affair – it would be unreasonable to expect him not to be. They would have probably still separated, but if he had been able to regulate his emotions, he would also have noticed that the situation was having a profound impact on the children. He would have seen that they were tearful and withdrawn. He might have realised that his rage was having huge consequences on their welfare and that if he didn't modify his behaviour there would be a long-term impact. If Dad had been able to step back and see the bigger picture, he might have understood that, despite what he and his wife felt about each other, if they had agreed to co-parent together, Alex and Martina would have felt more stable and supported during their childhood.

Good communication and working together to parent can make so much difference to how your separation impacts your kids. It's difficult to read that our conflict as adults affects our children, because we never want to hurt our children. But when we're feeling hurt ourselves, it can be really hard to untangle our parenting from our adult separation. Keep trying, because by doing that you'll better protect your children.

The Nuffield Family Justice Observatory carried out a piece of research that looked at evidence from both parents and children about their experiences of separation. One of its key findings was that separation is an ongoing process and not a single event, which means that there is often conflict before parents decided to separate and that conflict can continue into the separation and beyond. Importantly it states that 'for children . . . separation was never complete and evolved according to changing circumstances.'[5]

They also found: 'The separation of parents affected children both emotionally and practically in their everyday lives . . . Children and young people said they were not given information about what was going on, were not able to participate in decisions affecting them and did not feel listened to, leaving them feeling distressed.'

According to the Family Solutions Group, around 280,000 children experience their parents' separation each year in the UK alone and the way that this is managed will affect the rest of their lives and influence their long-term mental welfare and future life chances. The Family Solutions Group is a multi-disciplinary group with practical experience of working with separated parents and their children. In their core recommendations, they state: 'How parents handle separation will have a direct impact on their children, with lasting consequences which can endure throughout their lives.'[6]

Providing a stable co-parenting structure for your children will help them feel less distressed, more anchored, safe and protected even as they navigate into their new family system. The conflict in separation affects children, but if this can be managed, then the impact of that reduces. There are many of us working in this space who are striving to enable separating parents to reduce conflict to support children in different ways.

Speaking at a Family Solutions Group webinar in November 2020, Sir Andrew MacFarlane, the President of the Family Division of the UK judicial system, said: 'Those of us working in the system long for a better way of helping children, of helping parents to resolve what are, in effect, relationship difficulties when they break up.'[7]

All of this information can be hard to read. The fact that you are reading this book shows how important your children's mental wellbeing is for you. Using the techniques in the book and learning to communicate well without escalating conflict (step four) will help you put in place a way of co-parenting to help your kids stay emotionally well.

As parents we need to realise that whatever is happening to our relationship, we are still both parents to our children and that will never change. Our family system may not look the same, but all the same people are still in it. Co-parenting is about finding a healthy long-term way to make the new-look system work well for everyone – especially the children. We do that by remaining fully conscious of our children's happiness and welfare, and what's best for them. We do that by accepting *now* that our actions will have a ripple effect. Being parents at war is almost certainly damaging to our children and their long-term development.

Our children's mental and emotional wellbeing

Conflict, particularly prolonged conflict, can cause the deterioration of our children's mental health, which can have life-long effects. Reducing conflict between parents is an important way to protect our children's mental and emotional health following a relationship breakdown. Because we're going to be talking a lot about our children's resilience and emotional health during the book, I want to quickly zoom in on that. The National Institutes of Health in the US and the Royal College of Psychiatrists and the NSPCC in the UK all talk about the negative long-term impact of conflict on children during separation

> Emotional and behavioural problems in children are more common when their parents are fighting or separating. Children can become very insecure. Insecurity can cause children to behave like they are much younger and therefore bed wetting, 'clinginess', nightmares, worries or disobedience can all occur. This behaviour often happens before or after visits to the parent who is living apart from the family. Teenagers may show their distress by misbehaving or withdrawing into themselves. They may find it difficult to concentrate at school.[8]

Remember that happy and resilient kids are what we are aiming for – children who can grow up and speak their mind if they need to, who form healthy relationships, who can stand up for what's right and fair, who don't feel like they need to choose sides, and who can manage big emotions. To get all of that might mean that we personally have to do some hard things to win that amazing and hugely worthwhile prize.

Imagine this. You're walking along the pavement with your child. Someone accidentally bumps into them and your child's ball falls into the road. They take a couple of steps off the pavement without thinking.

There's a bus coming. What do you do? You instinctively run out into the road to protect them, right? You would automatically do everything you could to save their life. You would even put your own physical safety at risk to do so. It's no different with our children's mental health. If we don't try to co-parent, or we think that destroying our child's relationship with their other parent means we win, then think again. If we're doing that, then we're putting our child's mental and emotional health directly in front of the bus. I want to reassure you that starting to move towards thinking about the emotional wellbeing is really positive. This is a step-by-step process and it takes time and effort, and that's OK. All steps in the right direction are progress. Keep going.

Managing the immediate emotional effects of separation can be tricky, especially when we ourselves may be feeling like we're on a rollercoaster. The age of your child also has an impact on how they are affected by your separation. It's not just about young children, either. As adults we can be massively affected by our parents' separation, especially because they may share too much detail with us. It's important therefore to understand the potential emotional impact of separation on children by age so you know how to help mitigate those impacts and therefore protect your child's mental health. I've included one or two actions in each age bracket to support you.[9]

Age: Newborn up to 2 years old
Possible Reactions and Behaviours:
Even though your baby may not be able to understand words yet and won't understand that you and their other parent aren't together anymore, they still do react to changes in their environment and the people who care for them. This can mean they pick up on moods and atmospheres. Babies may become more irritable or more upset. Sometimes when babies experience a stressful environment, this can impact their immune system and they may get mild illnesses or

complaints including mouth ulcers. They may cry more when you're handing over to each other, especially if they're leaving their usual primary caregiver, and may be clingier than usual. Sometimes they might even reject one parent. They may have feeding and sleeping issues or may regress developmentally by a few months. The more stability you can both offer them at this time, the quicker they will adjust.

Action: Your behaviours and moods will directly impact your baby's response, so managing your moods and emotions will be key here.

Age: Toddler, 2–3 years old
Possible Reactions and Behaviours:
Your toddler will be able to express themselves more easily than a baby can, but their language is still extremely limited, as is their brain development. Making sense of things is hard when you're this small. Common responses to parents separating in children this young include separation anxiety and being very clingy. You might notice that they have more tantrums, they may regress in terms of sleep and potty training and they become very attached to an object. If they have a favourite toy, then make sure you have two of them, one for each of their homes.

Action: Communicating well together to make sure they have familiar routines and toys in both houses is essential.

Age: Pre-schooler, 3–5 years old
Possible Reactions and Behaviours:
Older pre-schoolers may be able to ask why their parents don't live in the same house anymore. It may be the first time that they have experienced big and uncomfortable feelings like sadness or insecurity.

Because language is still limited, watch out for changes in behaviour. Perhaps they might be mean to their play-mates or shout and scream more at home. They might have more tummy aches and more nightmares. They will possibly regress in their behaviour.

Pre-schoolers may have a little more understanding of the situation but may still struggle with feelings of confusion, sad-ness, and insecurity. Try to agree to name these feelings as they have them, rather than just focusing on making them feel better. If a child can learn to name their feelings and understand that big feelings are normal, they will become better at dealing with them. It can be really hard to see your child (at any age) experiencing distressing emotions. Being the grown-up and holding them close emotionally as they release these feelings is one of the best ways you can help them feel safe.

Action: Make sure you are telling your children that you will both still be their parents. Letting them see you talking together without any conflict is critical.

Age: 5–8 years old
Possible Reactions and Behaviours:
As your child becomes older and more aware of what's going on around them, navigating their parents' separation can become really tricky.

Developmentally, children may already be starting to experience feelings like loyalty and they can become con-cerned about the conflict they are witnessing and may feel the need to take sides.

It's really important as parents that you do not ask your child to choose sides. This is one of the things that can really affect how children form adult relationships in the future.

Because kids' brains haven't fully developed, they can very easily adopt the feeling that the separation is their fault and can experience a strong sense of guilt. So it's important that you both offer them constant reassurance that it's not their fault.

Trying to make sense of something that feels adult can be hard for children. You may notice that your child is suddenly acting very grown up. Or your child may be doing the complete opposite of that and, like younger kids, may be having temper tantrums, or being very clingy and tearful.

Action: There isn't a one-size-fits-all in this, but really look out for behavioural changes in your kids and help support them through as much as possible. Talk to your co-parent about what you both notice and come up with a support strategy. Perhaps agree that you'll inform each other as soon as you are aware of a new behaviour, or that you'll include it in your handover notes.

Age: 9–13 years old
Possible Reactions and Behaviours:
As your kids get older they may want to act in a way that replaces the absent parent. They may start acting like a carer or behave in a grown-up way that steps them out of their childhood. It's really important to keep an eye out for this and to notice if it's happening. Children who move into one of these roles lose out on their childhood and can unknowingly have the expectation of being a carer placed upon then. It's never appropriate for your child to become the grown-up or the carer. Their brains and their maturity just aren't equipped to handle the complexities of adulthood, even if they seem really mature. Kids at this age may also be starting to experience puberty and their responses to the changes in a family system can be made worse by an influx of hormones.

Children may withdraw or show signs of aggression or depression, they may have increased anxiety, or a sense of failure that they have not been able to keep their parents together.

Action: It's really important to explain to them that adult relationships are different to parental relationships and that your separation has nothing to do with them and no bearing on the fact that you're both still their parents and that you love them. If you can both reassure your children together, this can go a long way to helping them feel that their parents can still be parents.

Age: 14–18 years old
Possible Reactions and Behaviours:
Your teenager will have a more complex understanding of what's happening. This can be helpful in terms of explaining things to them, but remember not to overshare, as they are still kids and it may not be appropriate for them to know the details of your separation and the reasons for it.

They may feel torn between you both, their loyalties may be divided and they may feel they need to choose their favourite parent. It's very possible they feel a large amount of anger towards one or both of you and there is a real possibility that risk-taking behaviour will increase. This means sexual risk, drugs and alcohol as well as other things, including forming inappropriate relationships. They may also latch on to things they can control, such as exercise or the way they eat. They may also say, and act as if, they hate you.

Action: By keeping each other informed and telling your children that they have two parents and that it's important for them to have a relationship with both of them, you are reinforcing the understanding that the reason for the separation is grown-up stuff and they don't have to choose. Reassure them that the parental love for them hasn't changed and won't change, whatever is going on in the separation. Having a joined-up approach to any risk-taking behaviours is important, as is setting strong and consistent boundaries in both houses.

Age: 18–mid-20s
Possible Reactions and Behaviours:
As children grow into adults, parental separation can affect confidence. How you handle your own separation can have a significant impact on how your children form their own adult relationships.

Still be mindful of oversharing, as brains don't finish developing until we are in our mid-twenties. Your child might seem like an adult, but they aren't there yet.

Action: Even though it might feel as though you don't need to share much information with your co-parent about your children because of their age, please keep doing it. Look out for the emotional toll on them, and agree the language you're going to use about the separation, both around them and with the other significant people in their lives.

Age: Adult children
Possible Reactions and Behaviours:
Co-parenting often focuses on younger children, but it's really important to acknowledge that adult children can be significantly affected by their parents' separation. Perhaps you've picked up this book with younger children in mind, but have adult children that may be affected too.

As adults, when our parents separate, we can still experience a big sense of loss and we can feel very unstable as the foundations of our lives seem to unravel.

Adult children may express shock and surprise that you're divorcing and often disbelief, as though you are wrong in your decision, especially if you've waited until your children are grown up before you separate. This can also lead to them re-evaluating their childhood and questioning what was real and what wasn't. It can feel really destabilising.

They may well feel torn between their parents or caught in the middle, especially if parents have overshared the details of their separation.

They can also focus in on very practical issues, such as inheritance, the impact on lives if you've met someone else, or how they will care for you both as you age if you're not together. They may also worry about family gatherings and how they will now work.

Seeing their parents separate can bring a profound sense of grief and loss, so be gentle when you tell them the news. It can be very distressing even when your children are adults.

Action: Be honest with them about things that will impact them, but remember not to overshare or use them as a confidant. It's still important they have a healthy relationship with both of you. If you and your ex can agree that you won't make big events and celebrations an issue, this will be a relief for your children.

But I Don't Like My Ex – How Can I Co-Parent With Them Forever?

It might feel impossible today that you will have to continue to raise a child with someone you don't like anymore. It might feel totally overwhelming that you're going to be doing this with the person who you're not in a relationship with anymore. It might feel ridiculously complicated, you might be wondering about how you'll ever have a new relationship, or how to manage new partners on the scene. It can be very daunting to be thinking in the long term. I completely understand how that feels. I remember sitting with my brother one morning not long after my separation and realising that co-parenting was forever. My son was just one year old. It felt like a long-distance race that I just hadn't prepared for. I trained as I went and I didn't always get things right, but I was held in place by the knowledge that we needed to do this for our son.

When we bring a child into the world, it's a responsibility that stays with us for the rest of our life. In most cases our kids will adore both their parents, no matter what we feel about our ex-partner. Even if we decide to withdraw from our children, we don't get the option of not being a mum or a dad. For our kids we just become a mum or a dad who is no longer there – but we are still their mum or dad. It can be wounding for children to experience that withdrawal. If you're finding it hard to be present, don't be hard on yourself; this book will help you find a way through it. I've witnessed many parents manage this, so I know it's possible even though it might feel hard.

Co-parenting can feel like an impossible task when you don't get along with your ex. Finding a way through that to work with someone who you don't much like anymore is very hard. If our children are young, the idea of having to have regular contact with our ex can leave us feeling resentful and angry. Just reflect for a moment and accept that it's OK to be angry, resentful and upset. You may be feeling despair or sadness or grief and these feelings can at times threaten to overwhelm us. It's normal to have those feelings, and it's important for you and for your wellbeing that you process them fully.

However, it's really hard to feel angry, flooded with emotion, or sad and at the same time to make good and well-grounded decisions. When we are feeling like this, the practical and emotional needs of the kids can sometimes get lost amid the stresses and practicalities of separation. As a result, children can be left feeling confused, unsafe and unstable. This is why making a commitment to be a good co-parent is so important.

When we co-parent effectively it means that we consciously and deliberately put aside our negative feelings towards each other, refocus our attention on our children and take decisions that benefit them. This conscious focus is a key part of co-parenting. It's the very deliberate and sometimes difficult process of putting your children first. Putting their needs above your own discomfort so they can grow up in a safe and loving environment. That's what we need to do to become successful co-parents. Co-parenting can be hard, but it's incredibly important work for your children's wellbeing. It doesn't need to be perfect – it just needs to be good enough. You don't need to like each other – but you do need to be polite. The only way we can do that is if we move out of the short-term conflict and into the long-term wellbeing of our children and ourselves.

Co-parenting doesn't need to be perfect – it just needs to be good enough.

The Co-Parental Loop – the Biggest Principle for Long-Lasting Harmony

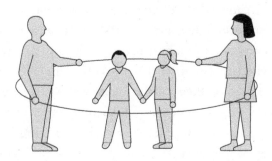

One of the ways we can help ourselves to remain in the long-term mindset is to understand a core principle of The Co-Parenting Method, and that is the Co-Parental Loop.

A Co-Parental Loop is an effective long-term parenting relationship where both parents are there for their children, and can communicate with each other respectfully about them. It's where they understand that they need to manage their own emotional response enough to make effective parental decisions together and show up and be unified enough parents even though they're no longer together as a couple. In order to make the Co-Parental Loop successful, we have to be thinking long term and not short term.

The loop provides a safe space for children who see their parents talking to each other and working together. Imagine the loop like an elastic band, with both parents standing inside it holding it taut. The children are in the middle. They feel safe because the loop is being upheld.

If one parent steps out of the loop then the loop becomes less secure. It's not providing a strong structure around the children. In the absence of a secure parental loop, our children will feel as though they're missing the influence of either one or both of their parents; they don't feel as safely supported by their parents, and this may show itself through behavioural issues. If your co-parent really won't communicate with you and they aren't reading this book, then don't worry. You can keep your side of the loop nice and strong for your children. You can give information to your ex and you can make sure that you are being polite and respectful to them and about them. It may not be a full Co-Parental Loop, but it will still provide safety and a stable structure from your side, which will be vital for your children. Often, when you're consistent in the way you hold up your side of the loop, then your co-parent will eventually pick up their side. As human beings it can take us different amounts of time to accept things, so having a patient mindset can be helpful if you're currently holding up the loop on your own.

(I want to be clear here that I'm not talking about single parents; that's a whole different parental system. I'm talking about upholding a Co-Parental Loop where children have an *expectation* of two parents.)

If parents are in the short-term 'I want to win' mindset and have stopped focusing on the overall aims of parenting, the loop is slack. It can be really hard to keep it secure when we are co-parenting, but it's super important we do. So how do we do it?

Crucially, it's not necessary to have a friendly relationship with your co-parent to establish a safe parental loop, but it *is* necessary to be able to communicate with them on practical issues. And it is necessary for you both to be polite and respectful to each other on the outside, whatever you're feeling inside.

Let me tell you about Jason and Helen. Jason had ended the relationship and for 18 months Helen was distraught. She didn't want the relationship to be over and was angry and fearful. She refused to think about the long-term need to co-parent. She tells us about the impact that had here.

'I loved Jason so much. I didn't want our relationship to end. Mark was only eight – too young for his parents to be splitting up. I found it so hard to see Jason without wanting to talk about my feelings for him. It became really hard for me to engage with him on a practical level, to talk with him and to make decisions with him, and I disengaged. If I'd engaged with him as a co-parent, that would mean we really had broken up.

'I think Jason had to manage a lot of the co-parenting on his own while I was feeling like this. He was certainly more there for Mark than I was able to be. He would try to get me to engage and make decisions about Mark, but I was just so sad that I found it really hard. He ended up taking most of the decisions without me and I think Mark could somehow sense that. I'd become disengaged and really distant. All I could focus on was wanting to get back with Jason. Mark started playing up at school, he was pushing other kids in the playground and shouting at his teachers. He was never normally like this and when I mentioned it to my best friend, she said that it was because he doesn't feel secure and that he needed his mummy too.

'I probably had a bit of a jolt when she said that and I saw that I needed to be a good mum to Mark and I needed to accept my relationship with Jason was over. We did The Co-Parenting Method online and

I could see that I was outside of what is called the Co-Parental Loop. I also understood lots of other things including what I was so afraid of. But Jason and I are in a better place now and, importantly, so is Mark. It's not easy, and I don't suppose it will ever be truly easy, but it's more stable for all of us.'

Photographs

In step one we've been looking at how to think longer term and why it's important to be in the Co-Parental Loop, and the Photographs tool will help you do just that. It will move you from just being able to think about the short-term mindset, responses and issues and help you think about the longer-term impact and how you want your children to experience their parents as co-parents.

To do this exercise, you need to find a quiet and calm space where you won't be interrupted. It'll take around 20 minutes. Somewhere to take notes is also useful.

In a moment, you're going to read a short scenario about your future. There are some questions following that, which will help form your thinking. After you've read the scenario and spent a few minutes reflecting on it, please answer the questions either on paper or just by thinking them through.

Get comfortable. Ready?

I want you to imagine that it's 25 years in the future. You're sitting with your grown-up children outside a café somewhere warm and sunny. The leaves are out on the trees and the birds are singing. Your adult children are looking at old photographs of themselves from when they were younger and they're talking very openly about their childhood.

I'd like you to think about the following questions and paint a vivid mental picture in answer to each of them. Pay close attention to how you're feeling as you think about your answers.

As you talk to your adult children outside the café:

- What do you want your adult children to say about their childhood?
- What memories and emotions do you want the photographs to evoke for them?
- What do you want them to say about the period when you separated from your ex and about how they were parented after that?
- How do you want your relationship to be with them now as adults?

If you'd like to close your eyes while imagining your café scene, then please feel free to do so. Spend as long as you like thinking about it – some people spend five minutes, some half an hour. Take the time you need and be gentle with yourself. Don't rush – this is important work. Once you've finished, open your eyes again.

You've completed the imagining part of the exercise. Take a couple of deep breaths now, feel your feet on the floor and wiggle your toes a little, which will help you to come back into the present.

Now I want you to answer the following questions. Either note down the answers in your notebook or computer, or simply reflect on them. It's whatever makes you most comfortable.

Looking Back

What do I want my adult children to say about how my ex-partner and I parented them?

Looking Forward

Which of my behaviours do I need to change going forward to enable my grown-up children to say those positive things about me and my parenting? (This is about *your* behaviours, not about the behaviours of your ex-partner.)

What are two small actions that I can take this week to enable my behavioural change? Write them down and make them happen. It might be saying hello in a polite way at drop-off, or not rolling your eyes when your ex's back is turned. It might be bigger – you may have realised that you need to stop being rude about your ex in front of your children. You can do this. These actions are within your control.

The Photographs tool isn't easy and it really forces us to take responsibility for our own role in our children's future happiness. You now have a vision of what you want your children to say about your parenting when they're adults, and a rough draft of what you may need to change to get there. You've just taken a significant step towards becoming a more effective co-parent.

Storing your Photographs tool

We're going to use our memory technique now to help us recall the tool and our visualisation when we need it. Remember, the more outrageously we can imagine something, the easier it will be for us to remember it. If you need a quick reminder about the memory techniques and what they do, you can find that on page 16.

Because we're looking into the future, we can store the Photographs tool in our eyes. And what helps us see? Yes, glasses. I want you to imagine putting on the strangest pair of glasses you can think of. Perhaps they're enormous or a very strange shape or made from an unusual material. Maybe they are bright green with pink spots on them. Through these glasses you watch your children at the café as they go through the photos of their childhood. Really summon up that image in your mind, feel it as vividly as you can.

If you'd like to label your Photographs tool on the eyes of your body outline, please do that now.

Throughout this step we've seen that it's fundamental to step out of the short-term thinking where we can get stuck in the detail of something we don't like. If we're in the short-term place then we are hyper focused on what is going on in the here and now, and this means we can't see the bigger picture. It becomes possible to see the bigger picture when we are in a long-term mindset where we are able to prioritise the wellbeing of our children through co-parenting. The longer-term mindset is all about holding on to the understanding that if we can get out of the win/lose mindset and step into a place where we see the arguing and disagreements as less important than our child's wellbeing, then we will be able to co-parent.

The benefits of being in the longer-term mindset are enormous. Even though, as we've seen, it can be so hard to do that when we're experiencing a lot of emotions, it will help protect your children's long-term mental health significantly. It's not separation that damages our children, it's the sustained conflict that they experience as a result of the separation. By taking action now, by taking even a small step towards positive co-parenting, you'll be making it better for your children in the long term. Even if you've been in conflict for a long time, moving towards a collaborative co-parenting relationship now will give them the security that they need for their long-term wellbeing.

Separation doesn't damage children; conflict does.

In the introduction I explained that we will use two memory techniques to help embed what you're reading so it becomes really familiar to you. When learning and tools are familiar, we can use them without having to think about them too much. We've already covered the outrageous imagery of the tools that help us remember them. The second way is through focused repetition. So, at the end of each step I will also summarise what we've looked at so you are able to easily recall the main points of the step. Feel free to revisit these small summaries whenever you need to.

STEP ONE SUMMARY

- You've learned about the negative impact on your children now and in their future if you don't move from a short-term mindset to a long-term mindset.
- You also learned about the Co-Parental Loop, that imaginary elastic that you and your co-parent loop around your children to keep them safe.
- You learned that co-parenting well, communicating respectfully and making good decisions together as co-parents is what provides that safe parental loop for your children to grow up in. We'll look at how to do both of those things in steps four and five.
- You learned your first two tools: Best Case, Worst Case and the Photographs tool.
- By using both of these tools you've built an outline picture of what you want your co-parenting to look like in the longer term and how you want your relationship with your adult children to be.
- You saw that if you don't invest the time now to have a good relationship with your children, then it'll be much harder to do so later, and you thought about which of your own behaviours you want to change to achieve that.
- You've got actions from both of these tools that you're going to take now in order to start to make that happen.

Storing your tools: You store the Best Case, Worst Case in your left hand, which carries your amazing best briefcase, and your store your Photographs tool in your eyes, with those crazy glasses that you're wearing. Take a moment to visualise both of those now.

Do you remember those feelings of fierce love and responsibility that you had the first time you set eyes on your child? The love and – importantly – that responsibility you felt then for your children's happiness never goes away. It's our job as parents *to be parents*. Just because we're no longer in a relationship with someone doesn't mean we stop being a parent with them; and following a divorce or separation, our children need us, perhaps more than ever, to show up as parents. It might feel like you need to climb a mountain in order to be able to do that right now, but you're not alone. Keep the end goal of resilient children in mind.

Co-parenting is not easy and it means we have to consciously take responsibility for our own actions to make it work. Becoming a co-parent and learning how to manage the powerful emotions we feel towards our ex is something we have to do for the sake of our children, even if we as adults might not want to. Managing the strong emotions that we might be feeling is very hard and one that we all battle with as co-parents from time to time. It is another essential step to take towards becoming a successful co-parent, however, and so we're going to look closely at that and give you the tools to do that in step two.

STEP TWO

Managing Strong Emotions

In step two of your journey towards understanding The Co-Parenting Method, we're going to learn about what happens to us when we experience strong emotions. Big emotions can affect our co-parenting in a few ways. They can stand in the way of us truly listening to our co-parent. They can mean we're not concentrating fully on our children. They may lead us to act impulsively and escalate conflict really quickly. When we are driven by our emotions it can often keep us in that short-term mindset that we learned about in step one, and this can prevent us from working well with our co-parent with our children's long-term wellbeing in mind. Experiencing big emotions makes it harder to take objective decisions, an essential part of co-parenting.

In step two we'll learn how to manage those emotions so we can bring up our children in a more stable environment. We'll look at the impact of those emotions on us as co-parents and on our children and you'll get three more practical tools that will allow you to move forward on your co-parenting journey. The tools will help you catch your emotions before they escalate, know what's causing the big feelings and give you a permanent ally to manage how you show up to co-parenting. Learning to manage our emotions gives us more control, which can significantly improve our communication with our co-parent. The importance of that is it means that you'll be able to make better decisions together about your children.

Sometimes, in step two, you might feel a bit overwhelmed. Managing our emotions when we're co-parents can be really difficult. It can feel like there is a lot at stake. If you are feeling overwhelmed at any point, I just want to reassure you that it's completely normal. Just go with it. Take some calming breaths, grab a cup of tea, have a break if you need to and trust in the process. I take parents through these steps all the time and it's right here in the mess where you can learn the most.

If you've had a break between chapters and feel you could do with a reminder of what you learned in step one, I'd encourage you to re-read the summary on page 53. Part of the magic of the method is being able to remember what you're learning and the small summaries at the end of each step are a great way to keep in your mind what you've absorbed so far.

How Do Strong Emotions Affect Us?

Let's face it – when we're co-parenting, we can have a lot of big emotions. It can feel hard to work with someone we're no longer in a relationship with to continue to raise our kids. We may feel anxious because we don't trust them, we might feel nervous around them, they may be angry at us. All of these things make it harder to do the job of co-parenting.

When the demands of our life become too great for us to cope with, we can experience high levels of emotion, anxiety and stress. Humans have quite naturally evolved to feel fear, stress and anxiety in certain situations. Thousands of years ago these were useful emotions that allowed us to survive in dangerous environments (think sabre-tooth tigers). But even though those ancient threats are long gone, our modern bodies still react to fear, stress and anxiety in the same way, and that's not always helpful. Our rational brains may know that, really, we don't need to be anxious because we're not in physical danger, but the response system is still the same. Having a physical reaction to being criticised, or running away from an argument because your ancient brain thinks you're about to be attacked by a tiger, doesn't help us, but can hinder us.

The ability to cope varies from person to person, and what one person finds stressful may not be a problem for someone else. Strong emotions, anxiety and stress can affect us in many ways, impacting not only how we feel, but also often how we think and how we behave. If we experience these effects for a long time, they may cause physical and mental health problems. So it's important to learn how they affect us, and in order to increase our resilience and our ability to cope. Co-parenting can bring with it some pretty big feelings, and sometimes you can feel as though it's difficult to know how to make decisions, or know what the best thing to do is. This can often be worse if you're in the early days, as everything feels as though it's been tipped upside down. It's important to know that these strong emotions can derail our co-parenting and understand how they do that.

> If you feel as though the big feelings involved in co-parenting are affecting you and you're finding it hard to cope or to focus, then please visit the resources section on page 255 and think about getting some extra support. It's really important that you have the right people around you helping you on your journey.

The Five Fs

The moment we experience a big emotion or a perceived threat or a danger, whether it's physical or mental, our bodies release cortisol and adrenaline hormones into our blood, making us ready to react. Our heartbeat and breathing become faster, we become more alert and our muscles become stronger. We become reactive and impulsive. It's an automatic and entirely natural reaction that we don't control. And, as with our ancient ancestors, it prepares us to fight, to take flight, to freeze, to fawn or to flop. Science tells us that both the sympathetic and parasympathetic nervous systems control these responses almost immediately, sometimes before we can even know what's going on. Our bodies and brains are incredibly fast and intent on keeping us safe.

This is the same in co-parenting. When something feels threatening, these fight, flight, freeze, fawn and flop responses come into play. They are our immediate, instinctive reactions to extreme stress and fear. Because it's easier to remember, I call them the five Fs. They are all completely normal and you can't choose which one to be in. Let's learn a little more about each of them in general:

- **Fight:** This is where we do battle with the danger. You might get extremely angry and be very reactive to a situation. In fight mode, you want to have the last word.
- **Flight:** This is where we run away from the danger by not being able to be present or engage with conflict. There are a lot of avoidant tendencies in this mode and we can often make ourselves too busy to engage.
- **Freeze:** This is where we shut down or become paralysed by the danger. We can give up quickly, and we can spend a lot of time procrastinating and catastrophising when we are in freeze mode.
- **Fawn:** This is where we actually move closer to the source of our conflict and go along with other people's perspectives to smooth things over. When we are in fawn mode, it's very hard to say no. Think of fawn like people pleasing.
- **Flop:** Many experts who work with trauma also add the fifth, less well-known response, flop. If you experience flop, you are mentally and physically overwhelmed and this can mean you are completely submissive or disengaged, or even disorientated.

Before we get into the impact of these modes on our co-parenting, I want to give you a tool that you can use in any situation that will help you put a little bit of distance between what's going on and your response. It's really useful to have something simple you can do that helps relieve the flood of adrenaline, so you can get back into control of a situation. Let's meet Finger and Thumb!

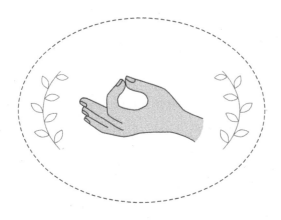

Finger and Thumb

The Finger and Thumb tool is an easy way to activate our rational brain by bringing us completely into the present. Being in the present moves us away from strong emotions and towards a calmer frame of mind. It slows our breathing and allows us to control our emotions rather than letting our emotions control us.

As a technique, Finger and Thumb is very simple, and when you're feeling anxious about your ex-partner – perhaps before a telephone call, or during a face-to-face meeting – you can use it to hold in check your fight, flight, freeze, fawn or flop responses. The technique is based on a mindfulness technique used all over the world in different guises. I first learned it from acclaimed coach Shirzad Chamine.[10] Chamine says that depending on our state of mind, our brain either sabotages us or helps us. I want you to be able to activate the state of mind that helps you, and the Finger and Thumb tool enables you to do just that.

The thing I love most about this technique is that it's very easy to practice. No one needs to know you're doing it, you can even do it in your pocket, and the more you get used to it the more effective it is. Parents who go through The Co-Parenting Method love it because it's simple and effective. Let me show you how to use it:

1. Very gently touch your thumb and forefinger together so they are barely touching. It should feel like it's tickling.
2. Move your thumb and forefinger together, noticing the light sensation. Let it tickle, feel the ridges on your fingertips, noticing the calm that comes.
3. Move between each of your four fingers for different sensations. Concentrate on the feelings.
4. Notice how all your attention is focused on the tiny spot of connection between your finger and thumb.
5. Notice how your breathing has slowed down.
6. Do it for 20 seconds to start with, gradually increasing the time you spend on it as you practise. Notice the sense of calmness as it brings you immediately into the here and now.

Once you get used to doing it, you can use it at any time – and no one even needs to know. Practise daily so it becomes a habit. Use it before seeing your co-parent or while you're meeting with them to help you remain in the moment and stay calm and present.

The Finger and Thumb tool is an excellent way to help us control our five Fs responses in the here and now, and you should use it whenever you feel yourself becoming stressed and anxious. It's also a great one to teach to your children if they're feeling anxious or stressed about anything.

Storing your Finger and Thumb tool

To help us remember this tool, let's find a place on your imaginary body to store it (see page 16). The Finger and Thumb tool we're going to store – unsurprisingly – in our finger and thumb. But how can you make them memorable? Are they a strange colour, or have they grown to be like giant bread rolls or sausages? Look down at your finger and thumb now and really imagine what they will look like. If you're filling in your body outline drawing, please label your Finger and Thumb tool now.

How Do the Five Fs Affect Our Ability to Co-Parent?

Stefan's Story

Let me tell you a story about Stefan. Stefan is 12 years old. He is in his bedroom with a pillow over his head trying to block out the sound of his parents shouting at each other. He squeezes the pillow more tightly over his ears as the sound of arguing increases. And he only releases the grip on the pillow, now soggy from his tears, when the front door slams.

For the next two years Stefan watches and listens silently as his parents call each other names, shout, talk badly about each other to their friends and family. Until finally, one day, his mum moves out of the house and back to Italy.

Stefan is now 14 and living with his dad, and he is angry. The last two years have been horrible. He has had to speak to various counsellors as his parents went through a really messy divorce. His parents don't speak and they are using him as a way of communicating with each other. He goes to visit his mum in Italy during the holidays. He likes it there. One day he comes home from school and his dad has some news for him. His job is taking him back to Washington D.C. Stefan needs to decide where he is going to live. Italy or Washington. He will need to change schools.

Stefan's anger intensifies. He starts smoking marijuana in the park with some older kids instead of going to school. He steals because it gives him a thrill. He feels invisible and full of emotion that he doesn't know what to do with.

Meanwhile, his parents are both lobbying him to come and live with them. They start to have discussions with each other about where he will go to school. Both of them think that schools in their country are better. They fight, they call each other names and they don't seem to mind if Stefan can hear them doing this.

They can't make a decision and time is running out to get him enrolled into the right school. The parents are at an impasse. Neither side wants to lose. And then Dad walks in one day to find Stefan in the bathroom with the door locked. He's not answering despite the hammering on the door. Eventually he unlocks the door, but doesn't even look at his father. He walks into his room and says he wants to be alone. Stefan's dad is fearful as he realises that his son might end up doing himself significant harm if things don't change.

After Stefan's dad had the scare with the locked bathroom, he calls Stefan's mum, and they engage us at The Co-Parent Way. We work with them separately to enable them to communicate with each other about Stefan so they can make a decision about his schooling and where he will live. A few months later both mum and dad, who incidentally still dislike each other, reach a decision with Stefan about schools and living arrangements. His mother moves back to the UK and Stefan remains at school here. Mum goes back to Italy in the holidays and Stefan to Washington and sometimes Italy.

Stefan is more settled. He knows and can see that his parents are able to communicate about him. He can see they are joining up their thinking about his welfare and are able to communicate with each other effectively enough. He can also see that they are managing their emotions and feelings towards each other. His erratic behaviour and his smoking are now irregular. At his dad's suggestion, his mum takes Stefan to the boxing gym twice a week. Stefan's parents are working together. They are co-parenting. And because of that, they are keeping their son safe.

Stefan's parents were both driven by a feeling of fear of not seeing Stefan enough and a fear of losing to the other parent. This fear caused them to be completely caught up in 'winning' Stefan and they were so upset and angry that they forgot to show up properly as parents. Both were in fight mode and it took a potentially catastrophic event to jolt them out of it and into a place where they could think longer term and also take responsibility for how they were feeling and manage their emotional responses to each other.

A separation often has some, if not a lot, of conflict, and when we are in conflict our bodies release adrenaline and we can experience fight, flight, freeze, fawn or flop responses as a result. We might see our ex-partner as a threat for any number of reasons: because we fear their power over us, or we don't trust them or we're angry with them. There are many causes. As a result of this fear, stress and anxiety, our responses are likely to show themselves in different ways. Through arguments if we're in fight mode; through disengagement if we're in flight mode; and through indecision and hiding away if we're in freeze mode. If we're in fawn mode we may become people pleasers towards our ex, which means we can suddenly find ourselves in a subordinate position, and in flop mode (which is often seen most during the break-up itself) we can behave as though we're not able to do anything for ourselves or others, like work, being a parent or basic self-care.

If we're in fight, flight, freeze, fawn or flop response modes, it means that the essential building blocks of a good co-parent relationship are absent. Due to the high levels of adrenaline in our system, we won't be feeling calm and won't be able to communicate effectively, and this is crucial to take well-thought-through decisions. Our mind may be racing, our heart beating faster. We may have butterflies in our stomach, our breathing may be shallow. We may be feeling aggressive towards our ex-partner or we may just want the contact with them to be over as quickly as possible with minimal conflict. We might not be able to stand up for ourselves properly in their presence and we might agree to things that we don't think are fair. We might be feeling frustrated or angry at them. They may irritate us unimaginably. Being in any of the modes makes it harder for us to react calmly, rationally and logically. It makes it more difficult for us to listen to or communicate with our ex-partner, or see their perspective. It's important to say that we can flip between the different modes depending on our situation, meaning we don't always react in the same way. It will depend on what you're experiencing.

What about the impact of us being in fight, flight, freeze, fawn or flop mode on our children? Well, most children are bright and will be able to see if their parents are struggling emotionally and aren't being fully present with them. They'll pick up on small changes in our behaviour, recognise that something isn't right and see that we have less time for them. Here are some of the ways the five Fs can play out in co-parenting:

FIGHT: It's normal to want to fight with your co-parent when you feel that you're being accused of things you haven't done or said. Arguing with your co-parent can feel like the only way through. But what actually happens is that it creates a toxic environment for children to grow up in. Children report feeling anxious and not in control when their parents are fighting with each other and not focusing on their needs as children. Remember Alex and Martina's story from step one? When parents are in these states it can be damaging for their kids' long-term mental health.

FLIGHT: When there's something big that needs a decision, but that decision needs to be made with your co-parent, it can just make us want to run away. It can just be easier to disengage or actively believe we are too busy to engage when we just don't want to talk about things. We're not only putting ourselves and the process in limbo, but also the lives of our children. When parents are in flight mode, they have flown the present, and their children need them in the present in order to feel safe and stable and grounded.

FREEZE: Freezing happens when we can't engage. When the emotion that we are experiencing is just too strong. When one parent freezes, they are no longer a strong presence for their children. It becomes difficult for them to take decisions about their children (procrastination is very present in freeze), about what to do during the separation, contact arrangements, holidays, parenting plans, and so on. When a parent shuts down like this, they are less able to protect their children from emotional harm because it becomes hard for them to engage with parenting, and that can have damaging consequences. Children of parents who are frozen say they're often left to their own devices and must find ways to look after themselves. They lose key parts of their parental support network.

FAWN: For some parents, it feels easier to let the other parent take control. It feels too hard to stand up for what's fair, because the wave of anger or emotion that comes your way is just too much. It's common for one parent to remove themselves from a difficult situation by becoming compliant and letting the other parent assume control. The child effectively is now functioning with one present parent, not two. In these circumstances children report feeling that they must become the grown-up to support the compliant parent. The children lose out on important parts of their childhood.

FLOP: If as a parent you flop, you're having an extreme reaction to stress and anxiety. Flop can mean that your body stops functioning properly, you become physically unable to do things and that you become incapable of making decisions or taking any action. It can be extremely difficult to be present for your children. If you feel you may have gone into flop, please call a friend or family member to help you. With help, it will pass, but while you're not fully present your children may need another adult around for them, as well as you. Please visit our resources section on page 255 for extra support.

Parents being in any of these modes can make our kids feel as though the foundations of their life are not solid. They can feel destabilised and less secure, and this is often during a time when they need as much security and stability as possible because their parents are no longer together.

When we experience strong emotions, we can shift our focus inwards, and our outlook can become narrow and short-term. If we are in this place, we can't be fully focused on the long-term welfare of our children. As parents, we don't want to hear that, but it's important to acknowledge this truth if this is where we are. It's so easy to find yourself here in the heat of a break-up or a tough co-parenting situation. In a moment we're going to learn one of the first tools that will help us manage those feelings. It's definitely possible, even if, right now, it doesn't feel like it. I've seen so many people learn to manage these emotions successfully. Not all the time (none of us are perfect), but more of the time. And practice makes progress.

Catastrophic Fear

Often what's underlying a fight, flight, freeze, fawn or flop response is something I call a catastrophic fear. It sounds very dramatic, doesn't it! Let me explain. It's a fear that is so overpowering, it colours everything we do; it's present in our behaviour, our decision-making and our communication. A friend might tell us that the thing we're fearing is irrational and very unlikely to occur. It's something that sits in our emotional brain and it becomes all-consuming and stops us from moving forward. We get stuck under the weight of it and this can get in the way of us being an engaged and well-balanced co-parent.

One of the common catastrophic fears of co-parenting is that the other parent wants to take our children away from us forever, and that's a really frightening thought. It's understandable because, by the very nature of separating the family, we see our children less. So parents are often well on the road to having strong and catastrophic feelings from the beginning of their separation. I want to show you how to deal with these fears. It's not necessarily about making them go away, but it is about learning to approach them more rationally. To do that first we need to identify them. And that's what our next tool will help us do.

By identifying our catastrophic fear, we're able to examine it, talk about it, reduce its power and use it to understand what's driving our behaviours. When we understand our catastrophic fear, we are more able to manage our responses and change our behaviours, which in turn helps the co-parenting relationship.

I want to help you to expose the thing you're most afraid of – that catastrophic fear that holds you back in your co-parenting. That's what we're aiming for, because only then can you deal with it.

I've done this exercise with clients who think their fear is that their ex will shout at them at handovers, or they'll end up arguing about Christmas holidays. I want to encourage you to go even deeper than this, because these aren't necessarily your catastrophic fears, they're often just the top layer. You need to find the fundamental and catastrophic underlying fear, which is something that will sit deeply within you. It may be something like this:

'If I argue with my ex, then they'll take me to court and take my children away from me forever.'

Or, 'If I'm listening and communicating with my ex then people might think that I'm letting them walk all over me and I've got no control over my life, that I'm a complete failure.'

It's deep fears like these that you want to uncover, because, although they might sound extreme or you might feel silly when you write them down or say them out loud, it's these fears that trigger your fight, flight, freeze, fawn and flop responses and stop you from stepping fully into the Co-Parental Loop.

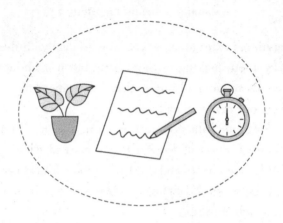

Speed Writing

So, you have a tool to use in the moment when you feel big emotions rising (Finger and Thumb), and now I want to introduce you to another tool that can help reduce your anxiety and manage your emotions in the medium and longer term. The tool is called Speed Writing, and it goes right to the heart of our emotional responses by uncovering your 'catastrophic fear'; the one that puts you into those modes.

Speed Writing is a powerful tool you can use any time you're stuck or unable to move forward or make a decision on any subject, not just co-parenting. It's the tool to use when you're feeling overwhelmed or when it feels difficult to make a decision.

Make sure you have some quiet time to do this task – perhaps about half an hour when you know you won't be interrupted. Grab your notebook or your computer, and at the top of your page write a specific question that will help us uncover our 'catastrophic co-parenting fear'. That question is:

'What's stopping me from stepping fully into the Co-Parental Loop?'

Before you start the speed writing, let me take a minute to explain how to do it.

I'm going to ask you to write for 20 minutes in answer to the question. Make sure you write for the *full* 20 minutes and don't end early. Note down whatever comes up for you. There are no right or wrong answers, and only *you* will see what you write, so there's no need to self-limit or self-censor. Write down everything. Even if you feel silly, or afraid, write it down. Just respond to the question, and even if you think you have nothing to say, write down that you think you don't have anything to say and keep re-reading and thinking about the question! Keep going for the full 20 minutes, because during that time your mind will clear, the fog will lift and your initial thoughts will give way to something deeper and you'll find something important and authentic emerging. You'll strip away the layers of the onion until you start to see more clearly what's holding you back from stepping fully into the Co-Parental Loop with your co-parent.

One of my clients found her fear when she started writing about going into mediation with her ex. He was so good at making her feel small, she was really afraid that she wouldn't be able to stand up for herself and be heard. And when she explored that more deeply, she had a deep-seated fear of not being listened to and, more deeply than that, not being believed. Eventually, she was brave enough to write down that her catastrophic fear was that her son would think that she was a bad mother, that he would never believe what she said, that she wasn't to be trusted.

If writing really isn't for you, then you can do exactly the same but by talking. Record yourself for 20 minutes continuously speaking in answer to the question. You'll get to the same results as long as you keep talking for the whole time.

At the end of the 20 minutes, you can stop writing or recording, or carry on for longer – the only rule is that you need to think about it for *at least* 20 minutes. Remember, only *you* get to know what you've written or recorded; no one gets to judge you on it, so be as honest as you can.

When you have finished, note down your fundamental underlying fear. If you're finding it hard, just ask yourself: is there something you know deep down that you don't want to write down? Is there something that's making you feel angry? What makes you feel as though you want to cry? What makes you afraid? My deepest fear is that my son doesn't want to come back to my house one day. What's yours? Read back through the instructions if you need to. Come back to step two when you're ready.

Go and find your timer, set it for 20 minutes and start writing or speaking. Good luck, and be brave.

How to use Speed Writing practically

Speed Writing is not an easy exercise. It can be emotionally tiring and thought-provoking. Stepping out of your comfort zone and giving it a go is a brave thing to do. What did you learn about yourself from that exercise? What is the fundamental fear that's holding you back in your co-parenting?

Becoming familiar with your catastrophic fear is a powerful mental shift. It will help you manage the strong emotions you may experience towards your ex-partner. It will also help you manage any emotional responses you may feel towards them. Over the next couple of days, be aware of your catastrophic fear and note down how it affects your co-parenting relationship.

By naming your fear, as you've done by uncovering it and writing it down, you move it from the emotional and overwhelming side of your brain to the logical and more practical side of your brain. When you do this, you are able to progressively reduce the hold that the catastrophic fear has over you as you can more easily think about introducing practical approaches to improve your co-parenting.

I want you to have a look around your home and find a small object that you can use to represent your catastrophic fear. You can use a travel clock, a paper weight, even a lipstick. It just needs to be something small and normal. When you've found something, I want you to look at it and name it aloud with your catastrophic fear. You might call it, 'I'll never see my kids again.' Or, 'I'll be out on the streets with no home and no money.' You get the idea. After you've named your object with your fear, I want you to put it out in front of you and see it objectively. This too will engage the more practical and logical part of your brain and help manage the emotional responses that are usually triggered by this fear.

On a piece of paper, while your object is in front of you, I want you to write down two things that you know are true that help alleviate that fear. So, if your fear is, 'I'll never see my kids again,' your truths could be, 'Even though it won't be for as much time, I'll still see my children,' and, 'I'm still their mum/dad/parent, even though they might have a step-parent in their lives now.' We'll call these truths and facts 'fear blasters'.

Truth and facts are the best ways to counter catastrophic fear. Keep a small book with you to jot down things you know are true, to help manage your big feelings and emotions. Refer back to those fear blasters whenever you feel overwhelmed or out of control.

Storing your Speed Writing tool

Let's go back to our outrageous imagery to be able to remember our tools. (See page 16.)

You're going to store Speed Writing, uncovering your catastrophic fear and your fear blasters wherever you feel fear. For me it's my stomach, so I'm going to store it there, imagining butterflies of all different colours, shapes and sizes flying around inside with a net to catch them. Where do you store your fear and your fear blasters, and what will you imagine in there? You also have your small object to help you remember this one.

On your body outline, draw your Speed Writing label now.

KEEP KIDS IN THE LOOP

Through my work I've found that children with two homes usually like to know where they are going to be, what they are going to be doing and when they are going to be doing it. It can be very grounding even for young children to know in advance what's coming up. As well as letting them know whose house they will be at and when, and if there are any changes this week, it's good for their stability to know where they will be for key events like Christmas. It's also important to let them know if they'll miss anything significant and tell them how you'll manage that. So if they're not with you for your birthday, tell them that you'll celebrate it the day before when they are with you. Be structured and neutral in how you tell them, without making it emotional, to help them take it in their stride. Some people find their children prefer it if there is a shared calendar that they can refer to themselves. Some parents put a schedule for the week on the fridge. Talk to your child, if they're old enough, to find out what will best support them.

Self-Management Avatar

We've seen already that being more mindful and understanding of what causes us to go into a five Fs response can positively impact our children, but how do we take it one step further and be able to manage how we interact with our co-parent on a daily basis in spite of these feelings? To do this we need to learn to do something called self-managing, which basically means we need to be able to recognise our feelings, understand the effect they're having on us and stop ourselves responding in a negative or unhelpful way to a situation. Having the ability to regulate your emotions and behaviours is critical to be able to build a better co-parenting relationship.

We are going to create something called a Self-Management Avatar which gives us greater control over our emotional responses. An avatar is a character we create who has exaggerated qualities and steps up to help us when we need this greater control. So, your avatar could be a warrior, a superhero, or someone in real life you look up to. It gets us into a powerful headspace and is a really useful ally on our co-parent journey. Stay with me – even if you think this sounds a bit 'out there', this is an incredibly powerful tool and can be game-changing.

When we build our avatar, it's important to create as much detail as possible. We imagine what it looks like, hear how it sounds, and know what words it uses. Our avatar has an 'energy' about it that's useful to us. So, for example, someone with a Yoda avatar from *Star Wars* can feel the wise energy of Yoda and experience that when they need it. In co-parenting, we need a Self-Management Avatar. Having someone wise and controlled by your side is a game-changer for people in terms of how they interact with their co-parent. In my coaching practice we've seen people build avatars from George Clooney to Queen Elizabeth II, from a Buddhist monk to a panda bear to a favourite aunt. It's your avatar; you get to choose what works for you.

You'll need to be in a safe and quiet space to do this with your notebook and it will take you about 15 minutes. So, get comfortable and hold off on any questions and thoughts you may have around this tool and simply follow the instructions. Let your imagination take the lead if you are able to. Don't let your brain tell you that it's silly. The more you can relax into it, the better.

Take a deep breath in for four seconds. Hold it for seven seconds and exhale for eight seconds. Do this two or three times. I'd like you to imagine yourself in a place that feels completely safe for you. It could be on a beach, or in a meadow with the wind rustling through your hair. It might be on the top of a mountain, or in your garden. Just make it up if you prefer, and imagine you can sense it or see it.

Now I'd like you to think of a person, or a type of person or even an animal, who's able to remain calm in any situation. Someone who's in control of their emotions. Just bring that person or animal to mind now. Take as long as you need to do that. Read the following questions and take some time in between each one to really think about the answers. (You'll be making notes at the end of the exercise, but if it's easier for you to make notes as you go along, please feel free to do that.)

- Who or what are they?
- What do they look like?

- What are they wearing?
- Are they standing or sitting?
- What do they sound like?
- Is their voice calm? Is it strong?
- Do they speak a lot?
- What do you notice about them?

This is your avatar. Greet one another and notice what it feels like to be near them.

Ask your avatar:

- What do I need to know about regulating my emotions and staying calm?
- What do I need to know about regulating my emotions and staying calm with my co-parent?
- How can I access you when I need you?
- And finally, ask your avatar – what is your name?

This is your Self-Management Avatar. Bring them to mind and talk with them whenever you need. Stay in the visualisation, thank them for coming and know that you'll see them whenever you call on them. It's time to leave the visualisation now.

Take a deep breath, wiggle your toes, and come back to the present.

In the place where you're keeping all your co-parenting notes, jot down the answers to the questions above. Write as much detail as you can, as this is what brings your avatar to life.

How to use your Self-Management Avatar

Great stuff – you've created your avatar! If you don't find visualisations easy and you only got a bit of information, that's completely fine. Just work with what you have, think of who you want by your side on this co-parenting journey and imagine them right there with you. You can build your avatar however it suits you best. Now let me explain how you use it.

Your avatar is there to protect you. It helps you to have a handle on yourself during stressful situations. It gives you strength and perspective and allows you to respond as your best self. When you use your Self-Management Avatar, you'll notice that conversations that might have become heated in the past no longer do so.

Your avatar is always there for you. Whenever you meet your co-parent, you're going to take it with you. You can build a strong connection with the idea of your avatar. Or, if it's easier for you to imagine, its energy. You can step into this energy whenever you choose. It will support you and give you whatever qualities you need. If you need calm, your avatar will give you calm. If you need courage, it will give you that, too.

To begin with, I want you to practise calling up your avatar at least twice a day, let's say every morning and evening after you've brushed your teeth. Close your eyes for a few seconds and bring it to mind. Really visualise the details. Go back to your notes if that's helpful. Recall the energy and feelings you've associated with it and stand shoulder to shoulder with it for a moment, drawing on those feelings and bringing them inside yourself.

Once you've got used to this, I want you to practise calling up your Self-Management Avatar during day-to-day situations. It might be when you're getting impatient in a queue. Or when you're on hold on the phone or stuck in traffic. You can always ask your avatar how you should respond to something. When you're fully comfortable with it, meet your co-parent with your avatar by your side. Your Self-Management Avatar will enable you to manage your feelings, your language and your emotions in conversations with your co-parent.

Always make sure your avatar is close by. And remember, practice breathes life into your avatar. The more you practise imagining it, asking it questions and listening to the advice it gives, the stronger the connection between you and your avatar will be, and the more natural it will feel to ask for its support when you need it.

Storing your Self-Management Avatar

Let's find a place to hang the avatar on our body to help us re-member it (see page 16). Bring your avatar to mind now. Since we stand shoulder to shoulder with our avatar, that's where we'll keep it – on our shoulder. Imagine your avatar standing right next to you with your shoulders touching. If you're using your body outline, then label your Self-Management Avatar now.

The Self-Management Avatar exercise might feel a little strange to put into practice at first. But I've seen the impact on parents time and again when they use their avatars in their co-parenting conversations.

Laura and Steven went through The Co-Parenting Method as they were struggling to manage their emotions when parenting together after a tricky break-up. Learning the Self-Management Avatar tool was a real turning point for them. Laura tells us why:

'Our relationship was tricky for a long time and when it finally exploded one day it turned out very quickly that both Steven and I had had affairs. We'd also been lying to each other for a long time that we still cared for each other, when honestly neither of us could stand the other one. We were both only staying because of the kids. Things got very heated very fast. We were awful to each other, vile in fact. I would say awful things to him about how he wasn't fit to be a father. He would call me a trollop in front of the children. Though thankfully they were too young to know what it meant. We made no effort to manage our emo-tions; they were running wild. We just didn't know how to work together. It was a hard time and when I think about what messages my children were picking up, I feel ashamed.

'What I didn't realise, until we went through The Co-Parenting Method, was how afraid I was of losing out on time with my children, of not seeing them grow up, of missing out on key moments of their lives. Realising this forced me to acknowledge that the way I was being with Steven was so emotional because I was so afraid. And it led me to think that it was highly likely that the same thing was going on for him. Thinking that Steven might be afraid, and understanding that I was afraid, immediately made me less reactive, but it wasn't until we built our avatars that things took a big step forward. We both knew we were in character [Laura's avatar was Kate Adie, the former newsreader, and Steven's was his neighbour George, who he would see calmly talking to his plants. Laura's was very straight-talking and unemotional and Steven's was very calm and serene], but somehow that didn't matter. It was such a relief to know we could have a conversation about the kids without it turning hateful.'

I can't emphasise enough how quickly our strong emotions can derail our co-parenting and therefore how important it is that we know how to manage them. By understanding the emotions we are feeling and by being able to name them, we become much better equipped to deal with them more effectively and stop them from having a negative impact on our co-parenting. By taking responsibility for managing these emotions using the three tools we've learned in this step, we will feel less overwhelmed, be more able to positively communicate with our co-parent and reduce the negative impact we have on our children when we have big emotional responses. Moving forward, taking responsibility for how your emotions impact your co-parenting is critical. It's a hard thing to do, but it will make a very big difference to how your child experiences their parents working together. I'm not asking you to not have those emotions, simply to manage how visible they are. When you can do this, you can create a space to co-parent well together.

Having two parents who can manage what they're feeling about each other and still show up as parents is vital for our children's short- and long-term wellbeing. As parents we have a responsibility to look after our children, and that may mean we have to do hard things like be respectful and polite to someone who we don't like anymore. I've seen and worked with parents who are viciously angry towards each other. It's not easy to reach parents when they're in such high states of emotion. One of the best ways to do this is by showing them the long-term impact on their children, which is why we have the Photographs tool early on. If this sounds familiar to you, please go back to your Photographs tool as many times as you need to. That's what it's there for.

When parents are angry it can be really hard for them to accept any responsibility for co-parenting not working. It's much easier to blame everything on their co-parent. However hard this might be to hear, it takes two people to create a conflict, and we all have some responsibility to take, even if it's only a little. Managing our emotions around our co-parent is the best way through the conflict. You've seen, and will see, in the stories throughout the book, that it's possible to do this even though it's really hard.

Not being able to make decisions, trying to win against your ex, conflict, and disrespecting your child's other parent are the reasons that divorce, separation and beyond are potentially damaging to our children. It's never easy to get divorced or to separate from someone who you have children with, but if it's done respectfully, being mindful of the impact on your kids, then it can be much less harmful for them. During and following your separation, if you can put your children front and centre, if you can understand your own fears, be conscious of your powerful emotions and the subsequent fight, flight, freeze, fawn and flop responses, if you can avoid stepping into these emotional states, and if you can remain as much as you can in the Co-Parental Loop, then you're providing your kids with a much safer environment to grow up in.

Let's move to our summary to help us remember what we've looked at.

- In step two we've looked at what it means to be in heightened states of emotion and we've thought about the fight, flight, freeze, fawn and flop responses that these strong emotions bring about.
- I've talked about how these emotions make us feel and the impact they have on us as co-parents, and on our children.
- You understood why these emotions are difficult to control and how we can better manage them.
- You learned the Finger and Thumb tool to help you step out of fight, flight, freeze, fawn or flop mode.
- You used the Speed Writing tool to answer the question, 'What's stopping me from stepping fully into the Co-Parental Loop?'
- You uncovered your catastrophic fear about co-parenting with your ex-partner and you have two truths to help you counter the fear and bring you back into a place of practicality and action.
- You also built an amazing Self-Management Avatar to help you be in control of your emotions around your ex.

Storing your tools

We'll store your new tools on your body now. The Finger and Thumb tool we store in our unusual finger and thumb. Our Speed Writing tool for uncovering your catastrophic fear and your fear blasters are stored wherever you feel fear. For me it's the butterflies in my stomach and the net that catches them. You also have your small object to help you remember this one. You stand shoulder to shoulder with your avatar, so that's where we'll store them. If you're labelling your body outline, you can do that now.

It's so much easier to blame difficult situations on other people than to look at how we are contributing to them ourselves. I'm going to challenge you to look deeply at yourself and notice what you're doing that is inflaming your co-parenting situation. Remember, we can't change other people, we can only change ourselves. I know that's a tough thing to do. And it's one to remember to circle back to if you find that you're getting stuck. Be kind with yourself when you're doing this. There is no perfect parent or co-parent. We just need to be aware that we can bring about positive change. Another useful thing to do is to be able to see our co-parent's perspective, just one of the things we'll be looking at in step three.

We can't change other people, we can only change ourselves.

Setting Boundaries and Recognising Your Co-Parent's Perspective

It's good to see you in step three. You've taken another step along The Co-Parenting Method and you're doing great. How are you feeling so far? What's working well for you? This is tricky work sometimes, but keep practicing and it gets easier. Practice makes progress.

So far we have looked at moving into a long-term mindset and managing strong emotions. Now we're going to turn our attention to the importance of looking at things from our co-parent's perspective and then how to set boundaries and recognise our co-parent's boundaries.

Seeing things from our co-parent's perspective is essential for building a collaborative Co-Parental Loop (see page 45). When you can take into account someone else's viewpoint, you get to see different sides of the same topic. This can help you get a sense of the bigger picture. In co-parenting, being able to see the bigger picture is so important as it helps your child feel as though both their parents have a handle on everything that's going on, not just what's happening in one house. It also helps your children believe that they still have two parents who can work together. At the same time, it's also just as important to have boundaries and know where the boundaries lie in co-parenting. Having boundaries makes us nice and secure, which means it's easier to feel comfortable enough to co-parent. When you're within your personal boundaries you will be comfortable with what's going on. Outside of your personal boundaries you won't be. It's exactly the same with how we make others feel too. If we cross someone else's boundaries we will make them uncomfortable. Being able to recognise that is another really important factor in helping our co-parenting along. When you know where the boundaries lie with each other, you're much more able to collaborate in appropriate and forward-looking ways.

You're going to learn three practical tools in this step. The first one is to help you do hard things, the second will help you to see things from your co-parent's perspective and the third will help you set clear boundaries between you and your co-parent so you know exactly how and when to interact and when to leave things be. Sometimes this step can feel challenging or difficult. Just go with it if you can, there's no need to put pressure on yourself. You can always revisit anything in the book whenever you need to – taking breaks is completely fine!

Why Is It Important to Be Able to Recognise Our Co-Parent's Perspective?

The first thing we need to acknowledge is that the biggest reason that it's important to see things from our ex's perspective is because it's one of the quickest ways to reduce conflict. When conflict is reduced, communication improves and helps build the co-parent relationship; this reduces those heightened states of emotion and most importantly supports the Co-Parental Loop, which increases our children's emotional stability.

I get that you might not want to see things from your co-parent's perspective. That you may be in conflict and the idea of giving them time and space to share something with you can make you feel powerless. But I want to demonstrate to you why it's so important.

When we acknowledge our co-parent perspective, we can start to get a more rounded picture of our children's lives and needs. We become more open-minded and available to new thoughts, which in turn has a positive impact on reducing conflict and improving communication (more on this in step four). When we're communicating better, we can be more collaborative. This reduces stress and worry for each co-parent – it helps us out of high states of emotion and back on to firmer ground. Communicating well and taking into consideration your co-parent's perspective about your child also reinforces your Co-Parental Loop and keeps your child feeling really safe and upheld. Keep in mind the long-term goal of wanting to create a lovely, safe environment for your child. This will really help.

Ideally both you and your co-parent will get to a place where you can both see each other's perspective, but here's the trick. Even when just one of you learns to do it, it goes a long way to stopping conflict between you escalating. How is this possible? Well, I'll explain later in this step, which is why I want you to keep reading.

Why Is It Hard to See Things from Our Co-Parent's Perspective?

You may be thinking about skipping this step. You may be thinking that you already understand your co-parent's perspective. Or you may just flat out refuse to even want to acknowledge that they even *have* a perspective. You might completely resent the fact that you even have to do this co-parenting thing with them. Stop. Don't go anywhere. I hear you. I see you. It's OK to think all of those things. And I want you to read this step because there are insights here that you really need to know.

When you're in a relationship that is working well, we see things from each other's perspective naturally. We might book a restaurant for dinner and check that it has things on the menu that our partner would like to eat. We might love rock music but our partner may love jazz, so we don't automatically book a hard rock gig to take them to. You think it through and adjust how you discuss things when you know someone might think differently about something than you.

When you're doing that with someone that you don't like anymore, the temptation is to dehumanise them, to not care about what they think because you're hurt or angry, or because you want a clean break. It's easier to be in the short-term mindset and discount them, rather than in the long-term mindset where you need to co-parent with them. If you take into account their perspective, you're making a long-term mindset move, and that's hugely important.

So, if the benefits are so great, why can it be so hard to think about things from our co-parent's point of view? Let's zoom out for a moment. In life, it's quite natural that we see things from our own perspective. We tend to see the world through our own filters. That's a normal part of being human. How we are raised and the people we are connected to play a big part too. We like being around people who are similar to us. It's comforting and safe and fun. Sometimes we have disagreements with people in our work and in our lives, but usually our main relationships are with people who are like-minded. These important relationships can usually echo what you think about things, including after you separate. It will be well-meaning, but they can also entrench your point of view, which can make it harder to see the bigger perspective. 'Confirmation bias' is a natural human behaviour, but if we aren't aware of it, it can make things pretty tricky in co-parenting. Confirmation bias is when we look for information that confirms what we already believe and makes us disregard evidence that doesn't support our opinions. It also means it can be really hard to see things from other perspectives and consider other viewpoints. When we're separating or when we are disagreeing with our co-parent, the people around us can agree with us and not challenge us to see things differently. This can fuel our desire to be right and to win and it can keep us in the short-term mindset. I first came across the idea of seeing things from another perspective through the work of CRR Global, an incredible relationship systems coaching company. Years later, as I was developing my own methodology, I was also reminded of my work in the international space between governments and NGOs about how important different perspectives are in moving forward away from conflict.

Separation from our partner (not always, but often) can be caused by key differences of opinion, and those differences can often be exacerbated as we move towards and beyond separation. We may be in high states of emotion or angry or resentful with our ex. We may not trust them anymore. We may think they are incapable or useless. We may think they've checked out. All of this pushes your perspective further away from your co-parent's, which in turn will affect how you work together as parents. I often see co-parents who have become entrenched in their own perspective, unable or unwilling to take on board another viewpoint either because it can feel safe and familiar to stick with what you know or because it can be convenient to take the opposite view of your co-parent when you're trying to win. Sometimes our position is backed up by the other important people in our lives, and this can help embed our position.

Take a moment to reflect on your own situation. How right do you think you are? How wrong do you think your co-parent is? What do you notice about yourself when you think about this? How is your breathing? Have you tensed up? If you want to note anything down in your notebook, please do so.

Listening to our ex-partner and giving them a voice may be the last thing we want to do because it can feel like we're letting them win. But we're not. Listening, hearing and seeing things from their perspective gives us information and knowledge, and in this there is strength because we become more able to guide a situation. The very act of listening helps uphold the Co-Parental Loop (see page 45).

It might be that your co-parenting is fairly relaxed and straightforward and you feel completely comfortable with seeing things from your co-parent's perspective. That's great, and so important for your children. Keep reading, however, because understanding the importance of seeing things from your co-parent's perspective will be essential if something changes. If you encounter a bump in the road along the way, it's good for you to have done that thinking so you have the right tools to be able to get past those bumps.

Several years ago, I was working with a woman called Zara. She was a senior manager at a well-known bank. She was powerful, and she was also angry. She tells us about the first time we talked about her co-parent's perspective:

'When I first heard the idea that my ex had a valid perspective, I was furious! So furious that I nearly fired Marcie! My ex had lied to me throughout the whole of our relationship and I'd had no idea until he told me he was leaving. I remember that I wouldn't even refer to him by his name in our sessions because I was so mad. He had betrayed me and I was shocked. I actually shouted at Marcie in the session that I would never listen to anything he said because he was a moron and he didn't deserve to see his kids. I didn't care at that point if a tree fell on his head. I was hurting and I wanted everyone to know about it. In my very strong opinion, he didn't deserve any access to them and I wasn't going to back down.'

If you're feeling like Zara, even just a little bit, then please read on. It's completely understandable that you may not want your ex in your life; you may really not want to have anything to do with them ever again. But you can't make them disappear. You have children together. And to be a co-parent we must consciously and deliberately acknowledge that our ex-partner is firstly still a parent, and secondly, has a perspective. By doing this you're taking a big step towards improving co-parent communications. And let me remind you that you don't need to be friends, and you're not giving away any of your power by doing this. We'll talk more about this later on in step four.

To be a co-parent, we must consciously and deliberately acknowledge that our ex-partner has a perspective.

We benefit from doing this too

Let's hear a life-changing example from Shauna. Shauna is mum to Billy and has been divorced from James for three years. Here she recalls the moment she first started seeing things from James's perspective:

'I remember really well the moment I started to see things differently. I was in the park and I saw a dad with his young kids and they were just messing around and having loads of fun. This was when I realised that whatever bad feeling there was between James and me, he loved Billy and wanted the best for him, just like I did. It might sound like a small thing when I say it now, but for me it was a really big shift – I was upset every time Billy went to James's. But when I started to see things from his dad's perspective, I saw that he loved Billy too.

'When I realised that, and looked at things from his point of view, I knew without any doubt that James felt the same way about Billy as me. And I started to accept, even embrace, Billy's relationship with his dad rather than fighting it. It made his moves between houses easier for me. It removed some of the competition from our parenting. And I could see Billy was happier too.'

Shauna managed to make that leap of perspective, and that was a key co-parenting moment for her. It completely changed her relationship with James. She didn't suddenly become great friends with him, but she did start to respect his relationship with Billy and recognise its importance for her son. She started to find the times when Billy wasn't with her easier to deal with.

When you accept that your ex loves your child as much as you do, co-parenting becomes easier.

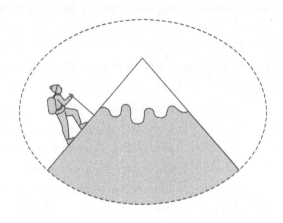

PRACTICAL TOOL #6

The Summit

The idea of something is often harder than the reality.

Before I show you an easy way to see things from someone else's perspective I want to acknowledge that you might be feeling a bit uncomfortable or fearful about that. To help with that, I'm going to teach you the Summit tool. This is a great tool that you can use in all areas of your life, and it's also another brilliant one to teach kids who are nervous about trying something new.

The Summit tool helps us understand that, even though it might be really hard to imagine doing something right now, the idea of something is often harder than the reality. Let me remind you of the Speed Writing we did in step two (see page 68). There we learned about catastrophic fear, and this idea can be applied to lots of things. As humans we often get sucked into catastrophic ways of thinking, and when we do that it becomes hard to see things from another perspective. It can also stop us from trying something different. Trying new approaches can open up new pathways for us that we didn't see before. The Summit tool will give you a practical way to do that so when you need to see things from your co-parent's perspective, you'll feel more secure about doing it.

So please grab your notebook and a cup of tea if you need it. Take a deep breath and just do Finger and Thumb for a moment to help ground you in the moment.

In your notebook I want you to draw a two-sided mountain. At the bottom left of the mountain, draw a stick person. This is you.

One third of the way down the right-hand side of the mountain, I want you to draw a line. This line is whatever new place or scary destination you need to get to. In this case, next to your line, we're going to write: 'Seeing things from my co-parent's perspective'. We are going to go on a journey. We need to get you over the peak of the mountain and a little way down the other side.

Here's the theory behind this exercise. When we don't know what something looks like, when we can't properly imagine it, or see it, it can make us fearful. The reason I use the idea of a mountain, drawn in this very simplistic way, is because I can get across the idea that we can't see over the top or round the other side of the mountain to the thing that is making us fearful. But if we can climb over the top of the mountain and experience whatever is on the other side, even just for a short time, then it becomes manageable. It's the not knowing and not having experienced something that leads us to make all kinds of assumptions about what it will be like. And when it's something we don't want to do, then those assumptions won't be positive.

If I tell you that you just need to visit the other side of the mountain a couple of times, to see what it's like, how does that feel? If I say, you can always come back to your starting point if you need to, does that help a bit? When we know we can always come back to our starting point, it can help the brain understand that this isn't forever. When the brain thinks something is all or nothing it can be quite hard to convince it to do something. But if it's just trying something on to see, then it's much more likely to be able to do that.

The other piece of information you need is to do with that line that's a third of the way down the other side of the mountain. There's a reason that this line isn't further down. If you over-extend yourself, if you do too much, if your new brave place is just too far out of your comfort zone, then the brain can go into panic mode. The line is there as your guide, to help you understand how far to go. If you go too far over and need to come back to the safe side of the mountain, you can also do that.

In the scenario of seeing things from your co-parent's perspective, we don't want you to take on board their perspective to the exclusion of everything else. Your perspective still has to be in there, and so does the perspective of your children, as well as an awareness of the bigger picture.

Try it for size

The way I want you to practise this is by doing it twice. Firstly, by thinking of something that is not to do with co-parenting. Do you have to do a work-related project that you keep putting off because you think you can't do it? Is there a physical challenge you want to do but don't feel brave enough to try it? Is there a hard conversation you need to have that you're putting off? Whatever it is, I want you to draw your triangle, and place whatever you're putting off a third of the way down the right-hand side. And now I want you to imagine yourself walking up that mountain. You get to the top and you know that down the other side is the thing you're putting off doing. Just imagine yourself peering over the top of the mountain. There it is, can you see it? What does it look like from up here? Take one more step over the edge of the mountain towards it. Hold on to the rail if you want to (yes, you can imagine a rail on the side of the mountain, it's your mountain!). Edge a little bit closer.

The next thing I want you to do is to imagine doing whatever it is you've written down. Imagine having the hard conversation, imagine starting to train for that physical challenge, imagine delivering the presentation. Whatever it is, just think it through calmly. When you're doing that, you're standing a third of the way down the mountainside and you're still

OK. All you're doing now is just allowing your brain to entertain the idea that it's possible. And that's all.

Now you've climbed your mountain and you've managed to go over the peak, you've seen and thought through what's on the other side. I know these things can feel daunting, but you did it, and by thinking it through once it becomes easier to do the next time, and eventually you can move from thinking to doing. You might try putting that scenario into practice in real life if the challenge doesn't feel too great.

Now I want you to do the same exercise, but imagining seeing something from your co-parent's perspective. It might be a conversation you need to have with your co-parent, you might be needing to challenge them on something they've done but you're concerned about how they will respond to you. Perhaps you need a date swap but are worried about what they will ask for in return. Whatever it is, remember this is all about getting more comfortable with doing hard things. Have a go now. Come back when you're done.

I want you to hold on to your mountain climbing gear as we move into the next part of this step and use it to help us be brave enough to see things from our co-parent's perspective.

Storing your Summit tool

You can keep the Summit tool at the very top of your head – perhaps you have a flag poking out of there to remind you of that. How vibrant is your flag? What colour is it? Is it bright, is it patterned? Bring it to mind now and remember the more outrageous it is, the easier it will be for you to remember it.

FILL IN THE GAPS

When your kids come back to their home with you it's really important to think about how you bring them up to speed with what's been going on in your house while they've not been there, especially after an extended time. Life events that become family reference points still happen even if your child isn't with you, and it's important that they know what's gone on, so they feel fully integrated and a part of things in your home. What this isn't, is a chance to make your home sound better than their other home. To make children feel as though they are missing out when they're with you is a deliberate attempt to sabotage their wellbeing. Instead, it's about calmly sitting them down when there's not lots of things going on, and asking them if it's OK to share with them some of the things that happened, because they were missed. You can reassure them that you were pleased they have had a lovely time at their other house. (If for some reason they've not had a good time, now might not be the moment to fill in the gaps – you need to judge the situation.) Maybe you want to scroll through some photos that you've taken so they can visualise what you've done. Make it about the key events that have happened rather than a running commentary about walking the dog and going to the shops. When my son comes back from his summer holiday at his dad's house, I run through in my head what significant things he's missed that we might refer to and I usually tell him over breakfast the next morning when it's just the two of us. It's a very light touch approach but it makes him feel included. Ensuring your children never feel on the outside is key for them feeling wanted and loved.

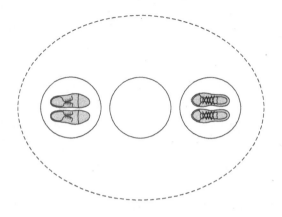

Standing in Your Co-Parent's Shoes

I've spent the last few pages talking about why it's so important to be able to bring in your co-parent's perspective, but how do we do that? The Standing in Your Co-Parent's Shoes tool will show you how to open up to the perspective of your co-parent and understand what's driving their parenting approach.

One of the great things about this exercise is that your co-parent is not required – you do it on your own! You get to see an issue from your perspective and your ex's perspective without them needing to be there to have a conversation with. You'll also get to see a bigger perspective of what's going on for you as co-parents and that's the perspective of your co-parenting relationship. That might sound a bit odd, but it's a trick to help your brain see the bigger picture.

To do this exercise, please find a quiet place where you won't be disturbed and grab your pen and paper. You know the drill! You'll need about 20 minutes to go through it and you'll be getting up and moving around if possible.

Firstly . . .

Firstly, I want to remind you that this is a great way for you to try to see things from your co-parent's perspective because it can't escalate into an argument – it's just you doing it! I want you to think of something in your co-parenting relationship that you and your co-parent are stuck on at the moment, a topic where there's some (but not too much) conflict. It could be something like how you're communicating with each other during drop-offs or your decision on what school would be best for your child. If you are thinking of a big topic, which piece of that could you focus on? So if you're thinking of 'our co-parenting' as a topic, narrow it down slightly. Perhaps it's how you make decisions together, or perhaps it's your general communication.

Some specific topics we work on with our clients are:

- 'Charlie's schooling'
- 'How we speak to each other in front of Eliza'
- 'Our different ideas around how much TV Akbar can watch'
- 'Prioritising Jacob's homework'

Spend a moment now bringing to mind the issue you'd like to discuss with your co-parent, and if you want to write it down, please go ahead. You should now have a specific issue you want to resolve with your co-parent.

Before you start, you can do the Finger and Thumb tool if you would like to, to ensure you are in a good frame of mind.

Secondly . . .

1. I want you to imagine three coloured circles on the floor about two metres apart. One is yellow, one is blue and one is green. The imaginary yellow circle is where you're going to go and stand and you're going to imagine your co-parent standing opposite you in the blue circle. Don't worry about the green circle for now.

2. When you're ready to start, please go and actually stand on your

imaginary yellow circle and imagine your co-parent in front of you. Look towards them and try to imagine that they're really there. It might feel silly or odd. Just go with it! There's no pressure here. Just try it on for size.

3. Now you're going to talk out loud about the topic you've written down. Make sure you start each sentence with either 'my brain tells me' or 'my heart tells me'. We use this phrasing specifically to bring in the different sides of our brain. 'My heart tells me' will help you look at something from an emotional perspective, and 'my brain tells me' will help you see things from a pragmatic and practical perspective. It's important we use both as this is when we can get to a more balanced outlook. Look at your (imaginary) co-parent and tell them everything that you know rationally and emotionally about this topic. Do it respectfully and do it out loud. I'm right here when you're done to help you through the next bit.

4. When you've finished saying what you need to say, I want you to physically move to stand where your co-parent was and really imagine that you're them. Stand as they stand. Be open-minded here – I know this might feel strange, and you might be angry and not want to do this right now, but keep going. Let's see what happens. If you can, please make sure you physically move between the two circles – the act of moving helps you shift your perspective. So you should now be standing on the blue circle, being your imaginary co-parent, and you're going to imagine you are talking back to yourself on the yellow circle.

5. Now, from your co-parent's perspective, I want you to respond to everything you just heard yourself say. You're still going to use the phrases 'my brain tells me' (rationally) or 'my heart tells me' (emotionally) before each point you make. Respond and say what you need to say. Some of you will find this difficult. When I do this with parents many will say, 'Well, my ex won't bother to reply,' or, 'I don't know what they will say,' or they will turn towards blaming

their ex before trying to get into their perspective. This is normal. I really want to encourage you past those natural responses to get into your ex's perspective and think about what might be going on for them and how to respond. Be open to new information. Remember, it's just you doing it, so although you're stepping into your co-parent's shoes, they aren't there. You've got this. Have a go – it doesn't need to be perfect. See what your co-parent has to say. You'll know when it's time to finish because there will be a natural pause, just like there is in a conversation with two people. At that point it's time to move back into your perspective.

6. Keep moving back and forth between your perspective and your co-parent's perspective a few times until either there is nothing else to say on this topic or much of the heat goes out of it. Usually two or three times in each perspective is enough. You may need more.

Thirdly . . .

Take a breath. How did you find the first part of the exercise? Did the heat leave the topic? Or did you exhaust it? How did it feel to be looking at the problem from your co-parent's perspective? Did you feel any shift in your mood as you did the exercise? Was it awkward or difficult? If it was, that's OK, it's normal for it to be challenging. Whatever it felt like for you, this first part of the exercise shows us that there may be good reasons for looking at a problem through a different lens.

For the next part of the exercise, please now go and stand in the green circle. You can think of this circle as 'the bigger picture'. Imagine this bigger picture knows everything about the relationship between you and your co-parent and deeply cares about you both. It cares that the co-parent relationship works for both of you as well as for your children. If it helps you to imagine yourself rising up and looking down on you both as co-parents, then feel free to spend a moment doing that.

You're going to now assume the role of the co-parent relationship. (And

I promise you, for the whole book, this is as whacky as it gets. But trust me. I've taken many people through this exercise and it's really interesting what happens in this next bit.) As the co-parent relationship, you're going to answer these four questions.

1. What are your emotions as you see these co-parents discussing their topic?
2. What is it about their relationship that is keeping these co-parents stuck?
3. What do you need them both to do in order to be successful?
4. What do the children of these two people need them to do differently?

Answer the four questions now before reading on – if you want, jot some notes down to help you remember. All of this information will be useful to you as you start to work on your co-parent relationship. Responses that I hear a lot from parents are that the co-parent relationship feels sad that parents can't communicate well; that the relationship can see what what's keeping them stuck is that parents have become entrenched and unwilling to look at things differently. Often the co-parenting relationship will be able to see clearly that parents need to be respectful, be calm and communicate; and when asked about what the children need their parents to do differently it almost always says it needs them to move aside from the conflict and work together. When you ask the co-parenting relationship the four questions in relation to your topic, your responses may well be different to those. The information that comes back to you from the co-parent relationship will be neutral and it won't take sides. There's a lot of value in that because it will help you see much more clearly and in a nice, balanced way, how to approach the topic.

Before we finish this exercise, there are four questions I have for you to think about. Make some notes to help you remember your answers.

1. What's new for you now as a result of standing in your co-parent's shoes?
2. Think about at least two practical actions you can take to help with the issue you have just discussed with your co-parent. What are the actions and when will you take them by?
3. What do your children need you to do differently to help resolve the problem you have just discussed with your co-parent?
4. How will you put that into action?

I know that for some people it's hard to get into the perspective of their co-parent, but it's important for our children that we practise doing it. Whenever you have a difficult topic to discuss with your co-parent, you can use this tool and the questions I've given you. Do it before you speak to you co-parent in real life. It can help to make the conversation run more smoothly.

The two practical actions you decided upon might be hard for you to do. But please remember that these actions are based in positive and collaborative co-parenting. And the reason we do these things is so our children feel safe and secure, resilient and happy.

Storing your Standing in Your Co-Parent's Shoes tool

We're going to store the Standing in Your Co-Parent's Shoes tool in our shoes. Let's imagine we're wearing very memorable shoes – perhaps they are sparkly shoes, or clown shoes, or shoes with ridiculous heels. How you imagine them is up to you, but please imagine something unusual, vivid and colourful that will be easy for you to remember.

When Zara (our senior manager from the bank, who nearly hit the roof when we talked about her ex's perspective) *did* do the exercise, she found it really hard to remain in her co-parent's shoes. But she persevered, and what resulted was really valuable.

'Moving between circles on the floor, between my perspective and my ex's, was not easy. I found it so hard to get into his point of view and really difficult to be polite and considered, even though he wasn't there! Getting into the perspective of the co-parent relationship was even harder. But I did persist and I came up with two actions. My topic was communicating at handovers. And I agreed to smile and say something mundane but polite and certainly not sarcastic! I didn't want to do any of it but I understood that it would have a positive impact on my son if I did do it and how it would be less positive for him if I didn't. Marcie asked me to try them just once. And I did. From that seed of neutrality, unbelievably, a respectful co-parenting relationship has grown. I would never have believed it. But a little bit of being polite by me has made the whole thing 100 times easier.'

Understanding Boundaries

Boundaries are present in all relationships in varying degrees. They are in our relationships with our loved ones, with our work colleagues, with our children and even with our pets! They are there with the people who we hire to help us, builders, cleaners, electricians, and they are there with the people who hire us to help too. Boundaries keep us safe; they are the things that we define ourselves by and the red lines or markers in the sand that we don't want to or let others cross. We have physical boundaries, when and how we let people touch us. We have boundaries about how we talk with people – you probably wouldn't walk up to a stranger and tell them something very personal about yourself. We don't let our kids paint the walls red, or walk on the sofa with muddy boots. Our pets aren't allowed to relieve themselves inside the house. You get the picture! Boundaries are different for all of us and your own will change depending on who you're with. It's important to have them because they mean that we can go through life knowing what feels OK and when to walk away from a situation because it doesn't feel OK.

Having boundaries with your co-parent is crucial. Your relationship has been redefined from being partners and parents to only being parents and it's because of this we need to make absolutely sure we get the boundaries right. Boundaries can be often be blurred when we're in the early stages of separation, particularly if you are both still living under one roof. As we unpick the stitching of our relationship and the infrastructure we have built around it, it can take time to rethink what your boundaries with your ex and for your co-parenting now need to be. Even if you're in separate houses already, the boundaries around how you interact will need to be set. For those who have chosen nesting arrangements (where the children stay in the house and the parents move in and out according to when it's their time with the children), boundaries become really critical. However you're living, respecting each other's boundaries is one of the most important things you can do to establish a mutual trust.

Boundaries can often be blurred when we're in the early stages of separation.

Parents Anita and Julia provide a really useful example of boundaries not being met in the early stages of separation. Julia tells us what used to happen:

'When Anita came to pick up our daughters from my house, she always stepped into the house as soon as I answered the door. This really used to wind me up. My house used to be our family home, Anita and I had our children in that house, and she still considered it her right to just walk right in, especially if the girls were there.

'But we had sorted out the finances and this was my house and she had her house. I didn't just walk into her space, I would always wait to be invited in. I found it really intrusive. She was always quite assertive and it made me feel as though she was trying to be more powerful than me, putting me in my place, by just stepping over the threshold into my home.

'I asked her several times to wait until I had invited her in, but she just laughed at me like I was being a silly girl. She said it was important for the girls to see us both in the same space.'

While Anita is right that children need to see their parents interact and be able to be in the same room together, it's not right that she should decide unilaterally how and when that happens. By not asking Julia's permission to step into her home, Anita was making Julia defensive and less able to collaborate in a trusting co-parenting space.

Setting the boundaries and rules for handovers is really important to keep things flowing as co-parents, as this is the place that your children will see you together the most.

HOW TO HANDLE HANDOVERS

Here are some quick tips to help make handovers smoother, while still maintaining your boundaries. Please remember that you should only follow this if it feels safe for you.

1. Open the door with a smile and wait at the door with a smile. Even if it's a bit fake – let your kids see that being around their other parent is OK.
2. Wait to be invited in or, if it's your home, invite your ex inside. The hallway is fine, they don't need a tour of the house.
3. Let your children feel able to show their other parent their bedroom. This is really important for your child and it's also really important for your co-parent. Even though you really may not want them to walk upstairs in your home, a one-off bedroom showing, if asked for, can be one of those things that keeps kids secure. Their room is their space, and they need some autonomy to be able to do this. Shut all the other doors if you don't want your co-parent peering into other rooms. That's completely fine. Set a time limit – 'Mummy's going to see your room for five minutes then we have to get ready for homework,' or something that is understandable to your children.

---

4. Make small talk. Have a few things ready to talk about that are not about parenting or separation so your child can see you are able to be normal around each other. This will go a long way to helping them understand that even when relationships break down, people can still be polite and civil to one another. The weather, sport, gardening and TV can all be neutral topics you can use.

5. Have everything your child needs to hand over ready for when your co-parent arrives. If everything is ready, then the handover will be quicker if you need it to be. Don't have your child waiting by the door in their shoes, but do make sure that you're not scrabbling around trying to find the maths sheet or a lost coat, as this can make everyone flustered and angry.

6. Make sure you have collected your thoughts before the doorbell rings. What information about your child do you need to pass on? Is there anything that your co-parent needs to know and is there anything that your child has experienced since they've been with you that it would be nice for your co-parent to know? Remember that information sharing provides continuity for your child and reinforces the Co-Parental Loop. Write a list that you can refer to if that's helpful.

7. Send your child off with a kiss and wish them a lovely time with their other parent. Use positive and affirmative language that reassures them that this transition is OK. 'Have a lovely time with Dad, enjoy watching the football together on Sunday!' You get the idea.

8. Before they go, it can be helpful for some parents to confirm when children are being returned. By doing this out loud, it can help prevent late arrivals, or absent-mindedness. It can also help remind parents who are deliberately late that you have an agreement.

It's easiest to keep boundaries with your co-parent when we have thought them through in advance. Have a think about any areas where you might need boundaries. Ask yourself what you need in place in order to feel safe, while still upholding the Co-Parental Loop. Write them down if it helps you. Here are some you may wish to think about:

- Talking about your separation – when do you talk about it and who do you talk about it in front of?
- Handovers – where do the handovers happen and how long do they take?
- Communication about new partners, new families and each other's private lives – what do you feel comfortable talking about and what's appropriate for you to know and not to know?

So how do we help ourselves set these boundaries? I want to show you a way that will mean you can be an active co-parent *and* your own person who has a private life that your ex is just not a part of. The simple knowledge that you can step in and out of co-parenting with your ex is a game-changer because it means you can be yourself, live your life and step into the co-parent space only when you need to.

If both you and your co-parent stick to these rules of engagement, then your discussions and decisions become purely business-like and child-focused. If you're worried about your co-parent not sticking to the rules and boundaries, then know that as long as you are firm and hold the lines, eventually this can encourage them to change as well. By being proactive about boundary setting, you have the power to influence the dynamic of the whole co-parenting relationship.

A reminder to those who are reading the book without your co-parent. Don't worry. I work with many individuals whose co-parents don't join them in The Co-Parenting Method. The brilliant thing about all the tools is that they still provide you with a structure and a process through which to engage your co-parent. For yourself, knowing what your boundaries are means you can keep your co-parent where they need to be, and if your co-parent tries to cross the line, you'll be more able to keep yourself emotionally safe by saying no, explaining that what they're discussing isn't necessary or appropriate and getting the conversation back on track to your children.

The Three Worlds of Co-Parenting

One of the easiest ways to set boundaries and to think about our new way of parenting together is to imagine that you've moved from one big world that you used to live in with your ex and your children into three worlds: 'my world', 'my ex-partner's world', and 'the co-parent world'. 'My world' is where you live your day-to-day life. 'My ex-partner's world' is where your ex lives their day-to-day life. And the place you meet to discuss your children is called the co-parent world. If you think of it like a Venn diagram, the place that crosses over in the middle is the co-parenting world.

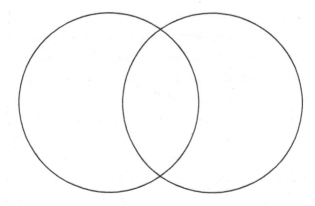

The three worlds provide a framework for our interactions as co-parents. By splitting our co-parenting into these worlds, we can choose to move between them appropriately. Each of the three worlds has clear boundaries, meaning we always know which world we're in, and the appropriate behaviour for that world.

When you're in your own world you're free of the influence of your ex-partner. Your own world is your own private space, and your ex has no say over what you do – unless it's harmful to the children, of course.

It's your personal zone, and you choose what you want it to look like. It includes your career, your friendships, your self-care, your creativity and other things. The more it's filled with things you want, the better you will feel in your own world.

When your ex-partner is in their world, they too choose what they want it to look like. And you have no say over what they do in their world – again, unless it harms the children. Although you don't enter your ex-partner's world, the fact that it exists reminds you that they're an individual, too, in addition to being an ex and a co-parent. It reminds you that they have a private life, and just like you, they're aiming to feel fulfilled.

The co-parent world is the space you step into when you meet. It's a calm and distinct space where you have unemotional discussions and take decisions about your children and their wellbeing. It's a business-like space that you consciously step into.

Having the three worlds gives you both some personal privacy, which is important in a co-parent relationship. The separation between worlds allows you to step into a neutral space when talking about your children with your ex-partner. You keep all the emotional side of things in your own world, where your ex doesn't need to see them, even if your friends and family do.

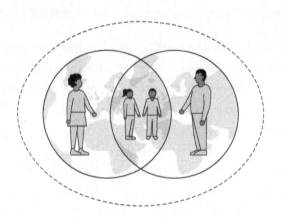

PRACTICAL TOOL #8

The Three Worlds

This tool will help you build your very own Three Worlds co-parenting system. You'll be able to use this to manage your co-parenting and keep it separate from your personal life.

The first thing I'd like you to do before you start is to find a place to do it where there are three different places to sit. That could be a table with three chairs, or a sofa that you can move along. If that's not possible, you can shift your body position on the seat you're sitting on. You'll need your notebook and pen too if you're using that. It will take about 20 minutes to complete.

Before we start I'd like you to make a commitment that you'll focus on staying positive in the creation of each of the worlds. When learning the tool, I want you to stay out of 'blame' mode, and try not to let negative thoughts about your ex-partner intrude. If you would find it helpful to use the Finger and Thumb tool to calm your thoughts (see page 59) then please feel free to do this now. You can also revisit your Best Case, Worst Case notes (see page 31) and the notes you took down from the Photographs tool (see page 49) before you start to help remind you that good boundaries are situated in long-term thinking and the kind of co-parenting that you're aiming for.

Ready? Then let's begin.

My world

Sit down in your first seating place. I want you to take a few minutes to really think about what you want your world to look and to feel like. Think about love, work, friends, holidays, family, money, and so on. Really visualise the detail. The more detail you can write down or think about what you want your world to look like, the more effective it will be. The only rule here is that your thinking should concentrate only on you. You're not allowed to write anything about your ex or your co-parenting relationship. The more ideas you come up with and the more specific those ideas the better, because it will allow you to visualise this world. You can be bold here. This is for your eyes only, it's all about you! There's no need to be shy or hold back.

So, for instance, you might include something like: 'I want my world to be a happy world full of laughter and fun and adventure. I want to be successful in my work, I want to be financially stable and I want to go on holidays near the sea. I want to have time to exercise and to socialise with my current friends and to make new friends.'

Take as much time as you need. When you've done the thinking, write it all down under a 'My World' heading.

My ex-partner's world

Now I want you to move to your second seating place. And it's really important, if you can, that you actually get up and physically move to a different place to allow your perspective to shift. Getting up and moving helps our brain to accept that we're going to be approaching something differently. That's really helpful for this exercise. If you don't have another seat or it's hard to move, then shift slightly so you're facing a different way wherever you are.

Your second seating place is where you're sitting in your ex-partner's world. When sitting here I want you to think from your ex's perspective. And I want you to do exactly the same thing for them. I want you to imagine what they would want in their world and write it down (or think it through) under the heading: 'My Ex-Partner's World'.

Really try to embody how they want to approach their life, love, work, friends, holidays, family, money, and so on. Don't write anything down in this section about co-parenting, or about you either. Be as fair, truthful and objective as you can, and try to keep your own personal feelings out of it. Again, take as long as you need. It doesn't matter if it's not exactly right and if you find it hard to imagine what your ex-partner needs, try to think more generally about what people need to feel happy and loved. That can help you get started if you're finding it tricky.

The co-parent world

For the next step of the tool, I want you to move position again to your third seating place or position.

This third place is where you're sitting in the co-parent world. There are two parts to completing this world. The first is to get into the perspective of your children, and think about what they would like your co-parent relationship to look and feel like. Please take some time to answer the following five questions and write down your answers.

1. How do your children want to feel when they are with their parents?
2. How do they want their parents to speak with each other?
3. How do they want their parents to make decisions about them?
4. How can their parents show them they are loved?
5. How can their parents keep them safe?

When you've answered all those questions, stay where you are – you're staying in the co-parent world for the second part of this section. Building on all the writing you've done so far, I now want you to think about what *you* want your co-parenting to look like in this world. When you're thinking about your own perspective, I want you to take responsibility for your own part in making the co-parent world a successful and neutral place. To make it easier to do this, please answer the questions below.

1. How would *you* like it to be when you meet your co-parent in the co-parent world?
2. How are *you* going to behave with your co-parent when talking about your children?
3. How collaborative will *you* be?
4. How will *you* approach joint decision-making?
5. What things can *you* do in your co-parenting that will make your children feel safe and held by you both?

You've completed the co-parent world section. Just have a re-read over everything you've written down. If you've written any negative actions or emotions, think about how you can flip them into positive actions or emotions.

So, for example, you might have noted down that you know your kids don't want you and your co-parent to argue in front of them, and you might turn this into: 'I will speak to my co-parent respectfully in front of my children.' Take your time to revisit both of the co-parent world sections to make these positive changes. While doing this, remember to stay fully in the bigger co-parenting perspective of what your children need from you.

Brilliant. You've now completed most of the Three Worlds tool. You've built three separate worlds. These worlds have clear boundaries between them. You know that all three are important, and that the success of the individual worlds impacts the success of the co-parent world, and the happiness of your children. You've created a blueprint for three distinct things: the good and positive things you want and need for yourself; the good and positive things your ex wants and needs; and the good and positive things your children want and need from both of you as co-parents.

Taking action in my world

You know by now that the tools work when we have actions to go with them. We're going to take your Three Worlds blueprint and decide on practical actions that will create real life change for you. Write a heading, 'Practical Action', on your paper. Underneath the heading I want you to write three or more actions that you can take to bring about the good things you want and need in your own world. What are you practically going to do to make these desires and ambitions come true? Are you going to reach out to old friends? Book a holiday? Join a club of some kind? Start doing sport again? Often when I take clients through the process of building their own world, they don't want to write actions down. They say they don't have time, or energy or money, to make themselves feel whole and good. I challenge that. We all have ten minutes to nourish ourselves, to do something for free, such as a walk around a short block, having a coffee on your front step, meditating, listening to a couple of your favourite motivational songs. Other clients use the building of their world to take on a new challenge, whether it's a physical challenge, or learning something. Remember there are going to be days when your children aren't with you. Filling that time with positive experiences is going to really help you thrive. More on that in step six.

Taking action in the co-parent world

We're going to do something similar now for the co-parent world. You might be feeling reluctant to write down practical actions that you can take to improve interactions with your co-parent, but it's important that you do this. By taking responsibility for your own actions in the co-parent world, you can directly influence how it works.

By recognising that your own actions impact the whole Three Worlds system, you can start to understand how you might steer the co-parenting ship. It's in your interest therefore to make small positive changes. For example, one change might be: 'When we meet to talk about the children, I won't bring up that my ex had an affair that ended our marriage.' Or another might be: 'I will approach co-parent conversations in a positive frame of mind to ensure they go as well as they can'. Even if your ex decides they don't want to engage with you in a positive frame of mind, by staying in yours, by not wavering, you are adding stability and solidity to the co-parenting, which is beneficial to your children. As you move into step four and we look at how we can use communication to influence co-parenting, this will become even more clear.

Implementation

You've reached the end of the exercise. Well, almost. For the changes to take place you need to implement the actions you've come up with, and I'd like you to commit to doing that now. Knowing what they are is only the first step! Being courageous and taking the actions you've written down is harder but it will help your own life become more fulfilled and improve your co-parenting relationship. Remember the Summit tool we did earlier in the step? If you are feeling like you need a helping hand to take a brave step with any of your actions, just go back to that diagram and use the tool to help you try something new.

If you're reading this book with your co-parent and things are amicable enough, then I'd like you to come together with them at the end of this step to find the similarities between your different versions of the co-parent world (only the co-parent world – not your world or their world). If you are able to go one step further and discuss the areas you will actively work on together, then you can start to co-design your co-parent world. This will be a positive and important step.

Before we complete step three, I want you to answer one final question. What new insights have you gained from building your Three Worlds? Spend a few minutes thinking about that and take some notes if you wish to. Your thoughts will give you further understanding of your own personal co-parenting dynamics and how to improve them.

You now have some thoughts and ideas about how to move forward and determine your co-parenting system. I want to leave you with a thought of my own. I know this is hard. I know it's challenging. Engaging with your co-parent only within the boundaries of the co-parent world requires self-management – it requires you to control any disruptive feelings you're having so you can focus on what you need to do in order to co-parent well. And it takes practice not to bring your own world into the co-parent world. It's a new skill, and I urge you to practise using it. The more practice you do, the more progress you'll make.

Storing your Three Worlds tool

We will keep the Three Worlds tool in our brain, because it took some thinking to come up with all of them. Imagine your brain slowly turning around as the world does. Maybe your brain looks like the earth from space? Or maybe it's like a glitterball!

Some of you will have co-parenting relationships that don't need such tight boundaries, where you can discuss your whole lives with each other freely. If this is you, that's great. If your co-parenting communication is this flexible and you feel comfortable with it, you don't need to tighten it and put strong boundaries around. You may still choose to, however, and knowing how to do this is important. For most of us there need to be clear boundaries. For instance, if your co-parent is constantly trying to find out things from your world, or overshares about things from their world, this can be uncomfortable and inappropriate. Please remind them that it's not appropriate to talk about those things in the co-parent world; if they're reading the book too, they'll understand what you mean. If they're not, you could suggest that when you meet you should talk only about the children and avoid talking about your private lives. To help with this conversation, in step five you'll learn a tool called 'the Meeting Framework' which will help you achieve this.

Boundaries, and using the Three Worlds tool, can also help you back on a co-parenting track when one of you is hurting after the end of a relationship. Jack and Konrad's relationship broke down soon after they had adopted their child. The process of adoption had taken its toll on their relationship and although the break-up was mutual, Konrad met someone else really quickly and that took Jack by surprise. It left him resenting Konrad and made their co-parenting relationship fragile.

'I was walking on eggshells the whole time,' recalls Konrad. 'Jack couldn't get over the fact that I'd moved on so quickly or that I wasn't hurting like he was. I think he felt cast aside and because he wasn't sorted out, that I didn't have the right to be sorted out. Really, it affected the way we interacted a lot. He stopped talking about our child and would always bring up my new partner and the fact that I seemed so happy. He didn't want to get back with me, but he didn't seem to accept that being happy was actually really good for me and our child. I wanted him to meet someone else too so he could experience that and then we would both be able to live a good life and co-parent together. But he was jealous and resistant.'

Jack found building his Three Worlds really important. 'I didn't want to go through The Co-Parenting Method with Konrad. I was down on myself because he'd moved on so quickly and I think I felt a bit worthless. His happiness completely distracted me from my responsibilities as a parent and I wasn't engaging properly in raising our child. Konrad picked up on this, he was always good at seeing the bigger picture. I'm glad he did to be honest. Even though some of the work was really hard, it helped me get a better sense of perspective.

'The Three Worlds tool was really eye-opening for me. I noticed two things. Firstly, that I was doing nothing to look after myself in my world when our child went to Konrad's house. I would just doom scroll on social media and watch a lot of TV. But more importantly, when I had to build his world in the exercise, I noticed that I was so annoyed at him that he had the right to this nice fulfilled life and that he was managing to achieve it when I was not. I resented that. When it came to building the co-parenting world I found it hard to get into that headspace of working collaboratively with him. And it was at that point I realised that I was focusing on the wrong place. If I worked on my world and accepted that he had the right to have his world and didn't obsess about it so much, then I'd be able to show up in the co-parenting world.

'Honestly, I'm still a little resentful that he moved on so fast, but I can manage those feelings enough now so our child can see me and Konrad interacting well. And I'm doing things that I like doing in my world, which helps me value myself. I got myself a kayak and have started to do water sports, which is something I always wanted to do. I'm looking forward to taking our child with me.'

Being able to see things from your co-parent's perspective and having the boundaries in place to aid your communication are both essential for building a co-parenting environment that best supports your child's wellbeing. Because both of those things reduce conflict, they also support your wellbeing, helping to take you out of high states of emotion. Step three may have felt challenging in parts, and I just want to remind you that the path to good and positive co-parenting isn't always a straight one and we just need to keep practicing and putting the tools we're learning into action in order to make progress. When the world around you is shifting it can be hard to keep our feet on the ground. Keep taking small steps forward and it will help you to feel more grounded. I've worked with parents and seen them taking regular baby steps forward. It's only when you look back to where you were that you can see how much progress you've made. Have a read of the summary below to help you retain what you've learned and bring your kids to mind while you're doing so; it will help remind you why you're doing this.

Seeing the bigger perspective can keep our co-parenting on track.

STEP THREE SUMMARY

- In step three we looked at seeing things from other perspectives and the importance of setting boundaries.
- You learned the value of being able to see your co-parent's point of view and the view of the co-parenting relationship.
- You understood how that bigger perspective can help you see more clearly what changes need to be made to help our co-parenting relationship stay on track.
- You learned the Summit tool to help you do difficult things like seeing your co-parent's perspective.
- You stood in your co-parent's shoes to really try to understand how they see things, an essential part of building a healthy co-parenting relationship.
- You built your Three Worlds tool, which is your new boundaried family system, and you now understand what's appropriate to engage with your ex about and what isn't.
- By creating your version of all the different worlds, you have a blueprint to remind you what you're aiming for to be happy.
- Your Three Worlds help remind you that your co-parent is a person too and whether you want it for them or not, that they are entitled to live a fulfilled life. If you're both making positive choices about your life as adults, then you'll be able to be more present for your children because you'll be standing firmly in the long-term mindset.

Storing your tools

You now have three more tools to add to your body outline: the Summit tool, which you keep in the very top of your head with your colourful flag; the Standing in Your Co-Parent's Shoes tool, which you keep in your memorable shoes; and the Three Worlds tool, which is stored in your brain. If you're labelling your body drawing, then do that now.

All the steps that you've been through so far will give you a strong grounding as you move into step four. The tools from the first three steps are aimed at helping you to get to a place where you can communicate well with your co-parent. Seeing things with a longer-term perspective, calming your emotions down and being able to see each other's perspectives are all going to help you be more positive in how you speak to your co-parent. In step four that's what we're zooming in on – communication, and specifically using how we speak to move us away from conflict. Ideally co-parenting is all about working together and finding solutions and moving away from focusing one each other's faults. Hold on to that thought as you turn the page.

STEP FOUR

Communicating without Conflict

For many of you, step four will be the most crucial part of the book. This is the step that has the most learning in it, so you might want to take breaks or pauses as you're going through it to give you time to reflect and digest. Learning how to communicate effectively is absolutely key to building a good co-parenting relationship. When we communicate well we reduce conflict and can start to make better decisions together. Both of these things are essential for the stability of your Co-Parental Loop (see page 45) because they mean you're working effectively together to raise your children. When your loop is robust your children are growing up in a secure parenting environment which has a positive impact on them now and in the future. Communication isn't just about what we say, it's also about how we listen, and that's one of the key parts of this step. It will be much easier to take all the learning from this step on board if you've completed steps one, two and three. You've built brilliant foundations on which you can now learn how to de-escalate conflict to have solid conversations together that reinforce your co-parenting relationship and support your children. If you've had to start reading the book at step four, because communication is your most pressing need, when you can, please read the first three steps, as it will make stepping into good communication so much easier.

Why Is Good Communication So Crucial?

Good communication is considered, thoughtful and open. It's choosing words sensitively so that you don't cause the listener to have an unnecessary negative reaction. It's about listening with an open mind and without judgement or preconceived ideas. It's about ensuring your body language is not conveying a message that's at odds with what you're saying. Good communication doesn't require you to be friendly. It's about how well you exchange information and opinions and thoughts with someone, so that what you're both saying is understood clearly and as you intended it. Think of it like a successful transaction. You know you've communicated well when both sender and receiver come away from the conversation with new information that they both understand and both sender and receiver feel they have been heard.

Good communication – calm communication – is the foundation stone of having solid and reliable relationships. When we have dependable relationships with our friends, our family and our loved ones, then we can focus on other things in life because we know we can rely on those relationships to be stable. Similarly in our co-parenting, when we communicate well with our co-parent we create a secure and easy passage for us to talk about our children. It's the basis of secure co-parenting.

Without it we are in conflict, and existing in conflict is exhausting. We wake up in the morning thinking about the conflict and we go to sleep at night worrying about it. Conflict caused by negative communication can consume us. We might be on high alert waiting for an email or a message or a phone call, we might be continuously revisiting our responses in the past and deciding how to respond to something in the future. Being in this state for any length of time is not a healthy place to be. Ongoing stress and high levels of adrenaline and cortisol can be destructive to our mental and physical health.

Renowned psychologist Dr John Gottman, in his fundamental research on making relationships successful, talks about communication as being crucial for achieving successful relationships.[11] His method is hugely relevant for co-parenting as well as marriages and partnerships, and workplace connections. His widely recognised and easily relatable metaphor uses the four horsemen of the apocalypse to talk about the four communication styles that can destroy relationships. They are criticism, contempt, defensiveness and stonewalling.

Criticism is not about making a complaint or offering a critique or feedback, it's about attacking someone at the core of their character. So for instance, if your ex is late to pick up the kids, a criticism would be calling them selfish. Contempt is when we mock others, or use sarcasm, or call them names, and goes far beyond criticism. Behind contempt is the desire to make someone feel worthless or despised. Defensiveness, the third horseman, is usually a response to criticism. However, when we're defensive it makes the other person feel as though we're not taking their concerns seriously and that we don't take responsibility for our mistakes. Stonewalling, the fourth horseman, is when the listener withdraws from the interaction and just stops responding.

If we're to have a successful co-parenting relationship then it's important to recognise that it's really common for us to find ourselves being one of these four horsemen. Step four will help us manage these responses so you can have positive and constructive communication with your co-parent.

Neutral and non-inflammatory communication is essential to maintain an effective co-parenting relationship for you and your children. If you're constantly criticising or arguing with your ex-partner, or can't hear their point of view, it's impossible to have a working co-parent relationship. And when children see their parents arguing, shouting or undermining each other, it gives them damaging messages that can have deep-seated psychological consequences. Children may learn that someone always has to be right, and compromise is unnecessary. They may learn that disagreements never get solved, and that can have important effects on their development, including finding it difficult to maintain long-lasting relationships themselves when they're adults.

Psychotherapist Adele Ballantyne confirms this. During my interview with her she noted, 'During therapy children who have endured their parents' conflict sometimes have skewed and distorted views about what adult relationships are like. Many feel that "all parents fight" and "unhealthy conflict is part of our relationships."'

Good co-parent communication, on the other hand, gives children positive messages about respect, negotiation, how we repair relationships and the importance of being civil. It shows children that even if people disagree, they can find a resolution and a way forward. Ballantyne says: 'Parents who are separating do well to limit the emotional distortion of adult relationships for their children when they seek help and learn strategies to resolve relationship breakdown conflict, including how they communicate with each other, leading to much more positive outcomes on children.'

Good communication lays the foundation for a more stable home life that builds children's resilience and sense of being loved. It also allows both households to be aware of what's going on in the children's lives when they're with the other parent, and whether there are any problems that need discussing. It means both parents can be a more joined-up parental unit for their children because they're both sharing news and information about them, and it also means therefore that they can be flexible in their parenting if they need to be. And finally, good communication allows for better decisions to be made about our children because we are able to have a conversation together about our children's needs and what's best for them. We don't need to be friendly with our co-parent to do any of this. We just need to meet up in the co-parent world (page 106) and be civil and polite. Consciously speaking and listening without letting past grievances affect the way you do it is what we are aiming for, and step four will show you how to get there.

Before we move on with this topic, I'd like to address an issue that crops up over and over again. You may be in a co-parent relationship where communication is a real problem, or you feel as though all the effort is coming from one side. Some parents fear that making all the effort, being conciliatory and building bridges, remaining calm and listening well, are signs of weakness. They worry that they are giving their power away by keeping things calm, or that they are being meek by not embracing confrontation. Remember the work we did in step one, where we saw the importance of having a long-term mindset that's focused on your children's futures, rather than a short-term view of winning the argument (see page 23)? Well, that long-term gain of keeping things calm has a profound impact on your children. You are not being weak by choosing this path. You are being a stable and present parent.

If you're reading this book on your own, I'd really like to acknowledge you, because by doing this work you are holding a safe, stable place for your children, even if your co-parent is not. Being open to engaging with them and communicating well with them, even if it is one-sided, will begin to improve your conversations and contribute to your children learning how to deal with conflict constructively. All of the techniques you're learning *will* improve the co-parenting relationship, whether you use them on your own or with your co-parent. It's certainly not a sign of weakness to use these techniques. In fact, it's a sign of strength. You've decided what your children need from your co-parent relationship and you're going to make it happen.

Let me give you an example of the power you have to influence how others respond to you. If I walk into a coffee shop and demand, 'GIVE ME A COFFEE NOW!' to the person behind the counter, how will they respond? Will they be gracious or grumpy? Will they make that coffee with love, or will they be tempted to spoil it?

On the other hand, what happens if I go into the coffee shop and smile broadly at the person behind the counter, ask them how their day's going, and order my coffee with a please and a thank you? I've changed the way I interact with the other person; I've given out something different, and therefore something different comes back to me. Now how will they respond? And how much more care and attention will they put into making my coffee? Whatever is going on for them, even if they hate their job and want to be anywhere else but making my coffee, it's harder for them to be annoyed at me if I'm being polite and respectful to them. If I treat someone with civility, then they are more likely to be civil back.

How people respond to us is at least partly in our control. And this includes your co-parent. When *we* change the way we speak with our co-parent, we change the whole dynamic of the conversation. And because of the changes *you* choose to make, your co-parent – without even realising – will also change the way they communicate with you. And that's why being a good communicator doesn't make you weak – quite the opposite. It gives you the power to positively influence your co-parent and to move them towards what your children need.

Being a good communicator doesn't make you weak – it gives you the power to positively influence your co-parent.

It can be really challenging to have good communication with our co-parent. Even after a lot of time has passed we can still find ourselves triggered when something big changes in our co-parenting system. You or your co-parent may be in a new relationship, maybe there is a new baby on the scene, a house move, an income change, it could be any number of reasons. At times like this we can find our communication falling back into negative patterns. In step two we talked about the high states of emotion we can feel when being around an ex-partner. The emotions around a break-up can stick around for a long time, even causing fight, flight, freeze, fawn and flop responses (see page 58) long after the event. In this book you've learned a number of tools that can help; you have the Finger and Thumb (see page 59) and Speed Writing tools (see page 68) for dealing with emotions, and your Self-Management Avatar (see page 73) to help scale down these reactions. Even with these tools, communicating well with an ex-partner can be hard. It's important to recognise this and keep in mind that the communication skills we're going to look at need practice and persistence. Be gentle with yourself if you don't get them right away or if you sometimes forget to use them.

The Importance of Listening

Most people tend to think that they're good listeners, but often the reality is quite different. Nancy Kline, author of *Time to Think*, underlines the importance of giving people the space to think and speak without interruption.[12] She notes that we can't usually speak for more than 20 seconds before we're interrupted or before we interrupt someone, so consciously not interrupting creates a safer environment where people can speak for longer periods. If someone is talking to us, we often interject with a thought, a disagreement, or a reference to our own experience. We rarely let people get to the end of what they're saying.

Interrupting doesn't help a conversation, it disrupts it. If we have something to say and we know we won't be allowed the time to say it, that influences how we speak. If we know we're going to be interrupted, rushed or ignored, we're less likely to remain calm. Conversely, if we know we won't be interrupted, that helps us speak both fully and calmly. So, what does this mean for us? It means that for someone to feel fully heard, we have to wait until they've finished speaking before responding, even if that takes longer than is comfortable. But it's worth doing, because when people feel fully heard, they feel calmer and communicate better.

If both you and your co-parent can let each other speak without interrupting, your conversations will become more constructive and collaborative.

Positive communication is less about what you say and more about how you listen. Just pause for a moment and reflect on that. We often focus on what we are saying, crafting every word and making sure we get the language right. But what if I told you that the single most effective way to create positive communication is about how well you listen? Listening to someone we don't like or trust is not easy. We may feel afraid, threatened or powerless if we let them have their say. It may make us defensive or dismissive or contemptuous when we are listening to them, which, if we allow it to, will escalate conflict.

Positive communication is less about what you say and more about how you listen.

Let me give you a non-co-parenting example of how it might help in practice. Have you ever been in a situation where you think you know what someone is going to say, and you end their sentence for them? Only for them irritably to say, 'No, that's not it.' The conversation perhaps becomes awkward. If you'd waited just a few seconds longer and allowed them to explain what they wanted to say in their own time, they would have felt heard, valued and fully open to your response. You've interrupted the speaker. You've not had an open mind and made assumptions about what they wanted to say and your impatience made them irritable.

So how can we listen well in a way that feels safe for us and how do we manage our emotional responses well enough to respond in a way that supports positive communication? Let me introduce you to something called active listening.

Active listening

Nate and Rosie have two sons. Nate left Rosie for another woman and their co-parenting was really toxic for a long time. They didn't communicate well and Rosie would not listen to him. She found it hard to differentiate between the Nate who left her and Nate the present father. Let's hear from Nate just before he and Rosie went through The Co-Parenting Method:

'Rosie is my ex. I left her for someone else and even though she pretends not to be, she's still angry. She can't listen to me without looking like she hates me. Rosie assumes that everything I say will be a lie. Every single conversation starts from a place of mistrust and quickly turns into a row. I have to brace myself every time we have to speak about the boys because it's always so draining. I should say that it's six years since we separated. She's with someone else now and I'm still with the woman I left her for. It's like she's moved on in all parts of her life, except in conversations she has with me. It's so frustrating. I know I made mistakes in our marriage but I find it so hard that we can't talk about the boys without her shutting down, or shutting me down, or having a row.'

For Nate and Rosie, it was really hard for them to move forward in their communication because all conversations were being coloured by their past experiences. It became really difficult for them to listen with an open mind and to hear the new information. That's where active listening comes in.

Active listening creates a level playing field for discussion that leaves behind previous experiences and starts afresh each time. That's why it is such a valuable tool in co-parenting. Shortly, you're going to learn how to do it. It's defined in various ways, but what all the definitions share is this: it's a way of truly listening and putting aside our preconceived ideas. And when we listen actively, we listen with our ears, of course, but also with our eyes, and with our intuition, and we notice how we're feeling. We're fully engaged in listening and not at all distracted. When we're listening in this way, others feel really heard. This allows them to feel safe enough to open up.

Listening well also allows for more collaboration. For example, our co-parent disagrees about a childcare issue and, using active listening techniques, we hear they have genuine reasons for disagreement, based on what's best for our child. Up to this point we may have presumed that our co-parent was disagreeing to be difficult. Being able to hear that it's not that allows us to communicate better and work more collaboratively. For some co-parents this will happen quickly; for others, especially if you're in high conflict, it's going to be a slower process. But if you use the active listening tool below, and park your emotions, then it will eventually make a difference.

Escalation needs two people and active listening prevents it. If you're reading this book on your own you still have the ability to create a positive change. Even if one of you practises active listening it has the power to prevent conflict. If you don't engage in adding fuel to the fire, the fire won't get hotter. If your co-parent doesn't want to be collaborative, then it will only turn into a conflict if you let it. Being able to control your responses will have a big impact on reducing disagreements. Be consistent and persistent. It may take some time, but by persevering, you will bring about change.

PRACTICAL TOOL #9

The Five Steps of Active Listening

To be a good listener we need to think deliberately about *how* we're listening. When we listen to people and we've formed an opinion on them based on what they're saying before they've finished speaking, we're making assumptions about them and may even be judging them. The underlying idea behind this tool is to learn to listen without assumption or judgement – a simple idea, but often hard to do in practice, especially when communicating with a co-parent. But it's an effort that's worth making. Listening to our co-parent without assumption helps us hear their point of view and allows us to understand the discussion from their perspective as well as our own. As a result, you get a better understanding of what your children need because you're understanding your kids' needs not just from your point of view, but also your co-parent's. If we're in judgement mode, blaming our co-parent for their latest misdemeanour, then we miss out on these insights and our children may suffer.

The Co-Parenting Method's Five Steps of Active Listening

Try using these steps in all your interactions, not just your co-parenting ones, and notice how much easier conversations become:

1. **Open your mind:** Keep an open mind during conversations. Try not to jump to conclusions straight away and see what unfolds. The conversation may go in a direction you weren't expecting.

2. **Give them your full attention**: Listen to the words and watch how they are speaking. Focus entirely on the speaker. You'll get a better sense of their frame of mind when you do. Eliminate distractions and show that you're engaged by maintaining eye contact, facing the speaker, and putting away any devices or items that might divert your attention.

3. **Be aware of non-verbal cues**: Pay attention to the speaker's body language, facial expressions and tone of voice. These can provide valuable additional information about their feelings and attitudes. Notice what you're feeling, as your feelings will have an impact on the other person. If you're irritable, then the other person is more likely to become irritable too.

4. **Don't plan your response yet:** Avoid formulating your response while the speaker is talking. Instead of thinking about what you're going to say next, focus on understanding their message. This prevents you from missing important information.

5. **Don't interrupt:** Wait until they've completely finished speaking, don't jump in and don't speak over them. Give the speaker space to say what they need to say and allow them to finish naturally.

Action and challenge

Without practice it can be hard to get into the flow of active listening. Indeed, it can feel a little bit awkward to suddenly change how we communicate with our co-parent. So I don't want you to start with your co-parent. Instead, start with your children (if they're old enough to have discussions with you). Use the five steps to really listen to what they're saying. It might feel strange at first, so take it slowly. Then (or if your children are too small) try all your five active listening steps out on your friends and work colleagues. Keep trying them. See what it's like to use them in meetings and notice how much more productive your meetings are. Also notice how well people listen to you when you speak after you've listened well yourself. I'll wager that when you do speak after listening well, people will stop what they're doing and really focus on what you are saying.

When you feel more comfortable with active listening, move into using it with your co-parent. At first you might need to just choose one or two of the elements – that's fine. As you become more confident in it you can add the others. Active listening is simple, but it has a really big impact. It can transform communication.

Here is Nate again, after he and Rosie learned about active listening:

'When we worked through The Co-Parenting Method I wondered how it would be when she got to the active listening bit. At first I didn't notice any difference. She would still stonewall me or sneer. I don't know if it's possible to have a sneer in your tone of voice, but she certainly managed it. One day it felt slightly different. Our oldest was doing end-of-year exams in school and wasn't very focused. I'd had an idea about how to help him that I braced myself to share with her. And she listened. I nearly collapsed because it hadn't happened for so long. The air between us remained calm. She didn't sneer. She listened to what I said and then unbelievably we agreed on a way forward. I didn't believe it would happen again, but it kept happening. Things became much better between us. Look, it's still not perfect, but we can align as parents again. We have joined up our thinking. It's been brilliant for the boys.'

Storing your Five Steps of Active Listening

The Five Steps of Active Listening we'll store in our ear because, well, we have to listen. What's going on in your ear to help you remember this tool? Do you have a soup ladle hanging out of it? Are there five steps leading up from your ear canal to your brain? Whatever it's like, make it ridiculous and you will remember it.

EXAMS

At some point your child will have to take exams. This can be a hot time. Your child is stressed, everyone wants them to do well, the pressure is piling up and because of this, tensions and emotions can run high. As co-parents, working together to give them the support and flexibility that they need at this time is so important. That might mean being flexible with your current arrangements. Your child might prefer being in one house over another when they're revising because of space or noise. Accept this. It's not a reflection of how they feel about you, they just want to do well. On the flip side of that, they may not want to study and you're going to have to work in close communication with your co-parent to set strong boundaries for your children to help them stick to their revision. Exams can bring about real mental health challenges for teenagers, so keep talking to your child and your co-parent about what's going on for them.

The Power of Pausing

One of the elements of active listening that we've just looked at is not interrupting. I want to look more closely at this, as this is a fundamental problem in co-parenting that I see time and again. Speaking over our co-parent and not allowing them to finish is a play for power. And plays for power are not helpful when we are trying to collaborate on parenting.

It's worth looking at what makes us want to keep interrupting our co-parent. We can find not interrupting difficult because we may not want to consider the needs of our co-parent. They might be about to say something that will make our lives harder, or be inconvenient for us. We might not want to hear them say something that we know is right because we know we will need to change our behaviour. We might simply not want to hear them because we think what they're saying is a load of rubbish. But here's the thing: if both you and your co-parent can let each other speak without interrupting, your conversations will become more constructive and collaborative, conflict will reduce, stress will be relieved. By pressing pause on your own need to interrupt, by holding the pause by letting them finish speaking properly, you will be enabling a much calmer space for your co-parenting communication.

Being able to press pause will give your active listening a turbo boost. Allowing your co-parent to finish speaking and being allowed to finish speaking yourself keeps a conversation in a positive flow. It keeps it calm, on track and moving forward. It helps prevent it from getting emotional and angry. I want to give you a tool that will help you press pause and give more space for listening.

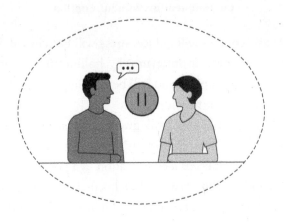

PRACTICAL TOOL #10

The Pause Button

Keep the Five Steps of Active Listening in mind as I introduce you to the Pause Button, one of the simplest and most powerful communication techniques you'll use in your co-parenting relationship. It helps conversations run more smoothly.

The Pause Button retrains our brain not to interrupt during a conversation. It encourages us to very deliberately pause for a few seconds and take a breath instead of cutting short our co-parent's thoughts, allowing them the time to put forward their point of view. Along with active listening, it allows us to fully focus on who we're talking to and what they're saying. Using this approach means your co-parent will feel more heard, and because you have more time to consider your responses you may also find better solutions to some of the challenges facing you, your children and your co-parent.

Simply follow these three rules to build your Pause Button.

1. **Choose your Pause Button.** Choose something that will remind you to pause. It could be a watch or a ring, but it needs to be something that you always have with you. Alternatively, if you need somewhere on your body to store it, put your thumb on the inside

of your wrist where you feel your pulse. This is your Pause Button. When you touch it, it'll not only remind you to be calm, it'll also remind you to pause during conversations. Some people rename it their 'Shut Up' button. If that works for you, then go for it.

2. **Put your finger on your Pause Button and pause while your co-parent is speaking and for five seconds after they have finished speaking.** If you need a few seconds longer then that's OK. Just ensure you maintain calm eye contact with them, or show them that you're thinking and considering what they've said, so they know you're not ignoring them. If they start speaking again before the end of your pause, then let them finish and wait again. Only when they've completely finished speaking should you speak. This can be hard to do and it may feel unnatural at first, but it'll start to feel more normal with practice. Persevere and you'll see how it starts to transform your conversations with your co-parent and others.

3. **During your pause, while the other person is speaking, use the Five Steps of Active Listening.** Listen fully to the person speaking. Use your ears, your eyes, and your intuition. Notice how they behave while they're speaking, and be open-minded about what they are saying. Notice how they are when they have the space to say what they need and to finish speaking at their own pace. Chances are they'll like it.

The next part of the Pause Button tool is all about how you respond.

When your co-parent has completely finished speaking, respond calmly and respectfully, having fully heard what they've said. Acknowledge what they've said – you can even summarise the main points back to them to make sure you've understood correctly. You need to respond, otherwise your co-parent will think you're blanking them or stonewalling and that's not helpful or useful when you're trying to build something together.

Stonewalling, as we heard earlier, is one of the four things that can break down positivity in a relationship. According to Dr John Gottman, when someone completely ignores what you are saying and doesn't acknowledge you, that can make you feel invisible, so be mindful that you need to respond.[13] Remember, using the active listening techniques is not at all about being passive or submissive. You don't have to agree with someone. You can say you need time to consider something. But your responses will be said in a calmer manner. Before you respond, consider the impact you're about to have, use your open mindset from active listening to be collaborative and try to use language that is positive rather than negative.

At the end of the conversation, ask yourself what using the Pause Button and the Five Steps of Active Listening allowed you to learn that you might not have noticed using your old listening style. Parents regularly report back that using these approaches quickly and significantly improves the quality of communication.

Reflection time

Now you have your Pause Button, I want you to imagine a conversation with your co-parent using both the Pause Button and active listening techniques. Bring to mind a conversation that might make you want to speak over them. Perhaps it might be that they are about to have an opinion about the children's behaviour. Maybe they're about to ask for a date swap, or more time with the children. Whatever it is, just bring it to mind now. When you're ready, think about what it would be like to use the Pause Button and *not* jump in and speak over them, and how that might make you feel. Think about how giving your ex more space to speak using active listening and pausing might make communication with them easier. Reflect on how it might improve your co-parent relationship. Write some thoughts down in your notebook about what emerges for you.

Sometimes that kind of reflection can make us feel uncomfortable. What happens if, when you give your co-parent space, they make a request that feels inconvenient or alarming for you? Well, in a successful co-parent relationship it's better when things are aired openly and honestly, even if they're uncomfortable. Just because your co-parent has asked for something doesn't mean you have to agree to it. Giving them the space to express what they need means you can then have a clearer and calmer conversation about it.

Now I want to put the shoe on the other foot. I want *you* to experience the power of the Pause Button. Think about what it would be like if, when *you* were speaking, your co-parent was using the Pause Button and the Five Steps of Active Listening, and they gave *you* the space to say what you needed to say. What would it feel like to have the time to speak without being interrupted? How would it impact what you're going to say? Take some time to think about it and please write some notes down.

Did you notice how powerful it is to experience the space of being listened to, and how it helps conversations run more smoothly? Many people who do The Co-Parenting Method say they feel a deep sense of relief when they imagine their ex-partner taking the time to listen to them. Well, that's a two-way street, and if our co-parent isn't making the effort to listen and to communicate effectively then, for the sake of our children, *we* have to be the ones to start that process. We have the power to influence the direction and tone of conversations. If we want to get something positive out of our co-parent relationship, *we* may need to be the wise and reasonable part of the conversation. Remember, this is quite different to saying we should be submissive and agree to everything they're asking. I'm absolutely *not* saying that. Be confident in your ability to remain calm and form a response that is thought through and structured and puts what you need to say across in a constructive way.

Storing your Pause Button

The Pause Button we've already placed on the inside of your wrist, so we'll keep it there. Imagine a big button with two lines on it there. It's bright red to remind you to press it. It's compelling to press it.

Every time you press it, your mouth clamps shut and it makes a strange sound. What sound does it make?

Inflammatory Language

What do you think of when you read the words 'inflammatory language'? Images of the tabloids with their screaming headlines? Well-known politicians being controversial and dividing the nation? It's not just politicians and pundits who can be provocative; we all have the ability to use words and phrases that really wind up other people. You'll know already what it feels like when someone says something to you that really makes you angry or incredulous. It doesn't feel nice, and it is highly unlikely that you'll listen well to someone who is making you feel that way.

Inflammatory language is language that escalates a situation – often (but not always) we know it's negative when we're using it and it invites an angry response. It's not thoughtful language, it's quick language, said in the heat of the moment, designed to bring about a reaction. Think of a time when you've been told that 'you wouldn't understand something' or when someone says you're 'overreacting' and to 'calm down' or 'you're imagining things'. All of these will make us want to retort and respond sharply. Being on the receiving end of inflammatory language makes us feel angry, frustrated, annoyed and upset. It's a way of speaking that increases tension and goads the other person to give you an angry response. It's often impulsive, and thrown into conversations without much consideration. We know if we've used language that someone considers inflammatory by how they respond to us. We can also tell if it's been used on us, as we might feel defensive or under attack. When we feel like this and when others feel like this, conflict escalates almost immediately.

Non-inflammatory language is generally neutral, considered, intentional language which deliberately keeps a situation stable, or de-escalates it. Using non-inflammatory language in a co-parent relationship is one of the most important actions you can take. As we know, the co-parent relationship needs careful handling. Even when we've been co-parenting for years, the relationship can feel fragile. Anything with our children involved is going to be emotive and it's important to recognise that we need to take care in co-parenting. It's a bit like walking on a frozen lake. It can seem solid, but may crack at any moment. Being mindful of each other and having a degree of respect between each other helps keep that ice nice and solid. It's only by communicating well that we can reach sensible conclusions and take good decisions about our children together. Using provocative language simply destroys this.

In our co-parenting we may have certain 'hot' topics that lead to arguments or things we do or ways of speaking that send co-parent conversations spinning off in negative directions. Hot topics are those conversations that can trigger us, or that we've always argued about. There's a high probability that we will use inflammatory language in these exchanges, whether we realise it or not. Sometimes it's just about using an inflammatory word or phrase that can cause conflict to rear up.

Just take a moment to bring to mind a word or words you use with your co-parent that cause them to react in a negative way. What are some of those things you say? What are some of the things that are said to you that you hate to hear? Write them down in your notebook now, or bring them to mind. Notice how they make you feel. The co-parent relationship is a challenging one. It's often built on frustration, anger and hurt, so you're more likely to use inflammatory language with your co-parent, especially if they provoke you and you feel the need to defend yourself.

Two parents I worked with, Angela and Vinny, came to me because they knew they wanted to co-parent and yet couldn't hold a conversation without it turning into an argument. When we unpacked the situation, we realised that Angela would always call Vinny's new partner 'HER' rather than by her name.

Vinny recalls: 'Angela was so disrespectful about my new partner. I saw red every time she was rude about Claire. I just got so mad. None of this was anything to do with Claire, but Angela was using her as a way to get at me. Every time she called Claire "her", whatever we were talking about would just dissolve into a shouting match. We couldn't make decisions about the kids. It was a nightmare. I couldn't focus, I would be agitated every time I needed to meet with Angela to talk about the kids. It was a mess, and it meant I didn't often agree to meet her because I knew it would end in a fight. I disengaged.'

Angela remembers: 'I was mad. Vinny had moved on so quickly after we split up. How could he do that? I couldn't hold my emotions in whenever I saw him. He had moved on and I was still picking up the pieces. And he had a new partner. I called her "her", which I know didn't help the situation, but it felt satisfying in the moment. It really wound him up – a bit like poking an angry bear with a stick. But I guess at some point I started to see that actually our parenting was just becoming non-existent together. And even though I was definitely angry and resentful, I needed to change what I was doing. I didn't want to. I remember really not wanting to. But I knew I had to.'

Working with Angela was a real privilege, because she really wanted to put her children first and she had so much self-awareness that she needed to modify her communication with Vinny. She could see her anger was causing her to be provocative.

As she began to understand that she had to step into the co-parent world when she spoke to Vinny, she was able to stop using the inflammatory language about his new partner, take control of her emotions and become more neutral and business-like. She used her Meryl Streep avatar (because for her Meryl is always poised and in control) to be in charge of how she spoke to Vinny. Ultimately she chose to do this not because she wanted to be Vinny's friend, but because she wanted a good co-parenting relationship to benefit their three children.

Inflammatory Language – the Impact on Your Child

The ideal state for children is with parents who offer them a secure and stable upbringing, and that includes how you communicate about each other in front of your children. Kids always need to feel that their parents are focused on them and have their wellbeing front and centre. When we separate, children experience an abrupt trauma – they realise that their world may not be as stable as they thought. If handled healthily this trauma can be largely healed, like a broken bone. Although it's painful, it's still mendable and can become strong again. On the other hand, bad-mouthing and criticism of your co-parent is much more likely to have a shattering effect. Like a shattered bone it's much less likely to heal properly, meaning the trauma of your separation may always impact your children.

I want to introduce you to Lara, whose story sums up really well the importance of not using inflammatory language or gestures. Lara was seven when her parents separated. Her parents were in high conflict and although their arguments weren't loud and volatile, they were sharp and pointed. Lara is now 19 and recalls the time when her parents were separating with a lot of sadness.

'I remember Mum rolled her eyes every time my dad messaged her. I hated that. That was my dad and I loved my dad so much. And Dad stopped calling my mum by her name. He started calling her "your mother" to me, or "you know who" to everyone else. It made me think that my dad was comparing her to Voldemort from Harry Potter. He wouldn't name her, and that felt scary. The days when I was not moving between Mum and Dad's houses were OK. There was some sense of stability. I could let myself breathe again because there was less opportunity for them to have a go at each other, but the days when I swapped I would be tense. I'd sit on the toilet for ages because I had stomach ache and my hands would get clammy. I would always forget things, which would make both of them mad at me, or worse, at each other. I felt under pressure to make everything smooth and calm, although I couldn't have said that to you when I was seven, it's how I feel I felt now, when I look back at it. Mum couldn't even look at Dad when she dropped me off. Every part of me wanted them to be able to have a laugh and a joke or share something silly, something that didn't matter, but they just seemed to hate each other so much. I'd cry at night, I'd hold my teddy, Brown Bear, really tight and whisper a wish to him to make it all better. He couldn't though. He was a teddy bear. The thing is, I still feel really connected to that teddy bear because he was the one constant thing I was allowed to take with me everywhere. He was my friend. Growing up I always felt like I had to split my loyalties. I loved them both, I didn't really understand why they couldn't just get along. Why they couldn't just lump it for my sake. Didn't they love me enough?

'Growing up with those feelings was really hard. I was quiet in school, and kept myself to myself. The only thing I loved to do, and still love, was to go running. I used to run for my county and one day both my parents came to see me. They stood together at the finish line and smiled at each other. That was the best day of my childhood.'

Lara's story always reminds me of why I do the work that I do. Why it's so important for all of us as separating parents to acknowledge the fact that it's really hard to be a co-parent and to try our hardest to do it well anyway, for our kids.

Children who experience this type of long-term trauma can become adept at compartmentalising. They hold things back. They may behave one way in one house and another way in the other. They may keep secrets because they feel disloyal sharing information between houses. They can feel pressured into having a favourite parent. It's damaging to their relationship with you, and it's damaging to their relationship with their other parent. But mostly it's damaging to them. Remember from step one, how the dad of Alex and Martina had a destructive way of talking about their mother and how it impacted the relationship initially between her and her children? Well, it also impacted the children's mental health too, and Alex became 'more aggressive at school because I was always looking for a fight with the other kids'. We heard how Martina became timid and started bed wetting.

Ballantyne talks further about the long-term impact of parental arguments on children. 'Even before they are born children begin to understand the world around them. They closely observe their parents and learn much from their behaviour as well as from their words. Destructive tactics such as name calling, physical aggression, stonewalling and capitulation, can leave children feeling confused and unprotected. In the long term children may carry mental health issues such as anxiety, depression, anger, criminal and anti-social behaviour, and poor performance at school to name a few.'

Managing our behaviour and how we interact with our co-parent at drop-offs, birthdays and school events is vital. Good communication with your co-parent is not just helpful, it's absolutely key to your children's long-term wellbeing. Using your avatar from step two will help you communicate well in these situations.

We're going to look at the idea of inflammatory language now, what it is and how it's used, and then we're going to look at it from a slightly different point of view. We're also going to look at how your children experience how you speak about and to your ex. We're doing this because this is one of the biggest challenges we face as co-parents. When we're angry at our ex and we show it to our children, we are breaking the Co-Parental Loop. Hearing you verbally attack your co-parent or undermining them when they're not there will upset your child's stability. It's the same when your children hear you speaking negatively about their other parent with friends, family members or professionals. In short, speaking positively about your co-parent in front of your children is crucial. Positive speaking also includes positive body language. Eye rolls and death stares have just as big an impact as words.

Controlling our language is not an easy thing to do, but it is possible. Doing this helps us move towards the ideal vision of the future you saw in the Photographs tool (see page 49) in step one, when your adult children spoke positively about being co-parented. Remaining calm, thoughtful and deliberate even when things are difficult with your ex is a powerful place to be, both for your children and for you. I've seen many parents manage to get to this place and be able to be polite with each other in spite of how they might want to act.

Remaining calm, thoughtful and deliberate, even when things are difficult with your ex, is a powerful place to be.

Avoiding Inflammatory Language

When we speak in anger we often know we're looking for a reaction. We speak in a critical, aggressive or judgemental way and we may use phrases like 'You always . . .', or 'You never . . .', or 'You promised . . .'. Our tone of voice probably changes too and becomes demanding, pleading, whining, accusatory. You get the picture.

At the same time, if we're being aware of what's going on in our bodies, we notice an increased heart rate, tightness in our chest, sweaty hands, anger. I hope this sounds familiar, because this is a fight response – remember we talked about fight, flight, freeze, fawn, flop (see page 58)? So, when you say provocative comments sharply, such as, 'You're always so negative,' or, 'You always put yourself before the kids,' or, 'You never listen to me,' you're probably firmly in a fight response. Being in fight response makes it harder to choose the calmer, sensible approach and it can make us want to lash out. By finding ways to manage the fight response, you'll find it easier to avoid using words that create conflict.

I've given you various tools to help you manage your strong emotions when you're in fight response; you could use the Finger and Thumb tool to calm yourself down (see page 59) or your Pause Button to remind yourself to listen without interrupting (see page 134) or your avatar to ensure you're meeting your co-parent in a calm and neutral way (see page 73). Another good way to get yourself out of fight mode is slowing down your breathing; you could try the 'four, seven, eight' technique: breathe in for four seconds, hold for seven seconds and exhale for eight seconds. This technique is really good for regulating the stress hormones that put you into the five Fs. You could also use your Three Worlds tool (see page 108) to remind yourself you're meeting in the co-parent world, which is a calm and neutral space where you only talk about the children.

By using these tools, you will have powerful shields from both your ex-partner's language and any fight response you may feel towards it. The shields mean that any provocations from your ex-partner can be dealt with more easily than before. Sometimes the situation needs a bit more, so we're going to look specifically at how to manage the language we use to decrease rather than increase conflict.

Reframing

If using inflammatory language is so damaging, how do we change what we say to make it more constructive? In a moment I'm going to introduce you to another tool that will reduce the likelihood of you using inflammatory language during a co-parent meeting. It's called the Reframe tool and the simple idea behind it is that there's more than one way of saying the same thing. Reframing is the process of taking something out of one wrapper and putting it in a different one. With our words, we need to get across a meaning or an idea, but if we're saying it in a provocative or angry way, then it's not going to land well or be heard properly. If we put the same meaning or idea in a calmer and more collaborative wrapper, we'll be better able to get our message across. Before we go into the tool, we're going to look at some examples of inflammatory language, and then think about how we could reframe them to say the same thing but in a calm and neutral way. It might feel a bit false or a bit forced, but just consider the alternative for a moment. Would you rather have a massive row, or would you rather say something that feels slightly awkward but has a constructive outcome?

> *Would you rather have a massive row, or would you rather say something that feels slightly awkward but has a constructive outcome?*

Common inflammatory phrases

Below are some common phrases that I hear a lot in my work, and underneath is a more measured approach that has reframed the sentence to make it more collaborative. Look at the first phrases. Notice how they can be very judgemental and critical. They can also be emotionally charged and needy and sometimes just downright aggressive. These are obviously not helpful responses to situations that are irritating you. What do you think will come back at you? At best an apology, more likely an irritated retort and at worst a full-blown argument that draws on your joint history.

Below the negative sentence is the reframed one, which is where we say exactly the same thing but without using inflammatory language. When we can reframe what we're saying to sound collaborative, you're much more likely to get a helpful answer that means you can resolve an issue.

'You're always so negative.'

When your ex is negative, pessimistic or doesn't like your idea, you say, 'You're always so negative' – this is inflammatory language, judgemental and critical. You'd expect your co-parent to react angrily if you said this to them. How might you react if it was said to you?

Reframe to: **'I see what you mean. Is there anything positive in this situation that might help us move forward?'** This is unemotional, helpful, and wanting to move towards a solution. Sounds a bit awkward, right? But again, focus on the long term. Being constructive means fewer arguments, it means a stronger Co-Parental Loop for your children and it means a better and less stressful co-parenting situation.

'You never listen to me.'

How about when you're frustrated with your ex and you complain, 'You never listen to me'? This too is inflammatory language: emotional, aggressive and needy. You can probably expect an irritable response to this.

Reframe to: **'It feels like I haven't clearly explained what I mean. Let me try again.'** This is a factual statement and largely without emotion. Again, it keeps the conversation on track. Remember to notice the tone of your voice. Sometimes it's easy to make reframing sentences sound quite passive aggressive. You need to make sure you sound neutral as well as making sure your words are neutral.

'You never understand me.'

A statement like this is aggressive and needy. It gives your power away.

Reframe to: **'We seem to be misunderstanding each other – can you explain what you mean, and then I can explain what I mean?'** This feels factual, helpful and focused on finding a solution.

'You never pick the kids up when you say you're going to.'

This is based in blame and criticism and your co-parent is likely to react irritably.

Reframe to: **'The kids get a bit worried when they're waiting for you. I understand sometimes it's hard to get here on time but is there anything that we can do that might help in the future?'** This latter statement is without emotion, is helpful, and wants to move towards a solution.

It takes a lot of self-control to move away from our habitual ways of speaking with our co-parent. But if you practise, the benefits are significant. Your brain is an amazingly flexible machine, and by practicing reframing you'll get better and better at it until you can do it naturally.

If you practise speaking in a way that breaks down barriers rather than builds them, then you're well on the way to a good co-parenting relationship with all the benefits that that brings.

When using reframing techniques, I want you to think of the conversation like constructing a building where co-parent decisions are taken on the top floor. You need to construct the conversation consciously and deliberately through each of its stages to make sure you get to the top. The top floor is where consensus is reached. Every time you use inflammatory language, you go back to the bottom of the building. However, if you carefully construct a conversation, you get progressively higher up the building and closer to the aim of making a mutually agreeable decision on the top floor. And that's the aim – it's not about winning, it's about working together for the children. Getting to the top is easier if you're communicating positively. Reframing is a useful way to do that, as is using the Five Steps of Active Listening, the Pause Button, and the other tools you're now familiar with. Reframing is quite a tricky skill and you'll have to spend some time practicing it, but when you understand its power to avoid conflict and to transform co-parent communication, you'll use it all the time. Let's give you the Reframe tool so you can start practicing!

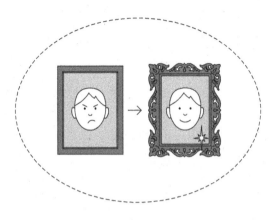

The Reframe

Below we've written some common situations with a possible inflammatory phrase and we have made a suggestion as to what might be a constructive alternative. Have a read through of these first.

ANNOYING SITUATION	NORMAL RESPONSE	CONSTRUCTIVE RESPONSE
Annoyed with ex's distraction when the children are spending time with them	'You're always on your phone ignoring the children'	'Molly is noticing that you're on your phone a lot. I know you're really busy. Shall we both make sure we have time for her when our phones aren't in use?'
Frustrated with ex, who doesn't respond to requests	'You always ignore me'	'It feels as though we are a bit stuck. Us not making a decision is affecting the children – shall we make a decision on this by the end of the day tomorrow?'
Not happy with ex, who never washes kids' clothes	'Are you incapable of using a washing machine?'	'Luca went to school with dirty clothes this morning and he felt really embarrassed. Shall we come up with a washing rota so he doesn't have to feel that again?'

Disagreement on what foods are OK for your child to eat	'Are you trying to make our child ill?'	'Jamie gets quite cranky after they have a lot of sweets. Shall we try and find a solution that means they can have more of a balanced approach?'
Your child is with their other parent and they've gone away, and you don't have any information about where your child is	'You can't not tell me where my child is. You're a psychopath.'	'It's important for Georgie that she doesn't feel she needs to keep secrets. It makes her stressed and it makes her feel guilty. I get that you might not want me to know where you are, or be involved in your time with her, so can we find a way through this to make her feel safe?'

Now it's your turn! In your notebook, draw a table with three columns. In the first column I want you to write down a situation where your co-parent does something that annoys or frustrates you. No need to hold back, put whatever you like in here. It might be: they send really long detailed emails when they don't need to; they leave making arrangements until the last minute; they are consistently late even when they know I have plans. Do that now before carrying on to the next part.

In the middle column, next to each of the things you've written down, I want you to note down what you might normally say in response to that. So, for 'they are consistently late', you might write down that you say, 'You're always late, you're never on time, you know I'm going out tonight, you're so selfish.' Fill the middle column in now.

Then in the right-hand column I want you to write down a new way of saying the same thing, but in a constructive and collaborative manner. It might not be easy – dig deep if you have to. Even if you're resisting doing this, remember it's your choice, you still have control over whether or not you use the new way of speaking, but the exercise of going through these scenarios and writing different responses will be helpful for you when you're building positive communication. Applying something that we've learned and putting it into action, or writing it down, helps us rethink how we approach things and opens us up to new ways of doing things, which might be more constructive for your co-parenting. Use your Self-Management Avatar to help you, if you need to (see page 73).

If you need some ideas for column three, here are some common constructive phrases that might be useful for you:

- 'Can you tell me more about that . . . ?' This is useful when you need more information from your co-parent.
- 'My perspective is different . . . ', or, 'I see that differently . . .' This is useful when you don't agree.
- 'The way I interpreted what you said was . . . please correct me if I'm wrong', or, 'What I've heard you say is X . . . did I understand you correctly . . . ?' These are useful if things aren't clear and you need clarification. They are also useful to check you are both on the same path.
- 'Would you consider . . . ?' 'Would you be willing to . . . ?' These are useful for when you want to test the boundaries of a new idea.
- 'What if we . . . ?' or 'It might be an option/beneficial if we . . .' These are useful when you want to put forward new solutions or ideas.

Phrases to avoid

Some words and phrases will set you straight on the path to using inflammatory language. Please try to avoid these. Here are the most common ones. You may have others.

Sentences that start with: 'You always . . .' or 'You never . . .' or simply 'You . . .' If possible, try to replace the word 'you' with the word 'I'. Let me show you what I mean. Reframe: 'You're always so aggressive' to

'I feel upset when I hear those words and the tone of voice and it's more difficult for us to take good decisions about the kids.'

Any comments about your ex-partner's emotional state. 'You're hysterical' or 'you're a control freak' aren't constructive in conversations, nor are comments that dismiss what your ex-partner is saying as irrelevant or stupid.

The word 'But' . . . This word is such an interesting one. When we use it, what it actually does is render everything that you have said before the word 'but' obsolete. 'I like the chocolate pudding but it would be even nicer with cream.' What the person hears is that the chocolate pudding isn't good enough. How about, 'The hotel is lovely, but the food isn't amazing.' The immediate impression is that the holiday isn't as good as it could be. Of course, sometimes we need to use the word 'but'. What I'm showing you is the impact it has on the rest of what you're saying. In co-parenting it can be such a trigger word and definitely inflammatory. 'You're a good dad but . . .' or 'Beth likes coming to your house but . . .'

Instead of using 'but', use 'and'. This joins up your words and keeps everything nice and present and also more collaborative. Let's have a look at how that works: 'It's an interesting idea, but it won't work' becomes 'It's an interesting idea, and we can explore whether it might work.' This latter approach gives you time to consider your response and means there isn't an argument in the here and now. It means you both have time to deal with the situation more calmly. You have not agreed to the idea, just said you could both think about it in more depth.

Storing your Reframe tool

For the Reframe tool let's imagine a picture frame that we are going to cram into our mouth to change what comes out of it. I like to imagine one of those very fancy gilt frames that you see in stately homes. It's not very comfortable! Remember, the stranger the image, the more likely it is that you will remember it. So go ahead and make your picture frame very unusual.

Using the Reframe tool

Moving into positive communication can be a hard thing to do. It can be really difficult to be able to pause and reframe things when your ex frustrates you. In the table you created you now have an idea of how to respond with positive communication in several situations you think are likely. If you can commit these to memory they'll be in your head when you need them. I want you to practise using them at every opportunity you can. You may feel silly and it may feel forced, but it will be game-changing in stopping conversations turning into arguments. Go back to the Summit tool if it feels difficult. I know you can do this.

Natalia used the Reframe tool with her co-parent Nico. Here's what she had to say about it:

'I knew the Reframe tool wouldn't work. There was no way it would stop Nico from shouting at me. He always shouted at me. I shouted back too, but he really went for it. It didn't work at first. I didn't want to try it, and then when I did try it I would follow it up with something provocative or mutter something under my breath. I think I was nervous to try it because I felt it kept me safer to be on the attack. But then I did try it properly and after a little practice I got better. The words would feel a bit weird to say out loud. It certainly isn't my natural way of speaking! But after a while Nico would be more open to hearing the positive stuff I was saying and unbelievably he stopped being sarcastic, or shooting back something angry. When he wasn't doing that, it was easier for me to stay calm.'

Slowly, very slowly in fact, Natalia and Nico built a way of talking with each other that probably sounded very forced and strange to anyone else. It was cautious, it was slow and it used stilted language. Importantly though, the language was positive, it wasn't inflammatory and they became able to talk to each other and sort out some co-parenting issues that had been there for a long time.

Natalia finishes off: 'I really was relieved. Actually, that is an understatement. I didn't understand really how something so forced could be so effective. But I don't care. I'm just glad it works.'

It doesn't need to be perfect. It just needs to be good enough. It needs to be better than it was before. Slow progress is still progress, so if you're feeling frustrated that it's not working straight away, keep trying, be persistent and be consistent. You will make progress.

By being in control of your communication and by responding in ways that don't inflame a conversation, you're being the steady anchor. You're choosing how you want to steer the conversation. Eventually, over time, your co-parent will notice a difference in how you communicate and they too will become more of a steady anchor, allowing you both to have functional conversations. These conversations may not be fun, but they will keep your co-parenting on track. And remember why you're doing this – not because it's easy, but to enable your children to grow up in a stable environment.

You're doing this not because it's easy, but to enable your children to grow up in a stable environment.

The Impact of Badmouthing Our Co-Parent

There are many reasons why it's not a good idea to talk badly to and about your co-parent. The most obvious one is the impact that your words and behaviours have on your children. Remembering that your child didn't choose to divorce or separate from you or their other parent can be really helpful when managing what we say about them. You may really want to say things about your ex that aren't complimentary. You may be coming out of a really tough situation and need to vent. I understand that, and if you need to do that then make sure there is simply no chance of you being overheard. Saying negative things or exhibiting negative behaviours about your ex where your children are witness to it is so harmful. Your children deserve for their parents to be respectful to each other and about each other, and they need you to do this in order to feel safe and loved.

These are the six most common situations where it might be easy to forget to manage what you are saying or doing in front of the children – I see these often in my work.

Talking about your co-parent to the children

This is the most obvious one, so we'll start here. Direct attacks on or about our co-parent when we're talking to our children, especially if we're trying to turn our children against them or discredit them, leaves our kids in a really difficult position because they don't know what to say or who to support. Big emotions and a sense of what is just can sometimes lead us to wanting to talk to our kids about where our co-parent has gone wrong. But your kids aren't the listeners you need for that. By being openly critical of our co-parent, we're asking our children to join *our* 'gang' and to choose us over their other parent. We're trying to win and are in a short-term mindset. We're showing them that we don't care about the fact that they were created or raised by both of us and we're giving them the message that part of them isn't worthy.

Let me ask you a very direct question: do you want your children to feel as though part of them is bad? If the answer is no, then you need to really think carefully about what you say and what you do in front of your children. When we looked at the example of Alex and Martina in step one, we saw exactly this. They were turned away from their mum because their dad was badmouthing her. This backfired in the long run because when they grew up the children saw that their dad had damaged their relationship with their mum. As adults Alex and Martina were angry with him and chose to see him infrequently.

Gestures are just the same as words

Rolling eyes behind a co-parent's back. Making hissing sounds, rude hand gestures, rude facial gestures, pushing, shoving, throwing things, breaking things, burning things, destroying your ex's property are all things that parents tell me have happened to them in front of their children. Whether it's in the heat of the moment, or in response to an email or a message from their ex, these gestures are clearly angry.

When a child sees their parent doing these things it can rock their world. It's sending them a very strong message about what one parent thinks about the other, and that can be damaging for them to witness. A good rule of thumb here is to think of your co-parent like a work colleague. What would we and wouldn't we do at work in front of others? The same boundaries should apply in front of children.

If you are experiencing this upsetting behaviour from your ex, a difficult but helpful question to ask is: 'What actions of mine are contributing to this happening to me?' Is there anything you can do to lessen this behaviour? Is there anything that you're doing that you think is OK, but that your co-parent might find provocative? Just have a think on that for a moment and see if it's relevant.

In my experience, these kinds of behaviours usually happen when a separation hasn't yet concluded and everything is still being unpacked. How you both handle yourselves through this time can largely determine how you work together as co-parents. Go back and get your Self-Management Avatar from step two and use it to support you through this. Charge your avatar with protecting your children by helping you remain neutral.

Being overheard in conversations with others

It's really tempting to talk about things we're going through and finding hard with the people who care about us. And of course it's really important that we seek support. When we do confide in our loved ones we need to be very mindful of where our children are and the language we use. When children overhear us being critical of our co-parent to friends and family it dehumanises them. It makes them feel as though the part of themselves that is their other parent is somehow bad. It can make them angry at you, it will certainly damage their opinion of you and it may even make them favour their other parent.

Children seem to have supersonic hearing and eyesight. They can hear everything, even when we think we are whispering, or making discreet gestures. Even if they aren't in the same room as us, children have a knack of hearing what we are saying. You need your adult space to talk about things when you're going through tough times, and you need to make sure that children can't overhear you. In some ways when kids overhear you talking about their ex it can be worse than when they experience it directly because it can make you seem dishonest. Think for a moment about when you're having casual conversations with friends, either face to face or on the phone. Can your children hear you? How about when they're in bed at night – are you sure they're asleep? Have you had a drink and lowered your guard? All of these things happen, and your children will internalise and be affected by the remarks they hear.

Professional settings

Cindy and Graham were at a meeting about their daughter's special educational needs on Zoom. Cindy was fuming as, before the call had started, her daughter had said that she had found some inappropriate images from pornographic websites on her dad's laptop. Cindy had had a massive surge of adrenaline and had gone straight into fight mode. As soon as the meeting started, Cindy exploded. She couldn't keep a lid on the emotions that were surging through her. She let out a tirade of anger, talking about how everything her ex was doing was damaging her daughter, and relayed in explicit detail the more unusual sexual preferences of her ex-husband. She was loud and she wasn't holding back. Cindy hadn't realised, however, that her daughter was just outside the home office listening to everything that was being said. She was exposed to the detail, the fury in her father's voice and the anger in her mother's voice, and the special needs professional who wasn't saying very much at all. She felt ashamed, she felt betrayed and she didn't know how to process it. Sometimes we have to speak to professionals about our co-parent, about our children and about our separation. Whether it's a family solicitor, doctor, therapist, teacher, mediator, coach or someone else, during this time we often need professional support. If you need to speak to them when your children can hear, then please do everything you can to use neutral language, be respectful and manage the strong feelings, you might be having. If you need some help managing the feelings then use your Finger and Thumb tool (page 59). Ideally you'll speak to them when your children aren't there, but I appreciate it's not always possible.

Manage your family and your network

Slightly differently, but still of crucial importance, is how your children experience members of their extended family discussing their other parent. Grandparents, aunts, uncles, cousins, close family friends will all have an opinion about what's going on in your life. It's really normal behaviour. What needs to be managed is how and when they talk about this with you. One tip that you can try is writing a messaging sheet about how you want the family to talk about your co-parent in front of the children. In its simplest form a messaging sheet is simply a piece of paper with all the key statements written on it about how you want others to handle talking about your separation or your ex.

Pressing upon your family and your network the importance that children need to keep their parents as heroes can make a massive difference to how your child goes through life. If you want to do that then sit down with your co-parent, or on your own, and write down the important messages that you want your child to hear consistently. You might write headings like: 'What they hear about our break-up'; 'How they hear us talking about their other parent'; 'How they hear us talking about the other side of the family'; 'How we all feel about them'. Adding the words that you want everyone to use under each of those headings is a really useful way of getting everyone to stay on message and that provides your children with an incredibly secure structure that they can rely on.

Amrita and her co-parent were doing a great job of co-parenting. It had been a messy separation that could have descended into a big blame game, yet they had managed to put parenting first and even though it was all a little bit strained, they were doing well. Amrita's mother, however, was furious with her ex-son-in-law and didn't want to miss an opportunity to let him know that. Amrita could see this coming. It was their daughter's confirmation and everybody on all sides was going to be together for the first time since the separation. The children had no inkling of what was brewing under the surface but Amrita knew she had to do something. She wrote a short messaging sheet that she and her co-parent sent out to their relatives. It had simple things on it like:

We talk respectfully about each other at all times, and we take extra care to do this when the children are around.

We don't attribute any blame for our separation.

We uphold each other as parents all the time in front of our children.

Please help us help our children by doing the same.

This was well received. Some people may have thought it a bit strange, but it was important to Amrita and her co-parent to take control and steer the ship and prevent it from going off course.

Amrita's mother, however, needed a little bit more. Amrita sat her down and explained that the impact on the children could be really big if they felt that Grandma didn't like their dad. She explained to her mother that whatever her feelings were, she knew she could be a good grand-mother and look after the children. Amrita said to her mother that there was no expectation to speak to their dad and her mother agreed to not say anything rather than say anything negative. The day passed smoothly enough and everyone focused their attention on Amrita's daughter.

It's really important that all extended family members are giving children the same message: 'You are loved and both your parents love you and we support that.'

What you say about yourself

What you say about yourself can also have a profound impact on your children. Something that is much more common than you might think, is taking on the 'victim' role in front of our children. Talking about how hard it is, how upset you are, how you're not a worthy parent, talking about your mental health, sometimes even telling children that they would be better off without you, are all things I've heard from my clients when they are in their most fragile states.

Co-parenting, divorce and separation can deplete us terribly. If you feel vulnerable, please seek help from a professional and your friends. You'll be better protecting your children by doing this. Going through a separation and living through a tough co-parenting relationship is really hard. I see those tough times and I acknowledge that it can feel all-consuming and overwhelming. I also need you to know that the effect on your child if you look to them for emotional support is huge. You might be inadvertently looking for help and someone to lean on and finding you are expecting that from your kids. A child needs to be a child. Your kids need to know you are the adult and in control enough that you can seek help if you need to. Don't tell your children that they would be better off without you. Don't break their hearts. If you're reading this and it resonates with you, please pause your reading now and call a family member, a friend or a professional to ask for help or turn to the resources section (page 255) to find support. It's OK to ask for help.

Literal Language

Language is a funny old thing, and the phrases we use that emerge from day-to-day life are often very unusual. 'Keep your eyes peeled for a parking space', 'I made a pig's ear out of that', 'I laughed so much my sides split'. Well, I don't know about you, but keep away from my eyes when you're parking, and don't make me laugh as I don't want my sides to split.

Language can be confusing. Understanding nuance and what someone actually means to say can be 'mind-blowingly' hard. Neurologically, brains don't finish fully developing until we are in our early twenties. All those little nuances, phrases and inferences that we understand as adults are lost on children, and are sometimes even confusing for those in their teens and early adulthood. This is so important to bear in mind as we communicate with our children and also about our ex with or in front of our children. Using simple and literal language that has no possibility for misunderstandings by our kids becomes crucial when we are separating because those misunderstandings can lead to a sense of instability or mis-interpretations of you or your co-parent. And for your child, it can mean they don't feel as though their place in the family system is secure.

I often hear things like: 'I wish I'd never met him,' 'She makes everything so difficult,' 'He's crazy,' 'She won't stop until she takes everything.' We need to be careful about saying things like this within earshot of our children. Even very young children can understand more than we think. They understand names and emotions, so if their mother is angry and they hear her say the word 'Daddy', they may put two and two together and work out that Mummy is angry with Daddy.

Children can also be very literal. Throwaway comments that you might make like 'I wish I'd never met him' may be taken at face value and internalised by them. So, what impact does that have? Well, if you hadn't met the father of your children, then they wouldn't have been born. Children up to the age of late teens might read into this 'you don't want me' or 'you'd be happier if I wasn't here'. Because what they're hearing is: 'If I hadn't met him and hadn't had children with him then I'd be happy.' I know that's not what you meant – and other adults will know it too – but it's how your children interpret what you say that's critical. Even older children don't yet have an adult experience of the world and are therefore more likely to misinterpret the ideas behind their parents' words.

Let's think a little bit more about how children interpret language. What about this: 'She makes everything so difficult . . .' A child might interpret this as 'it's bad to make things difficult, so I should try to please people'. This people-pleasing message is harmful for children to pick up, yet it's something that we see time and again in the children of separated parents. Children are extremely good at internalising messages that they have inferred incorrectly from what we are saying. If we can mitigate this or reduce it by thinking about the language we use around our children and the attitudes we model, then we can go a long way to helping them become more resilient adults.

There are many phrases and examples that we can list here. Particularly common criticisms of co-parents are based around money. A financial settlement can be very destructive (I call them the 'F bomb') and words like 'money grabber' and 'greedy', when associated with a parent, are hard for children to hear. I had a client whose child thought that her mum was taking all her dad's money. Dad would say to anyone who would listen, 'She's taking everything, she's cleaning me out.' To a child, even a young teenager, that phrase can be taken quite literally. Meaning Dad might be left with nothing, not even anywhere to sleep. Think how scary that would be for your kids. What would be the impact on them? The next tool will help keep us on track with our language to make sure we are being mindful of not using phrases that can be misinterpreted by our children.

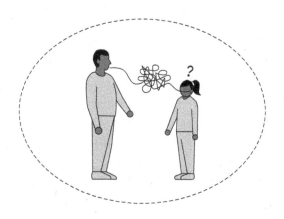

What's in a Word?

We've seen how easy it is for children to misinterpret our language. We've learned that the more literal and specific we can be the better. I want to give you a short and simple tool to help you remember how to do this.

I want you to make three columns in your notebook. In the first column, think through the words and phrases that you find yourself saying a lot. Here are some of the most common ones that I hear in addition to the ones I've already shared with you. The genders used are interchangeable.

- 'There's something wrong with her mental health'
- 'She only thinks about herself'
- 'Crazy, that's what he is'
- 'She is so selfish'
- 'He doesn't know how to parent'
- 'How will the children be safe with him?'
- 'I wish he would disappear and not come back'

When you've done that, in your second column, make a note of what, in the worst-case scenario, your children might understand by that phrase.

So if you've written, 'He only cares about himself,' your children might take from that that their dad doesn't care about them. How would that be for your children? It would be devastating and have a long-term impact that could affect them for the rest of their lives.

In the third column, please write down what you can say instead, that leaves your children no room to worry or infer anything catastrophic from your words. So you might change 'He only cares about himself' to 'In this specific case John is not considering the consequences of his actions.'

It might take some time to get used to, but I want you to only use your third column going forward. Practise using the new phrases that you've written so you can get used to how they sound. What you may notice is that the phrases that are confusing for your children are actually catch-all phrases for the way you're feeling. So, you might feel that John is selfish and only cares about himself, but it might be triggered by a specific event. Let's make sure we look at the detail as it can help us phrase things in a way that is less catastrophic for our children.

Storing your What's in a Word tool

What's in a Word we're going to keep on your throat, because this is how your words have sound. Imagine a beautiful necklace or scarf around your throat. Is it full of precious stones? Is it a silk scarf with animals on it? Perhaps it's a stripy, brightly coloured woollen scarf. Take some time to imagine it now.

How are you doing? Check in with yourself for a moment. How are the tools helping you? What are your biggest learning points that you have taken away so far from this step? Before you carry on reading, take a moment to reflect on that.

You have just completed the longest step in The Co-Parenting Method. Co-parenting is a marathon, not a sprint, and each step you complete in this book is helping you be marathon fit. One of the fundamental pieces of successful co-parenting is effective communication, because it reduces conflict and enables you to find a way through a conversation without it being derailed by an argument or unpleasant language or gestures. This keeps the Co-Parental Loop nice and stable, which is essential for the secure parenting environment you need to create for your children and enables you to start making better decisions together.

The tools and techniques you've learned in step four are probably the most fundamental ones in the whole process. They can also be the hardest to implement. The more you practise, the easier it gets. Keep moving forward one step at a time, that's all we're aiming for. Let's move to our summary now to help you really hold on to what we've learned in step four.

STEP FOUR SUMMARY

- Good communication is so important and isn't just about what you say, it's also about how you listen.
- You learned the Five Steps of Active Listening tool to help de-escalate conflict and listen well.
- You learned the Pause Button to help support that listening.
- By listening well we enable our co-parent to feel heard, and this simple technique means that they are less likely to keep coming back to conflict. We saw how powerful that was in helping keep conversations on track.
- We looked at the power of words and how they can quickly inflame a situation. What we say and *how we say it* has a profound impact on how it's heard and what comes next – the words we choose can make or break a situation and turn it into a positive direction or a negative one.
- We also looked at how the language we use about our co-parent can impact our children and how they often understand things in really different ways to how they were intended.

- The Reframe tool is how you turn negative and unhelpful language into something more neutral and forward-looking.
- And finally the What's in a Word tool is to help you remember how your children hear what you say.

Storing your tools

It's time to hang your new tools on your body outline! The Five Steps of Active Listening we store in our ear. The Pause Button we placed on the inside of your wrist. The Reframe tool is crammed into your mouth and What's in a Word is on your throat. If you want to label your body outline, then please do that now.

When you communicate using these tools, you'll lay a smoother foundation that you can both stand on to move your co-parenting forward. I mentioned at the beginning of this step that good communication helps us make good decisions, and that's where we're going next. When we've got a lot going on and we're feeling a lot of emotion, it can be hard to take practical decisions. Planning ahead can really help us. What's a decision you're struggling to make with your co-parent at the moment? I'll see you in step five and we'll work on it together.

STEP FIVE

Making Good Co-Parenting Decisions

In step five we will be building on what we learned about good communication in the previous chapter to look at how we ease decision-making with our co-parent and make durable decisions for our children's present and futures. The decision-making part of co-parenting is why you do all the rest of it. Parenting requires lots of decisions to be taken and if you have a reliable formula for doing that successfully, then you will probably be doing a good job as co-parents. Every day as parents we have to take decisions, from what we feed our kids, to the amount of TV they watch, to whether they're well enough to go to school or if they really are sick. Having to make decisions with someone you're not with adds another layer into the mix and you need to know how to resolve disagreements in order to keep your co-parenting on track for you and your children. If you can't make decisions with your co-parent, your parenting can end up in a state of limbo, which is not a good experience for your children.

As we move through step five we're going to look at how to take your child's perspective into account in your decision-making process and we'll also cover how to build a Co-Parent Charter and a Co-Parenting Plan. A Co-Parent Charter is the agreement you'll make with your ex on how you both show up to your co-parenting. And if you're doing the method on your own, it's the commitment you take about how you engage with your ex in co-parenting. It helps keep you accountable and gives you a nice strong anchor to lean on. Your Co-Parenting Plan is the document that houses many of your co-parenting decisions so you don't need to keep revisiting them with your ex. Before we build those for you, it's important to understand why decision-making with your co-parent can be hard.

Why Is It Hard to Make Decisions with Your Co-Parent?

For all sorts of reasons, it can be hard to make good decisions with your co-parent. By the very nature of separation, we are usually already in some kind of adult disagreement or discord. Having to work together, communicate with each other and make good decisions together about our children can be difficult when emotions are running high. When we talk with our co-parent we may be in the grip of a fight, flight, freeze, fawn or flop response (see page 58) or, because we're angry, we might just not want to consider our co-parent's point of view. Or we may be trying but not yet be fully comfortable with some of the tools we've already learned around listening and communicating, so that conversations are still frayed. In this context, making good decisions about our children can be tough.

What's more, when we take decisions as co-parents, we often have to juggle the needs and views of our children, ourselves *and* our co-parent. On top of that, we have to think about new partners, school, work, other family members and more. Decision-making gets harder to do when you have fundamental differences of opinion, or if you have different parenting styles, differing views about pocket money, social media, after-school clubs – the list is endless. Decisions that have weight and emotion attached to them, such as school choices, where your child goes and when, and who holds the passport, are all hard to navigate with someone who you may be in conflict with or don't want to be around. By now you have enough tools to manage the resentment and communication difficulties – and with practice they will make a real difference – yet when it comes to getting decisions over the line, the process can still be derailed.

When decision-making works well it is a relief for everyone and it provides your children with the stability that they crave. When you're making decisions well with your co-parent you're listening to their point of view, you're seeing things from your child's perspective and you make the decision with your child as the focal point and work outwards from there. Even if it's hard to reach a decision because you're taking into account your child's perspective, you'll find a point of alignment between you as co-parents to use to help you over the decision-making line. A point of alignment is simply something, one thing, relevant to the decision that you *do* agree on.

Edward and Sami had been separated for just over a year and were struggling to make a joint decision about when their children could watch TV or go on screens. Edward was happy to let them go on whenever they wanted. Sami on the other hand thought they should only watch at weekends. Edward and Sami used the tools from The Co-Parenting Method to hear what each other thought was important. Sami tells us how it worked for them:

'Edward loves TV and so he never minded when the kids wanted to go on screens. I felt like it was impossible to achieve anything with the kids, or do anything different, because they always wanted to watch TV or go on their iPads. We couldn't agree and we were both convinced that we were right. When we learned the Active Listening and Pause Button tools, we weren't able to interrupt each other anymore. We were always interrupting each other. And suddenly we had to really listen! That was eye-opening. We both definitely like to be vocal. But having to listen meant that amongst all the disagreements we found something that we both agreed on. And that was homework. All the watching was getting in the way of the kids doing their homework, so that's where we started from. We were able to decide together that getting homework done before the children were allowed on their screens was a rule we would implement across both houses.'

From there they grew their discussion and ended up deciding the children would be allowed 30 minutes of screen time every weekday and more at weekends. What in the past would have caused a row about each other's parenting became a constructive, business-like conversation that led to an effective decision. So, you can see how important it is to find that key point of agreement that you can build on.

Seeing things from your child's perspective

Seeing things from your child's perspective is crucial for making good co-parenting decisions. By approaching your decisions from your child's perspective you're much more likely to find common ground and less likely to descend into disagreement or familiar unhelpful patterns of communication.

Before I go on, let me be really clear: I'm not saying here that children should take big decisions. Letting children make inappropriate or big decisions when they are too young can be damaging for several reasons. Firstly, because it puts pressure on them to have responsibility that they're just not ready for. Kids who are asked to decide about what they want are outside of the parental loop, which means they have lost their parental anchors. That's not an emotionally safe place for a child to be. Secondly, kids can also develop a conflicting sense of loyalty when they are asked to choose.

Leah was eight when her parents asked her who she wanted to spend Christmas with that year. Her parents were progressive and they had a great co-parent relationship. Leah had always thrived within the Co-Parental Loop. But being asked to choose who she wanted to be with for the holidays was so destabilising for her that it turned everything upside down. She was like a rabbit caught in the headlights, according to her parents – she simply looked from one parent to the other, burst into tears and fled the room. Unsure what was going on, her parents ran after her and tried to explain that they really didn't mind, that they wouldn't feel bad whoever she chose. But the act of making your child choose something may be too much for them to bear emotionally. Because remember this: even though you're not together, it's more than likely that they will wish that you are. They can't, nor should they, choose between you. You need to set a framework of rules and decisions that they fit within. You can take into account their point of view, but you don't need to consult with them to do that. Especially if they are young.

Making decisions that take into account your child's perspective isn't about asking them what they want, it's about *thinking about* what they want and need. It's about asking yourself what your child would choose and what's best for them, and then it's about looking at the impact of the decision on your child. It's about being really honest with yourself while you're doing this, so you are genuinely seeing it from their perspective and not making their perspective fit in with your own. It's about getting enough information that is relevant to your child for you to use in your co-parent decision-making.

CLUBS – EVERY OTHER WEEKEND

Weekend clubs or after-school clubs are one of those hot topics that can make co-parents fight. When you book a weekend club for your child it's ideal if you and your co-parent will both commit to taking them there. However, that's not always possible. Some parents may live too far away, others refuse to take them because it's 'their time' with their child. So the parent that is footing the bill feels frustrated because their child is only getting to go half the time. Unfortunately, clubs don't do discounts for children who can only come 50 per cent of the time.

If you're experiencing this, I want to invite you to remember that this is your child's club. If they want to go and they get something out of it, then try to take them, even if it's a little tricky. Their time with you is about real life, not being with you every second of every day. Go and watch them play football or dance and teach them that commitment to something is important. There's no perfect solution to any of this, but focusing on your child and their needs will help you find a way through.

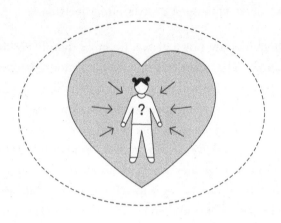

Child-Centred Questions

It's easy to say all this, but how do we do it? You'll know by now that I always want to give you the tools to do the job. This tool is all about how to see things from your child's perspective and taking that into account in your decision-making.

Below are four questions that will enable you to do that. If you ask the four questions as they are written, with your child in the third person, they are easier to answer. This is because by asking them in this way you disconnect much of the emotion from the situation and you're able to see more objectively what is needed and you're more likely to find a point of agreement that you can build on. You can use this tool with or without your co-parent when it's difficult to take a decision and need to figure out the best course of action.

The first question asks what your *child* would choose, and the next three questions allow for a more adult perspective. Together, the four questions allow you to understand your child's point of view. They help you to break down a problem and come up with practical actions. Use the questions when you need to take difficult decisions about your child, especially if decision-making becomes emotional. It's a useful way to structure your thinking and find a way forward, while keeping the needs of your children front and centre.

1. If our child could choose, what would they choose?
2. Never mind us as parents, what's best for our child?
3. What's the impact of our decision on our child?
4. What's the impact of not reaching a decision on our child?

You can see that the questions show your child's perspective, what they would choose and what you as parents think is right for them. They also force you to think about the impact of your decision and the impact of *not* making a decision. The questions help find solutions that are right for our children. They can help to break a deadlock between co-parents. Even if it's just you going through the book, then the questions are hugely helpful to aid decision-making about your children.

When using these questions, remember to make your answers honest, trust your instincts, and note down practical and positive actions that you can take. I'm now going to give you an example of how to use them.

Mia's parents can't agree which after-school club she should attend. One parent says it should be swimming and the other says art class. Let's see how useful the questions are for resolving the issue.

Question 1: 'If Mia could choose, what would she choose?' The answer may be, 'Well, actually we haven't asked her, so let's do that. Or maybe we already know the answer – we know that she'd prefer to do swimming.'

Question 2: 'Never mind us, what's best for Mia?' Here we put aside our own interests about diary clashes, logistics or cost issues and ask, in a perfect world, what's best for Mia? Are her best friends doing one or the other? In the longer term, is it more important that she can swim or draw? Note that there aren't correct answers to these questions, and of course practical issues remain important, but the questions themselves allow us to break down our decision into smaller chunks.

Question 3: 'What's the impact of our decision on Mia?' How will it feel for her? Will she feel as though she's been consulted and listened to? If we decide on art, which isn't her chosen option, how's Mia going to feel about that? Will she feel unheard or forced into doing something she's less keen on? Or will she accept the decision because we've explained it's difficult to attend swimming classes this term? We'll want Mia to know how we took the final decision, and importantly that both her parents agree.

Question 4: 'What's the impact of not reaching a decision on Mia?' It's going to be tough for her if we can't agree – in that case Mia may do neither. We'll have to explain that we as her parents couldn't come to an agreement and that will be upsetting for her. It'll make her feel as though her parents can't work together co-operatively to support her inside the Co-Parental Loop.

Action

OK, now we've looked at it together, I want you to do it yourself. Have a think about a co-parenting issue where you're struggling to reach an agreement, and write it down in your notebook. If you're able to, you can do these questions with your co-parent and you can use them in the Meeting Framework tool which you'll learn shortly.

Underneath your co-parenting issue consider each of the four questions and write your answers down. When you've done that, please write another heading called 'Practical Action', and note down any practical action you'll take as a result of your new insight.

These four questions are the ones I use most often to help co-parents reach decisions in a more child-centred way. There are other questions that can be helpful too, if you're struggling to come up with a clear, practical action. Here are some of those:

1. What has worked well for our child in the past that we can learn from here?
2. What is it that makes our child emotional or angry or upset?
3. What feels fair for our child?
4. If our child were to reveal their true feelings, what would they be?

5. What's best for our child in the long term?
6. What's best for our child in the short term?
7. What will help our child thrive?
8. When our child is 25 and looking back, what would have been best to do?

Storing your Child-Centred Questions tool

We'll associate the Child-Centred Questions tool with a question mark attached to our belly button in the centre of our body. How will you make your question mark memorable? What colour is it? What's it made of? How is the question mark attached to your belly button? By ribbon or a string of pearls, or something else?

How to Have Good Co-Parent Meetings

Meeting with our ex may be the last thing we want to do. Handovers are bad enough, right? Having to actually arrange a time to sit down and have a discussion can fill us with dread and worry. Yet short, regular meetings about co-parenting are really important. Being able to come together in your co-parent world to figure out what needs to happen for your child is a cornerstone of co-parenting. I also know that for some parents this is really hard to do. It can mean sleepless nights in the run-up to the meeting; some of you will be really nervous and perhaps even fearful. Where there is a lot of unprocessed emotion it might take a bucket-load of taking charge of yourself to be able to do it. I hear you; I see you. It's hard. Not all of you will feel like this, but for many of you it will be somewhere on the scale of uncomfortable to terrifying.

Jamie recalls having to meet their co-parent to talk about their son:

'We used to meet every couple of months. Somewhere neutral, like the park, somewhere outside if possible, as that was better for me. It made me feel like I could just escape, leave, walk away if I needed to. I don't know why I couldn't do that inside, but that's just the way it was. Often we used to meet in this outside café and I can still picture it really clearly. I would be nervous for days beforehand, grumpy with everyone, and I wouldn't sleep well. Not because I was physically afraid, but because I was terrified I was going to have a hard conversation, that it would descend into an argument, that I would get all muddled up or bamboozled. That was one of his ways of asserting power over me, to make me feel stupid.

'As I would walk to the café, my heart would literally be pounding, hammering in my chest, and my palms would get really sweaty. I would concentrate really hard on looking relaxed and composed but inside my nerves were shot. We would sit down and have a conversation about Barney and talk through any decisions we needed to make. My ex would often go off on a long monologue – he liked the sound of his own voice. I just needed to get through it.

'The meetings were often unsatisfactory, they would go round in circles as we couldn't agree on a decision, or it would descend into a row about something from our past. It wasn't particularly pleasant. But that all changed when I did The Co-Parenting Method and learned why I was in pieces before these meetings. Then when I learned the Meeting Framework everything became manageable from that moment on. I still hate meeting my ex. I still get nervous and sweaty-palmed, but I am much more able to focus on making the decisions. It's polite and transactional and I don't let us go off topic. We even have an agenda that we stick to. It's crazy, but it works.'

Thank you, Jamie, for introducing us to our next tool, the Meeting Framework.

PRACTICAL TOOL #14
The Meeting Framework

The Meeting Framework helps reduce the amount of time you need to spend with your ex-partner and can therefore help to reduce stress. It sets clear boundaries because you only meet to communicate about your child and nothing else. The Meeting Framework helps us organise successful co-parent meetings by giving them structure and focus, and allows us to prepare for them. Because we pre-agree the logistics and agenda beforehand this means that meetings become more predictable, contained and stable, and as a result we have more constructive conversations about our children. In your meeting you can use the Child-Centred Questions when appropriate. The Meeting Framework is a helpful way to approach meetings because it is structured and timebound. In my experience parents in a lot of conflict rely heavily on this approach because it keeps things contained. Parents who are in less conflict find it useful because it prevents conflict from escalating unnecessarily, which is fundamental to making good co-parental decisions.

I recommend that you schedule in regular meetings to discuss your children with your co-parent. I suggest a minimum of two to four meetings per year, although you may need more, especially if your child has specific needs. These meetings focus only on the children and nothing else. They concentrate on the practicalities of your child's life and their emotional wellbeing and any decisions that need taking.

How to create your Meeting Framework

To create your Meeting Framework you need to do four things:

1. Decide on a date and time for the meeting.
2. Agree a neutral location. This should not be somewhere you used to go as a couple. Try to choose a venue that works for both of you, and make sure alcohol isn't served. A video call is fine if you don't live near each other.
3. With your co-parent, agree agenda items in advance and agree that only these topics will be discussed during the meeting. Topics that appear on the agenda are *the only things* you'll talk about, so think carefully about what you want to discuss, and what you don't. Agenda items should be about your children and nothing else. They must be specific and not include things like 'any other business' or 'miscellaneous' or 'general catch-up'. (If setting the agenda is hard, then use a principle of fairness to help you get over the line. Either both add the same number of items to the agenda, or take it in turns to set the agenda. If you're taking it in turns, then limit the agenda to one or two items only.)
4. Agree a set amount of time for the meeting, and stick to it. Limiting the amount of time you have means that other topics are less likely to creep in. Think about how much time you need and then reduce it by 10–15 per cent. This keeps you completely focused on the agenda items. When your time is up, agree to end the meeting and come back another time if things aren't resolved. This has the added benefit of teaching you both to reach decisions quickly and effectively together.

Here are two suggested agendas. Feel free to adapt them by adding or removing topics according to your needs.

Agenda One: 40 minutes

School progress in maths

Steven's eczema – treatment and handing over medicines

Homework – how much time do we want Steven to be spending each week on it?

School trips – upcoming trips – what stuff does Steven need in what house for each trip?

Friendships and/or playdates – how to manage with What-sApp groups for birthday parties?

Agenda Two: 20 minutes

Sara's issue with A-Level choices. What are the criteria she should be using to help her decide?

Joined-up plan to get her to revise more for **GCSEs**. What can we do in both our homes to enable the best possible outcome?

If during the meeting your co-parent moves away from the agenda and starts talking about personal issues, or wants to revisit the story of your break-up, remind them why you're both there – to talk about the children – and that you've agreed to stick to the agenda. Be polite and respectful and focus on making decisions and agreeing practical actions.

Your Self-Management Avatar from step three, that you built to help you manage strong emotions and meet your ex in a calm and helpful way, will help you approach these meetings in a grounded and less emotional manner. This is really important when we are taking decisions about our children. Take the four Child-Centred Questions from the tool earlier in this chapter (see page 172) with you so you can make sure you remember to see it from your child's perspective. This will help keep the adult emotion out of the decision and this means your meeting is much more likely to stay on track and focused on the agenda.

For those of you reading and going through the method on your own, it can be helpful to explain the Meeting Framework to your co-parent as a way that you can make decisions together in an efficient way. Helping your co-parent see that parental decisions are unavoidable and that there will be points when you need to put your emotions aside to focus on those decisions is important, and the Meeting Framework is a way to do that.

Storing your Meeting Framework tool

To remember the Meeting Framework tool, we'll imagine storing it under our bottoms, because we put our bottoms on a chair while having a meeting! You could imagine it as an interesting, memorable chair. What kind of chair is it? What does it feel like sitting on it? Is it comfy or hard? Is it zebra print or fluffy?

When we make decisions it can also be really useful to consider the pros, cons and impacts of those decisions. It can help lessen the emotions around decision-making and enable you to consider it in a more open-minded way. Looking at the pros and cons means you might need to think about benefits and drawbacks that you hadn't previously thought about and that can allow you to see the bigger picture. Your next tool is a formula to help you do this. It's a good one for preventing us from slipping back into that short-term, wanting-to-win mindset too.

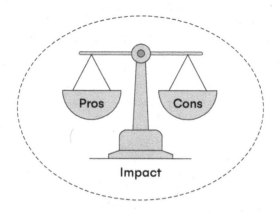

Pros, Cons, Impact Formula

If you and your co-parent need extra support to reach an agreement or if you're in any way worried about the impact of your decision, then you can use my Pros, Cons, Impact Formula. Sometimes we need to be guided in a very structured way through a decision and this formula will help you with that. I still want to urge you to trust your instincts too. If you get an answer that doesn't feel right, then please listen to yourself. You are the parents and this is simply a guide to help you get from point A to point B.

If you're doing this tool with your co-parent, then try to agree the scores together so you only have one set of values for each section. If you're both at opposite ends of the scoring spectrum you might want to consider meeting in the middle. If you're doing it on your own without your co-parent and you're using the tool as a decision-making support, try to think about things from your co-parent's perspective too.

Grab your notebook and pen and follow the steps below. Before you start, take a couple of deep breaths and feel your feet on the floor. Both of these things will help ground you and put you into a more neutral frame of mind.

1. Write down what decision you need to make.
2. Decide on how long you want to spend making this decision.
3. Now write down all the pros for the decisions.
4. Now write down all the cons (try to have the same number of pros and cons).
5. Now score all the pros (out of five) as to how much of a positive impact they will have.
6. And do the same with all the cons. Score them out of five as to how much of a negative impact they will have.
7. Add up your pros, and then add up your cons. Which score is higher?
8. Consider using the higher score as the basis for your decision.

So it might look something like this:

Decision: Whether or not to limit Ruby's time on her smartphone

Pros

It's better for her mental health – 5
She will have more time for homework – 5
She will interact with the family more – 5
(total 15)

Cons

It means I get less time to work – 4
She loves learning from things that she watches – 4
She gets less down time – 4
(total 12)

Now you have your scores, you can see that one way of deciding will have more impact than the other. Use this information to help feed into your decision-making as co-parents. Remember you are still the parents, so if something doesn't feel right then you need to listen to those feelings too.

Storing your Pros, Cons, Impact Formula

We'll store our Pros, Cons, Impact Formula in our right elbow, as we can really impact something when we elbow it. Think of your elbow as having a hammer on the end of it, to really hammer home that impact.

What Is a Co-Parent Charter?

Imagine a document that represents our intended way of behaving towards each other as co-parents. A Co-Parent Charter does just that. It sets out ten behavioural agreements or commitments, and it acts as the foundation of our future co-parent relationship. You can do this on your own if your co-parent isn't going through the six steps with you – I'll explain how further down.

By setting out your intentions of how you will co-parent together you will have a greater degree of accountability as to how you behave with each other. It helps remind you what you will do if you disagree, and it gives you a plan of what to do when things go wrong, or when there are bumps in the road. It can be one of the tools that enables your child to grow up in a non-hostile environment where parents act towards each other in a respectful and co-operative way.

The Co-Parent Charter is a series of statements that you and your co-parent will agree on together. You can amend the statements as they exist in the example I've given below, or you can write your own (more on that further down). The important thing is that you have a statement for each section.

The Co-Parent Charter

It might feel strangely formal to have a charter with your co-parent about how you are both going to act and behave with each other. That formality might mean you want to skip doing this tool. But let's take a step back for a moment. When we write something down and when we agree to it with someone else, it adds in a new level of accountability. Accountability is one of the things that helps us keep showing up to doing something. So by writing and agreeing on your charter you build in another layer of commitment as co-parents that you'll stick to co-parenting well together even if things get tough.

Below is an example template version of the Co-Parent Charter so you can see what it looks like in practice.

Sample Co-Parent Charter
[Insert parent names here]

This Co-Parent Charter covers how we work together to bring up [insert name of child]. It deals with how we interact as parents and how we respect each other as individuals.

[Insert name of child] is/are our priority. All our interactions, decisions and agreements will acknowledge this as the overarching principle.

This is not a legally binding document, but we have both agreed to it and want it to inform how we parent [insert name of child] together.

1. We will make our co-parenting impersonal and transactional.
2. We take responsibility for the way we communicate with each other in regard to our co-parenting.
3. We commit to uphold the Co-Parental Loop for our children, and to consciously manage our emotions in order to make the loop secure for them.
4. We recognise that co-parenting won't always be a smooth process and when it gets difficult we will remember that this is not about us and that the primary focus needs to come back to our children.
5. We respect each other as individual human beings and will respect each other's privacy. We agree that anything that happens in each other's private worlds is not our business unless it concerns our children.
6. We trust that both of us want the best for our children and that all decisions we take will be from this place.
7. We respect each other as parents and the different strengths and experiences we can bring to our children.
8. We will never say a bad word about each other in front of, or within earshot of, our children. We will uphold each other as a parent and, in doing so, we will uphold the part of our children that comes from each other.
9. We will encourage and support each other in our co-parent duties and meet each other at pre-agreed times to

discuss our children. We will discuss how we feel our children are getting on, and will promptly deal with any issues that need dealing with.

10. We are aligned on these points.

Signed

[Parent Signature Here] [Date Here]

[Parent Signature Here] [Date Here]

[Witness Signature Here] [Date Here]

Creating your charter

There are three different ways you can create your Co-Parent Charter.

First, if the charter template above works for both you and your co-parent, use that. Simply type it up and print it off and both sign it.

Second, if either of you wants to make changes to the template to make it more specific to your situation, do that. I'll walk you through how to approach that just below.

Third, if you're reading the book *without* your co-parent, speak to your co-parent about creating a charter together. If they are not open to this, independently create a charter that covers your own commitments to the co-parent relationship. This is a really good way of keeping you in a long-term mindset even if you're not getting much engagement from your co-parent. Again, you can use the template version or adapt it to your needs.

Signing your charter, whether you're doing it together or on your own, is really important. Putting your signature on something is a signal either to yourself or your co-parent that you are committing to living by the statements that are written down. Signing it helps us strive to stick to our charter. If you want an extra layer of accountability, consider getting a third party to witness and sign it too.

Make sure you keep the final document somewhere you'll see it regularly. You can put it on the fridge, near your toothbrush, or in the loo!

Having it on public display is a good reminder for both you and your friends and family that your role as a good co-parent is non-negotiable.

Personalising your charter

If you want something more from your charter, then personalising it is the route for you. Whether you need to be specific because of your children's needs or because of your situation, or simply because it feels more right for you, having a personalised charter can be really helpful to keep everybody on track. A personalised charter can also feel more meaningful to parents and more relevant to them, which makes it more likely that you will stick to it.

The charter is split into sections, and each section has a need and a behaviour that needs to be met. I'm going to take you through each section so you know what you're aiming for and are clear about how to add in detail in a way that works for everybody.

Before we get into each section of the charter, you'll notice the introductory text sitting at the top. This reads:

[Name and Name's] Co-Parent Charter

This Co-Parent Charter covers how we work together to bring up [insert name of child]. It deals with how we interact as parents and how we respect each other as individuals.

[insert name of child] is/are our priority. All our interactions, decisions and agreements will acknowledge this as the overarching principle.

This is not a legally binding document, but we have both agreed to it and want it to inform how we parent [insert name of child] together.

Action: All you need to do is to put your names and the name of your children in there. This text is there because it's important to remind ourselves of what the charter is and what the guiding principles are.

Now let's move on to the ten statements in the charter. There need to be a minimum of ten statements and a maximum of 18. Any less than ten and you're not going to be covering enough situations, and I find that any more than 18 and it becomes hard to stick to as there are just too many things to remember.

Below you'll see what each statement is about, and a specific statement from a real-life charter so you can understand how to modify it while keeping the language neutral and collaborative. Sometimes there needs to be more than one point under each area, but ideally not more than two.

Statement One

This is all about managing your emotions and removing the emotion from the co-parenting. Which, as we saw in step two, is important for staying on track with co-parenting.

I suggest: We will make our co-parenting impersonal and transactional.

From a real Co-Parent Charter created by one of my clients: We will make our co-parenting polite, kind, respectful and neutral and focused on decision-making.

Statement Two

This is about how you intend to communicate with each other. How we choose to communicate is critical to make our co-parenting positive and effective.

I suggest: We take responsibility for the way we communicate with each other in regard to our co-parenting.

Real-life Co-Parent Charter: We will aim to have easy communication with regards to making arrangements to spend time with Bobby and Sue.

And:

We will commit to managing our emotions in order to take decisions about Bobby and Sue, together, and respond in a timely way.

Statement Three

This is all about committing to uphold the Co-Parental Loop. Staying in the long-term mindset is so important in our co-parenting, and as we saw in step one, upholding the Co-Parental Loop is our constant reminder of this.

I suggest: We commit to uphold the Co-Parental Loop for our children, and to consciously manage our emotions in order to make the loop secure for them.

Real-life Co-Parent Charter: We commit to upholding the parental loop for James and Samantha, and consciously managing our emotions in order to make the loop secure for them. We will do this by communicating with each other respectfully in front of them so they can see that we are still able to do that.

Statement Four

This is about when it gets tough. Which it will do at times. Being able to use our tools to get back on track with our co-parenting shows great commitment and desire to stay in the long-term mindset overall.

I suggest: We recognise that co-parenting won't always be a smooth process and when it gets difficult we will remember that this is not about us and that the primary focus needs to come back to our children. We will use the tools we have learned to help us.

Real-life Co-Parent Charter: When it gets difficult, we will remember that our primary focus is Maya and that by parenting collaboratively we do the best for her so she can grow up in a stable, nurturing and loving environment.

Statement Five

This is about how you respect each other as individual human beings and acknowledging that you are leading separate lives. It also refers to the Three Worlds tool and we are reminded about the boundaries we need to make that work well.

I suggest: We respect each other as individual human beings and will respect each other's privacy. We agree that anything that happens in each other's private worlds is not our business unless it concerns our children.

Real-life Co-Parent Charter: We will respect each other's boundaries and worlds. We won't cross over the boundaries into each other's worlds, including work, our private space, finances and other life choices, unless there are worries about the children.

Statement Six

This one is about trusting each other as parents. It's a hard one for many co-parents to include, but it's about reminding ourselves that our co-parent loves our children even if the parenting might look a bit different.

I suggest: We trust that both of us want the best for our children and that all decisions we take will be from this place.

Real-life Co-Parent Charter: We will trust that our co-parent wants the best for Ben and Sarah and that all decisions we take will be from this place of trust. We will enable our co-parent to trust us by sticking to schedules and arrangements.

Statement Seven

This is about recognising each other's contribution as parents. It's about drawing on the tools you've learned to recognise that we have different perspectives as parents and different roles to play.

I suggest: We respect each other as parents and the different strengths and experiences we can bring to our children.

Real-life Co-Parent Charter: We will respect each other as parents and will respect the different strengths, qualities and experiences we can both bring to our parenting.

And:

If we mess up, we will apologise and recognise that we all make mistakes but not let it escalate into something that can damage our co-parenting relationship.

Statement Eight

This is all about how you communicate with your children about each other. As we saw in step four, it's crucially important that we endorse each other as parents in front of our children. Our kids are part us and part their other parent, whether it's nature or nurture, and we don't have the right to diminish that side of them. It can also be about how you share big pieces of information with them.

I suggest: We will never say a bad word about each other in front of, or within earshot of, our children. We will uphold each other as a parent and, in doing so, we will uphold the part of our children that comes from each other.

Real-life Co-Parent Charter: We will commit to uphold each other's status in front of Frances. We understand that positive behaviour and communication about each other is the best way to keep them safe in this respect.

And:

When we are ready to introduce a new partner, we will make sure each of us has an opportunity to meet the new partner in a neutral location for a short period of time before we introduce them to Frances. We understand this is important so Frances doesn't feel that they need to keep information secret.

Statement Nine

This is all about mutual co-parenting support and good decision-making. It's about continuing to parent actively and sharing information with each other to support each other as parents. For your children this can mean the difference between experiencing you as joined-up parents or separate ones. They will feel more secure if they know you're communicating about them even when you're not in the same place.

I suggest: We will encourage and support each other in our co-parent duties and meet each other at pre-agreed times to discuss our children. We will discuss how we feel our children are getting on, and will promptly deal with any issues that need dealing with.

Real-life Co-Parent Charter: Until we've decided who is going to live where and made all our arrangements, we will work together to find a way to share information about the children. We can do this via a hand-over email or WhatsApp. We should make sure there is detail about what they've been doing in these messages. We should continue to share information with each other once our arrangements have been resolved.

Statement Ten

This always needs to say: We are aligned on these points. By stating this, it is an active choice you are taking to commit to the charter and your acceptance of your role in it.

So now you have your charter, and if you've spent some time personalising it then it should really speak to you and your co-parent and how you want to be around each other in relation to your co-parenting. Let it be your guide on this journey. Remember that if you're doing this on your own it will serve as your reminder of how you will be with your co-parent to uphold your part of the Co-Parental Loop.

Storing your Co-Parent Charter

To help us remember the Co-Parent Charter, let's do something a bit different this time. Rather than storing our charter on our body, let's put it on our fridge! Place it right in the middle, where you'll always notice it. We need it to be visible to remind us to follow it.

A Co-Parenting Plan

Parenting comes with having to make a huge number of decisions. Every day we need to decide things for and about our children. When we're co-parenting it's hard to make those decisions in isolation and making them together can often be a contributor to conflict. Having a place where many of those decisions are made in advance reduces the need for decision-making between you as co-parents and therefore reduces the risk of conflict. That reduction in needing to communicate can be really helpful for some parents on their co-parent journey. A Co-Parenting Plan is a practical written agreement between two parents that sets down how you want to manage your child's time, and how you respond to, and deal with, certain circumstances. The plan helps you decide the arrangements you need to put in place to care for your children after separation. It provides a structure that allows you and your co-parent to agree the many practical questions around bringing up your children following separation. It's like your own personal co-parenting guidebook.

Why is a Co-Parenting Plan important?

For many people the plan is their main co-parenting tool. Having the plan reduces the need for contact between you and your co-parent, because many parenting decisions have been pre-agreed.

A Co-Parenting Plan is a fantastic tool to help you handle a range of practical questions. These include things like: how does handover happen when children move between homes? How much time does your child spend with you and how much time with your co-parent? How do holidays work? What are the rules around food, or TV time, or homework?

More than that, the plan also serves as a day-to-day reminder about how you as co-parents have agreed together to raise your child. Think of it like rules of engagement, or the blueprint you can both refer to for your parenting decisions. Together, you both write and agree to the

Co-Parenting Plan so no conflict should arise from any actions you take based on it. When you use it alongside the charter, you have both practical and behavioural bases covered.

Even if you're not writing one with your co-parent, the plan is still super useful. Louisa remembers writing hers:

'According to a couple of my friends, going through The Co-Parenting Method on my own was daft. But in reality what it gave me was a solid framework about how to handle and show up to my particularly difficult situation. I didn't know it at the time, but one of the most useful pieces would be the Co-Parenting Plan. Even though Brett (my ex) wasn't interested in getting things sorted, for me, having one place where all the information was kept was invaluable. When I filled it in I was calm and relaxed; and so under the health section I was able to write down my decision that I would tell Brett about medical emergencies as they happened. Same with the passport. I wrote down that I would keep the passport, but I wouldn't hold it back as a weapon if Brett asked for it. I was very reasonable when I wrote it and those reasonable decisions helped me stay accountable when things got really tricky between us. We were in the middle of one battle when one of the kids got very sick and had to go to the hospital. I knew I had committed that I would call Brett if this happened and so I did just that. I hadn't called him on the phone in a long time and he was surprised but relieved that I had. In a funny way, that phone call, which showed I could put the needs of the kids before my own, helped us start to get better at communicating again. So, if you're doing The Co-Parenting Method alone, then still fill it in. It really helped me.'

The Co-Parenting Plan

The Co-Parenting Plan is divided into distinct sections. It's written this way to help you think about specific areas of your children's life and some of the co-parenting decisions that need to be made in each area. You'll probably find some sections of the plan easy to fill in, and some less easy. Even if you find it difficult, try to answer all the questions as thoroughly as you can. Robust Co-Parenting Plans can help stabilise difficult relationships. For the parents of Stefan, whose story you heard in step two (see page 61), having a Co-Parenting Plan was very helpful to manage the interaction between them. The plan worked as an important point of reference to keep everything functioning in their co-parenting family system.

Some of the questions in the Co-Parenting Plan may not seem relevant yet if you have younger children, but please do try to answer them all the same. Having made a decision about how you will react before you cross those bridges means you're more likely to remain calm and business-like when you do. And even if circumstances have changed, your prior thinking will still be helpful.

There are various ways you can complete your Co-Parenting Plan, and how you do it will depend on your circumstances. Firstly, it's important to say that however you choose to fill in your plan, please have your

Self-Management Avatar (see page 73) next to you when you do it. Your avatar will help you manage your emotions and make it easier to keep in mind what's best for your children and make a commitment to upholding the Co-Parental Loop (see page 45).

OK, let's think about how we create the Co-Parenting Plan in practice.

If you can, you should arrange a meeting with your co-parent and work through the questions together. If you fill in the plan with your co-parent, make sure you use the Meeting Framework to pre-agree the agenda of the meeting, and remember to ask Child-Centred Questions. This will help you if you have a difference of opinion. If you do find yourself disagreeing on a section, move onto another section that you will agree on first. It's helpful to pick the low hanging fruit as it creates a good collaborative basis for the plan. Approach filling in the plan in sections to keep it manageable. So, aim for two sections per meeting. It might take a while to do this, but it will help you manage any emotional response and keep those boundaries nice and secure.

If your relationship isn't strong enough to sit down and discuss the plan with your co-parent, there are other approaches. Some co-parents fill in their plans separately and then come together to compare and discuss. Again, we recommend you do this spread over a number of meetings. Ideally, you'd do this face to face, physically or online.

Others work on a shared file and make comments and suggestions directly on the document. If you do that there is more room for misinterpretation, so please make your language neutral and collaborative.

For those of you going through the book alone, please still fill in the template. When the time is right, it can act as a discussion document with your ex, and it can also be an important guide for you on how you want to raise your children. Completing it alone may feel strange, but it will help you address things you've not thought of before and prepare you for the future.

However you fill in the plan, whether with your co-parent or individually, be as business-like, practical and unemotional as you can be. Give your plan the best chance of working by being honest with yourself about what's best for your children, as well as what will work for both you and your co-parent.

We're going to go through each section of the plan and look at what it's there for. Under each section are the questions that will help you make your decisions under that topic. Feel free to add your own if you would like to. I've included an answer to the first question in each section to help give you a feel for how to fill in the plan.

Introduction

This Co-Parenting Plan aims to help you navigate the many practical questions that arise about bringing up your children when you separate. You can use the following three reminders at the top of your plan to remember some fundamental points and to help you keep you on track when you're filling it in.

Remember at all times that we are both parents to our children.

Remember that our children love us both.

Remember that our children want to see us both.

Who's in the plan

The first section is about putting down who the plan is being written by, who it is written for and other people who will have a direct impact on the plan.

Questions

Parent names: *John Adams and Lucy Berman*

    Children names and ages:

    Teacher, carer, support worker names:

Logistics

The logistics section covers where the children will live, school pick-ups, after-school activities, school holidays, who looks after the children if one parent is sick, where the important documents are kept, laundry, summer camps and more. Following a relationship breakdown, many co-parents start with this topic and it can quickly lead to friction and aggressive communication. By going through this book, you now have the skills to manage this. When discussing logistics with your co-parent, remember to keep the welfare of your children front and centre of your mind and you can use the Child-Centred Questions tool from step four. Agreeing on logistics means that both of you know what your kids are doing, when they're doing it, and who's responsible. It reduces the need for interaction with each other, which for many co-parents is a huge benefit. Strong logistical arrangements will really help you on your co-parenting journey.

Questions

1. How many nights a week will the children stay with each of us? Which nights will those be? (consistent patterns are helpful here)
   The children will stay with Lucy every Monday, Tuesday and Thursday and every other weekend (including the Friday of that weekend). They'll stay with John every Wednesday and every other weekend.
2. When and how do handovers take place?
3. How will we divide the school holidays?
4. Will we review this arrangement? If so, when?
5. Will the children go to summer camps and clubs and activities?
6. How do we manage school pick-ups and drop-offs?
7. What clothes and belongings will be taken and returned at changeover and what will we have at both houses?
8. Who will be responsible for making sure that clothes that are changing houses are washed?

9. Who will take them to regular sporting engagements on weekends and after school?
10. Can the other parent come if there is a match or prize giving?
11. Who will be responsible for organising routine doctor, nurse, optician and dentist appointments?
12. If one parent has to go to hospital for a period of time – who will the children stay with?
13. Will anyone else look after the children (for example, childminders, babysitters, relatives, new partners, friends and neighbours)? If so, when?
14. How will we cover bank holidays and inset days at school?
15. Where will the children spend significant holidays, festivals and dates – Christmas, New Year, religious festivals, birthdays, Mother's Day, Father's Day?
16. Will we aim to spend some time together as a whole unit on those days?
17. How often will we meet as a family unit so the children can see us together as parents?
18. How will we plan for taking the children abroad?
19. Who will look after the children's important documentation such as passports and birth certificates?
20. How will we determine how the year looks in terms of holidays? (For example, will we meet in October to set a plan for the year ahead? Such a meeting can also be an annual chance to rediscuss any issues in this Co-Parenting Plan if necessary.)

Communicating with Each Other

You already know that how you talk to each other is fundamental if you're trying to build a co-parenting relationship. In this part of the plan, we take all the work we did in steps four and five and put it into practice. We look at how often we'll meet to take decisions, how we'll work out disagreements, how to communicate with each other in an emergency.

Questions

1. What will be the one primary medium we use to communicate with each other (WhatsApp, messages, email, through a co-parenting app)? *We will use WhatsApp to communicate with each other the majority of the time.*

2. How will we share important information with each other (school reports, trips to the doctor)?

3. How often will we meet face to face to discuss our children and our parenting?

4. Where will we meet?

5. How much do we include the children in our decision-making?

6. If we decide to include the children in our decision-making, how will we do it?

7. When is it OK to call each other and when isn't it?

8. How do we work out our parenting disagreements?

9. How will we communicate with each other in an emergency?

10. When big decisions are needed (such as around schools, careers) how will we work together to make those decisions or give advice to our children?

Communicating with the Children

This section of the plan sticks with communication, but focuses on the children and how you communicate with them when they're not with you. It's not about how you actually talk to your children, but rather about how you stay connected with them when they're with their co-parent. Staying in contact with our children when they're not with us is really important for their emotional growth and safety. For children, knowing they can access both parents whenever they want without feeling ashamed, guilty or afraid is so important. Allowing regular contact with the other parent upholds the Co-Parental Loop and increases your child's resilience.

In this section of the plan, you'll agree how and when your co-parent speaks with the children when they're at your house and vice versa. It also ensures there are respectful boundaries in place so that when children are with one parent the other parent isn't constantly calling or messaging them.

Questions

1. When they are not with us, how will we communicate with our children, how often and at what time?

   We will video-call them every 48 hours at a time that we agree with our co-parent in advance. Usually 5pm is a good time, but we understand that this may change, especially on holidays when we may have plans. We'll have a maximum of ten minutes on the phone with them and the parent that they're with will help to make it a positive experience.

2. When they are not with us, when should we *not* call to speak to them?

3. If we are separated for longer periods of time, what else can we do to ensure that our children maintain meaningful contact with the parent that they are away from? (You can include things like story time, small gifts, postcards, online gaming platforms where you can play together.)

Rules

Section four of the plan looks at rules. Underpinning everything we do when we bring up our children are house rules, boundaries, things they can do and things they can't. Aiming to have similar rules and guidelines in both houses is important to keep children feeling held and safe. They don't need to be exactly the same, but the more similar they are, the simpler it will be for your children. It may not be possible to have identical rules – especially if there are new relationships with partners who have their own children and ways of doing things. But if there can be some central rules that are similar, that's helpful. To help with this process, the section on rules looks at things like screen time, bedtimes, food – and consequences for breaking the rules. It also encourages us to think about how we keep our co-parent informed if our child has broken the agreed boundaries.

Questions

1. What will be our agreed rules that cover both houses? (These could include screen time, sweet treats, bedtimes, social media, homework, and other areas.)

   The children will have 30 minutes of screen time a day and two hours a day at the weekends. Sweet treats won't be given before meals or before lunchtime on a weekend. Homework needs to be done before screen time. As they age we will put social media restrictions in place. We will make sure when they're old enough for us to do this, that we put keeping them safe online at the heart of our discussion.

2. If our children break the rules and we need to put in place a consequence – what will that be?

3. How will we keep each other informed about what has happened?

Expenses

When separating, money is often a hugely difficult topic. I want to be clear that in the Co-Parenting Plan we're talking about extra expenses related to your children only. This Co-Parenting Plan doesn't cover your wider financial settlement, and it doesn't cover your child's maintenance agreements. The money section of the plan is focused on things that aren't covered by your other financial plans, like pocket money or costs if your child takes up a new interest that needs some equipment.

Maintenance agreements end when your children reach the age of 18, so you may also wish to discuss any costs beyond that age – for example, who will contribute to the children's college or university costs?

Questions

1. How will we share day-to-day expenses that fall outside of our child maintenance arrangement?
   Here is a list of things that we agree fall outside of our child maintenance agreement:
   - *Pocket money*
   - *Savings*
   - *Equipment for hobbies*
   - *Going out with their friends*
   - *We agree to split these costs equally.*
2. How will we give out pocket money and how much will it be?
3. What will we do if our financial positions change?
4. How will financial arrangements change as the children grow up (for example, making provision for college or university)?

Education

Education is an important one to get right. Schools are usually willing to email information to both parents if you're separated, so make sure you contact your children's school to let them know about your separation, and to find out what's possible. Schools will also usually send out two copies of reports and will see you both separately on parents' evenings if you request that. If you can, it's great if you can get to parents' evenings together – you can use it as an opportunity to have a short co-parent meeting afterwards to discuss your child's progress in school and talk about any red flag areas that may have come up. If you're going to do so, remember all that you've learned about neutral communication and make sure the meeting takes place using the Meeting Framework in the co-parent world (and remember to take your Self-Management Avatar!).

Schools and teachers also play a vital role providing a stable environment for children including spotting when our kids are not doing well or are struggling. So, as co-parents, having regular discussions with teachers can be very useful. Your children may have special educational needs, so dealing with the school to support those needs will mean you also need to have open channels of communication with each other and the school. It is your responsibility to make it as easy for the school as possible to keep you both updated about how your child is getting on.

Questions

1. How will we communicate with the childcare providers/school and the relevant teachers about our separation and the impact it may be having on our children?
   Lucy and John will send a joint email to the school to arrange to have a face-to-face conversation with the children's class teachers. After that Lucy will be the main school contact and will send John anything that comes from the school immediately. Any emails that Lucy sends to the school she will copy John into.
2. Where will reports, notices, pictures and other things related to our children's progress be sent?
3. Will it be possible for school to send some of these to both houses?
4. How will we handle school reports? Who will go through them with the children?
5. How will we approach parents' evenings?
6. If our child has additional educational needs, how will we communicate around that with each other and with the school?
7. If your child has health needs, how do we keep in regular touch with the school?

Wider Family Contact

When you split up from your partner you often also split up from your partner's wider family. This can be really difficult for kids.

Children are most likely to flourish when they receive consistent messages from everyone who surrounds them, including those in both your and your ex-partner's wider family. It helps reinforce the feeling for children that everyone – including grandparents, uncles, aunts, and so on – are playing their roles correctly, and it makes them feel more secure. And, as we've seen throughout the book, feeling secure is really important for children's mental wellbeing. This part of the Co-Parenting Plan helps you decide together as co-parents what you want your separation 'story' or 'messaging' to be, so you can inform your wider families what you want them to say to your children. When everyone is on message, children feel held and secure. If Grandma is talking to your children and starts saying awful things about their mum, then that's going to destabilise their family system. Everyone in the family has a responsibility to keep children mentally safe.

Questions

1. How will we make sure that both sides of the family are talking to the kids about our divorce in the same way?

   We will write a messaging sheet for the family about how we want them to talk about our divorce. We will each take our own families through that sheet and ask them to commit to using the sheet when talking to the kids about their other parent.

2. How will we make sure that both sides of the family are being respectful about us in front of the kids?

3. How will we make sure our children stay in contact with friends and relatives from each other's side of the family?

Health

Your children may have health issues that mean you need to have regular communication. This is the part of the plan that will help you address how you're going to approach that. Be kind to each other; your child's health is a very emotive topic and needs to be treated with care and sensitivity. If medication needs to be passed between houses it will be essential for you to be able to maintain a dialogue to care for your child properly.

Questions

1. List the details of any health conditions and medications.
   Danny has a penicillin allergy but is on no medication for this.
2. List the details of the medical professionals your child is registered with (doctor, dentist etc.).
3. How do you manage any long-term health needs of your child, including appointments, medication and treatment?
4. Who is responsible for making appointments with the GP or specialist medical appointments?
5. Who is responsible for making appointments with the dentist?
6. How will you deal with medical emergencies?
7. How will you communicate about medical emergencies and general medical and dental updates?
8. How will we pass medication between houses and what happens if that medication needs to be specifically stored, e.g. in the fridge?

Other Areas

And finally, this part of your Co-Parenting Plan is the place for any other topics and questions you want to consider that haven't been covered elsewhere in the plan. These could be choices about religious upbringing; arrangements around family pets; and the huge question of how to introduce new partners to children and what a future 'blended' family might look like.

Questions

1. What will we agree about any religious practice and upbringing? *Neither of us have any religion that we follow so this isn't relevant to us. However, if either of us meet a new partner who does observe religious practice then we shall both be curious and respectful of that and we will be mindful to talk respectfully about it with the children.*

2. Are there any cultural traditions that we will need to uphold?

3. Will we need to make arrangements around any pets that the children have?

4. How will we introduce new partners to our children's lives? See page 221 for some thoughts on how to do that.

5. How often will we review this plan?

So, as you can see, the Co-Parenting Plan is a massively useful tool for airing, discussing and resolving lots of different issues, sometimes before they arise. By making it clear what's been agreed and what hasn't and by deciding parental responsibilities, it can be a vital step towards a successful co-parenting relationship. The many tools you've learned while reading this book will help you when you're discussing the parenting plan with your co-parent. Remember to use them!

Take your time filling in your Co-Parenting Plan and try to put in as much detail as possible. It will be a really solid guide for all of you moving forward. If you need to add other parts to your plan that fall outside of these areas, please agree those with your co-parent and make the decisions accordingly.

Storing your Co-Parenting Plan

Like with the Co-Parent Charter, you won't store the Co-Parenting Plan on your body. Instead, I'd like you to print it out and put it where you can get hold of it easily when you need it. Perhaps it's near the house phone, or near the front door. Wherever you know that you can easily reach for it, that's where I would like you to store it.

Having ways to make decisions more simply means that it becomes easier for your co-parenting to remain on track and your Co-Parental Loop stays nice and secure for your kids. Using the tools you've learned in this step means that decision-making becomes a less emotional and more focused process, leaving less room for conflict to emerge. By doing that, you're providing a parental structure for your kids that is grounded, secure and one that they can rely on. Growing up with two parents who don't live together, but who can achieve this, is what we're aiming for. Having the Co-Parent Charter and your Co-Parenting Plan is an important part of this security because you are both agreeing to how you will behave around each other and you've looked at and thought through many of the decisions you'll need to take about your children. Minimising the opportunity for conflict is at the heart of both these tools and together, with the practical approach of the Meeting Framework, you have most of what you need for your successful co-parenting relationship. To help you remember what we've looked at in step five, here's your summary.

STEP FIVE SUMMARY

- Robust decision-making is one of the cornerstones of keeping your child feeling nice and stable.
- We looked at why it's hard to make good decisions with a co-parent – sometimes the practical elements can be really onerous and you may not want to deal with them.
- We also looked at why it's really important to be able to do it and how to get a handle on decision-making to keep co-parenting on track and your children's lives moving forward.
- You learned the Meeting Framework tool to have laser-focused meetings with your co-parent to increase the effectiveness of your decision-making discussions.
- And you learned the Child-Centred Questions tool, to be able to take into account the perspective of your child when you're making decisions.
- You also learned the Pros, Cons, Impact Formula to help with your decision-making.
- Your Co-Parent Charter will help remind you of your behavioural commitment to each other as co-parents or to yourself with your co-parent.
- And finally your Co-Parenting Plan will store all the decisions you've made with your co-parent or for yourself.

Storing your tools: The Meeting Framework we'll keep under our bottoms that are sitting in a chair. The Child-Centred Questions tool we'll associate with a question mark attached to our belly button, and the Pros, Cons, Impact Formula we will store in our right elbow.

Instead of storing the Co-Parent Charter and the Co-Parenting Plan on your body, we will be physically printing them out and putting them somewhere you can see them. Both of these tools have so much information in them that a visual reminder will help you revisit what you have written more often than if they are in a drawer somewhere. Print out your charter and put it on your fridge or somewhere you will regularly see it. The same goes for the Co-Parenting Plan. I'd like you to have this somewhere you can just reach for it when you need it to help keep you on track in your co-parenting. Having these two tools to hand so you can remind yourself of the content will be really useful for you.

For children who switch between two homes, life can be complicated. Even if the rules are the same in both houses, they still have to adjust. The home is different; their bedroom is different; things are kept in different places; the food and ways of doing things at mealtimes are different; the plates and cutlery are different; people dress in a different way, behave in a different way; things smell different. These might sound like small things, but they all add up. Most of us are used to being in the same home all the time. We don't move between houses and so there is no adjustment. Kids with two homes have to constantly adjust and that can be tiring and sometimes upsetting for them. We know that children who move between houses can compartmentalise. They often feel like a visitor in both houses, and they may cover up and manage their feelings to protect themselves. All of these things have an effect on our children's mental health. But if we as parents can create strong and stable foundations for them by making good decisions about them, then this will give them the grounding and the resilience to transition between houses more easily.

Decision-making with your co-parent can be one of the things that we find draining. It's hard, and we need to use all the tools we have learned along the way to help us. If you're feeling depleted and drained, it can be difficult to show up to all the different aspects of co-parenting in the way that you want to. But it is possible! And as we move into step six we're going to be focusing on you and boosting your resilience to help you thrive in your own world so you can find it easier to stay on track with your co-parenting.

Beyond Surviving to Thriving

It's crucial for your children to see you thriving and not just surviving. When you are thriving, you're fulfilled, you feel happier overall and you have high levels of resilience. As a thriving parent you're passing really positive messages to your children and achieving this as a co-parent means that your children can see and learn that being able to thrive is normal and possible even after a relationship breakdown.

We all know that being around people who are fulfilled feels positive, and it's the same for your children. If they experience you as a happy and productive adult who is able to parent them with their other parent, then having two homes and separated parents will be manageable for them. In this step we're are going to look at how we achieve this. This is the icing on the cake in terms of managing their wellbeing and enabling them to grow up into flourishing adults. However, even when we're thriving there will always be bumps in the road. We'll look at how we deal with events that might derail you and I'll give you some tools that will help keep you in a strong place, allow you to stay in control, manage any tricky co-parenting times that may come your way and move towards a fulfilled life. I want you to feel good about yourself and your co-parenting. You've done hard things and you deserve this!

How to Thrive

In step three, when we built your Three Worlds system (see page 106), we focused on making sure your world had a good number of parts in it that were just about you – elements and activities that build you up and make you feel good about your life. You committed to making some of those things a reality even if that was hard. I want to take that a little bit further now.

I want you to thrive in your life and in your co-parenting, and in order to thrive in co-parenting we need to be happy and nourished and not depleted and drained. It's now time to move you firmly into a place where you smile, you feel great and happy. When you feel all these things you can also apply yourself more positively to co-parenting, and when your co-parenting is on firmer ground then your children will thrive as well as you.

One of the key elements of feeling fulfilled, happy and on track in life is how you deal with problems. Life is a series of different events that we experience and it's how we deal with those that matters. The more resilience we have, the bigger our ability to deal with things and bounce back, and the easier it is therefore, for us to thrive.

In order for us to be resilient, we need to make sure that we are looking after our physical and mental health. That we are having nourishing experiences, that we are doing things that bring us joy, and crucially that we are moving forward with our lives. We need to be putting enough effort into doing that so we are balanced. Having positive things in our lives is not a nice-to-have; it's essential. A lot of us struggle with this concept. Recall for a moment when you last did something just for you. What was it? How did you feel afterwards? How long did you carry that nice feeling with you? Whether it's going to a concert, going on a run, meditating in a field, reading a book in the daytime, going out to the pub with your friends or going on a holiday, doing things for yourself gives you a feeling of a sense of self, of being an adult, not just a parent or a co-parent. This improves our sense of resilience. And when we are resilient it means we can cope better, we bounce back from knocks more quickly and we are happier and more flexible in our approach to life and to difficulties. When we don't have much resilience, then we are more likely to snap, shout, be brittle and find it difficult to be joyful.

The Resilience Bucket

That feeling when you come back from an amazing experience and it stays with you for several days, is the feeling of your resilience being filled up and your self-care being seen to. When you feel good, when your resilience is high, you are more flexible, less breakable and you can do hard things. Having resilience means you can better deal with anything difficult that might come along. We need a place to store all this lovely resilience, and so in a moment I'm going to ask you to imagine a bucket, your Resilience Bucket. You can personalise your bucket and make it look appealing to you; if you like the look of your bucket then you're much more likely to remember to fill it up.

Helen's bucket was a shiny purple bucket with a jewelled handle that she bought from a very posh department store. Her bucket looked beautiful and it made her smile when she looked at it. David's bucket was black and bullet proof. His bucket would never rust. It was durable and it was big. Your bucket can be however you want it to be. Please close your eyes and imagine your bucket now. Open them when you're ready. This is your Resilience Bucket. If you want to draw it in your notebook to remind yourself of what it looks like, then please do so.

We are going to fill up your Resilience Bucket with positive things.

Think back to the Three Worlds tool. Your world had lots of things in it that nourished you. (If you want to revisit the notes you took then, please feel free to do so.) Those same things are in your Resilience Bucket, except in your bucket they're going to be much more specific. The more specific you are, the easier it is for you to take action.

Here is Jonno's specific Resilience Bucket list:

- Running three times a week on a Monday, Wednesday and Friday at 8am.
- Intermittent fasting during the week from 8pm at night until 11am the next morning.
- Friday night five-a-side football followed by drinks with the team.
- Days out with the kids in the fresh air on weekends that they're with me.
- Tidying the house before I go to bed each night.
- Installing a window seat in the office so I can look at the view. I'll do this in the next three weeks.

Before we go any further I'd like you to write five specific things that you do already or will do that fill up your Resilience Bucket. Are you going to do more sport? Are you going to go on that cocktail-making course? Are you going to get that kitten you've always thought about? Deciding what to put in your bucket is up to you, but it should be about you and not about other people in your life. So if you've never wanted a cat, but your kids have, this doesn't fill up your bucket. It's nice to have but it's not a desire of yours. Write down five things now that are achievable and stretch you but that are not out of reach. So for instance if you're on a tight budget, a six-week holiday in the Bahamas might be nice to have, but not realistic!

Now I want you to imagine drilling a hole in your bucket. A small hole maybe, but you can see the resilience starting to leak out. How does it feel to watch your leaky bucket? The holes are caused by stressful things in our lives. Co-parenting may be one of those things. The less there is in your Resilience Bucket, the less resource you have to cope with the difficult things. Sometimes in life we can't plug the hole, so we need to do more to fill up the bucket, which is why I want you to keep doing the things that you want and putting things in your bucket that make you feel purposeful, happy and fulfilled.

It's easy to put ideas in the bucket but it can be harder to action what's in there. I want to help you take action so you can feel as good as possible. Have another read of the list that you've just written of the things that are in your bucket. Are they all manageable? Can you achieve them? Then I want you to write next to each one when you will do it by. Be as specific as possible.

Now I want you to stand up and look down at the floor. Imagine there is a line in front of you. This is your commitment line. On the other side of the line is your Resilience Bucket, and by stepping across the line you are committing to doing the things in your Resilience Bucket and achieving them and prioritising them when possible. When you step over this line it means you are committing to self-care and accepting its importance to your world and your co-parenting and therefore your children. Without committing to looking after yourself it will be harder to thrive. So off you go, step over that line. I'm right here with you and you're worth it.

Congratulations! You've committed to keeping your Resilience Bucket regularly topped up. It will help you live a fulfilled life and by doing that you'll benefit your children. Physically stepping over an imaginary line might seem a bit strange, but psychologically it's important. Maybe you felt a flutter of nerves before you did it. By stepping over the line, you're making an agreement with yourself that you'll do something.

Probably, the time you'll have to do the things on your list will be at those times when your children are with their other parent. The very nature of co-parenting, as we know, means that you won't have your children with you all of the time, and that can be really difficult to accept. I want you to really focus on nourishing yourself when they aren't with you. Put things in your bucket that are for you as an adult only and that can only happen when your children aren't there. Perhaps it's a night out without needing to pay for a babysitter, maybe it's an evening art class, or an exercise class? Those times when your children aren't there can be really tough. Filling them with things that can simultaneously fill up your bucket and distract you can be helpful.

Storing your Resilience Bucket

To remember our Resilience Buckets, we will imagine storing it in the other hand to the one holding our best briefcase from chapter one (see page 31). In your right hand imagine carrying your personalised Resilience Bucket. Imagine it bumping gently against your leg as you walk down the street. You can't forget it when it's constantly banging into you!

Dealing with Bumps in the Road

Even when we're thriving and feeling great there will still be moments when something happens in co-parenting that trips us up. In order to keep you in your thriving place we need to know how to deal with those bumps in the road that can destabilise us and our co-parenting relationship. Being able to keep in mind the bigger picture as we are on our co-parenting journey is fundamental to it succeeding. We've talked all the way through this book about remaining focused on the long-term goals of having strong and positive relationships with our kids as they grow up. We've also referenced those times when it might be harder to stay in the long-term mindset when something or someone new arrives in our co-parenting system that rocks the boat. I want to help you ride out those storms in a way that has minimal impact on your co-parenting relationship, so you can stay on course for your children and continue to thrive.

Grace and Joseph had been co-parenting for several years. They had three children who were all teenagers. Joseph recalls when he found out that Grace was having another child with her new partner.

'I was happy for her, but on some level it must have made me feel angry. I don't really know why. I think it was because it was going to upset our equilibrium that we had found. Now we were going to have to adjust everything to fit in around the new baby and the boys were going to be focused on their new baby sister. Things started to get fractious between Grace and me and it suddenly and unexpectedly became hard to co-parent with her. I noticed myself getting annoyed when I got a message from her and I started to take days to reply. That definitely made her mad and things just escalated from there. It wasn't until her daughter was born that I could see I was being unreasonable and causing waves where there really shouldn't have been waves. But it taught me a lesson. That emotions are funny things. They don't always feel logical and if we're not expecting them, they can catch us off guard and make us react in unexpected ways.'

There are certain things in long-term co-parenting that we regularly see making it harder for parents who have been doing really well at working together. These bumps in the road are commonplace, not just because you're co-parents, but because we are going through life. It's important to remember that life is a series of events that we either make happen or that happen to us. How we experience them and show up to them is what is important.

Sometimes when we're co-parenting we might wrongly think that all our life problems are due to our difficult co-parenting relationship. If we're in that mindset and blaming our co-parenting relationship for the things in our life that aren't going so well, it's not helpful for the co-parent relationship and it's also unlikely to be true. Whether you're co-parenting or not, over the course of a year, you may experience a health issue, a promotion, a bereavement, a big celebration. All of these are completely normal. Over the course of five years, ten years, twenty years, you'll have good and less good experiences. By realising and taking on board that things happen to all of us, regardless of whether or not we are co-parents, we can change our approach to how we react to things that affect us when we *are* co-parents.

It's the same with our children. Look at two sixteen-year-old boys. They are both doing their GCSEs, they both have an influx of hormones and they both eat a lot. They are both stressed because of their exams. Perhaps they aren't sleeping and are worrying about taking the exams. Maybe they're talking about the pressure they're under and how much they're feeling it. If one of them has parents who are together and one of them doesn't, it could be easy to think that it's worse for the one that doesn't. Assumptions might be made that the boy with separated parents isn't getting the emotional support he needs and that's why he's floundering and feeling anxious. But probably and most likely, it's just a stressful time for them. Life happens, and separation and co-parenting doesn't always make it worse, but it can be an easy excuse to reach for if we're having a hard time in life.

Whoever you are and whatever you have experienced, it's likely that your life has not just been one difficulty-free experience. Our resilience and our outlook, whether we are co-parents or not, is what makes us able to deal with life.

Common bumps in the road

Having said all of that, as co-parents there are definite trigger points that can derail our stability. Let's look at four of the most common ones, how we might feel about them and some ways to approach them to keep us on track and in the long-term co-parenting mindset.

Introducing kids to a new partner

This is such a big trigger point that I wanted to address it first. At some point in your co-parent relationship a new partner will probably come on the scene. This can have an extraordinarily destabilising effect if we don't handle it well. For the co-parent with the new partner, the temptation can be to rush into introducing them to the children. The idea of building a new family unit can be appealing and a common mistake I see is that this happens too early and in an unstructured way. For those of us whose ex has found a new partner, this can put us on very shaky ground. Of course, the new partner may be why we are separating in the first place; whether or not that's the case, we can feel very put aside, and importantly it can tap into our fears that we are going to be replaced as a parent. (Remember the catastrophic fear from step two?)

Even though you now have ways of managing strong emotions, it doesn't mean that there won't be emotions. I want to say that if this is you, I have no doubt that your feelings are real, they are big and they are destabilising. I want to urge you to revisit the approaches to managing your emotions in step two (page 55) if you're finding the idea of a new partner hard and remind you that you can't be replaced as a parent. Even if you're not seeing much of your children now, remember to be consistent with them and work towards your relationship with them as adults. Go back to the beginning of this step and look at what actions you can take to fill up your Resilience Bucket. It all helps you to feel more grounded.

A new partner may well be on the scene permanently, so it's really important that we manage this in a constructive way. How we bring them into our children's lives is really important. Have a solid plan in place to introduce them to the children in an appropriate way.

HOW TO INTRODUCE A CHILD TO A NEW PARTNER

I usually encourage parents to work towards the following approach: firstly, introduce a new partner when it looks like it's going to be a long-term relationship. It's hard for your child to get used to several 'special friends'.

Ideally, let your ex meet the new partner *before* the children meet the new partner. This only needs to be for a couple of minutes and should be in a neutral place. If it's you meeting the new partner, remember that this meeting should not be an interrogation, nor a job interview. Think of it like meeting someone who will be on the outer edges of your life. It's best to make it polite and respectful and courteous and to remember that if they're going to be in your children's lives then it's sensible for you to be able to communicate with them in a positive way. It's important for your children.

When it's time for the new partner to be introduced to the children I would always suggest moving slowly and thinking of building a relationship between your children and your new partner as though it is a layered approach. Build it one layer at a time. If your children are young, then just introduce the idea of a new friend gradually. If your kids are older, you can explain that you have a new partner but they are not taking over the role of parent. This latter point is critical. Always reassure your children that your love for them will not change and that love as a couple is different to parental love. Please tell your co-parent when you will be making those introductions so the children don't feel as though they need to hide anything.

If it's possible, let the meeting between the new partner and children be outdoors. Meeting outside can be helpful for reducing stress levels and removing some of the pressure from a situation. It also gives you a focus of a playground or a walk that can be less awkward than sitting around a table having a drink or a meal.

Build up the meetings gradually. Remember your children, like anyone else, take time to trust people and build new relationships. You might have known your new partner for a long time, but you need to give your children (and your ex) time to do this on their terms and in their way. Patience is everything here.

Your ex is getting remarried

Naomi had been in a new relationship for three years; she was happy and settled, but she still remembers clearly the day she found out that her ex was remarrying. It was her new partner's birthday and her ex was coming to pick up the kids for the weekend. She recalls here:

'As the kids were running around finding their shoes and their school bags, he just dropped it into conversation. "I'm getting married to Sara." "Oh, congratulations," I said. "Let me know if you want me to have the kids when you go on honeymoon." And then he left with the children. I started shaking. I was literally trembling from head to toe and I couldn't control it. I knew he was in a long-term relationship – his girlfriend was pregnant. I was pregnant with my new partner and so it wasn't as if I wanted to be with him anymore. It was more complicated than that. It was a shock and probably on some level I felt really put aside in a very final way. I was amazed at myself that I had been able to be so polite. I went in the garden and sat at the end so my partner couldn't see me and I shook for about 15 minutes. And then slowly it started to pass and I walked back into the house. I found out later that shaking is a really normal response to shock and it's caused by adrenaline and a fight, flight, freeze response. But I had not a clue at the time why my body was doing this. I didn't much feel like celebrating a birthday now, but I still did. I was flabbergasted that his announcement had affected me so much but I was super proud that I'd remained calm in front of him.'

When your ex decides to remarry, it can be very triggering. Like we've just seen in Naomi's story, thinking long term can help. Your ex being in a long-term relationship is more likely to provide stability for your children, and this can be a useful mindset to take. Even so, you might feel rage or sadness, or you might have an unexpected reaction. It can be complex. It's OK to have mixed and strong feelings about this. If you can refocus your reaction and think forward to focus on your kids and how you can support them through this stage, that can be constructive. Being consistent, being supportive and showing your children that moving on through life is OK will provide them with the stability they are searching for.

If you're getting married or moving in with your new partner, be mindful of how and when you tell your ex. Try to do it when they are in a safe environment. Give them space to react and don't let it escalate into an argument. If you are able to make a joint plan about how to tell the children, that will also be helpful. Your ex shouldn't be telling the children that you're getting married, but please do them the courtesy of letting them know when and how you will do that.

One of you is having another child

Let's start with an obvious statement. Newborn babies are blameless. I want to start with that because it can help us remember that even if our ex has had an affair and a new baby is on the way, that it's not the fault of that baby. Earlier we heard Joseph's story and how even though things were fine in their co-parenting, the news of the new baby was still derailing for him.

Bringing a new baby into the picture can be hard. Whether you're the proud parent-to-be or it's your co-parent who's expecting, the first thing to focus on is how to integrate your original children with the new child. This newborn will be your child's half sibling and it's really important that you help build a relationship for them. It may or may not be easy, but what you need to think about aiming for is an amazing system where all the children can consider each other siblings of a sort and can take these relationships in their stride. Use all your communication techniques to build bridges with your co-parent. Be inclusive, not exclusive.

One of you wants or needs to move

Sometimes, for whatever reason, co-parenting happens at long distance. After a separation one parent may return to where their family is based, or work may take you abroad or far away. The conversations around moving are highly destabilising for us as it's a big upheaval and a big change. How you approach the conversation very much depends on where you are in your co-parenting relationship. Ideally, open conversations, putting the children at the centre of them, is what to aim for. But for the parent who's going to live far away from the child, it can be heart-wrenching. Approach these conversations with care and gentleness, keep the best interests of the children in mind and find ways for everyone to see them. Video calls are one of the tools that can be helpful here.

From all of these examples there are several common approaches. Communicate well, listen well and be collaborative. It's the quickest way through the mess to get back to living a more peaceful life. I know this can be easier said than done, but the more you focus in on the things you can control, the easier it will be. And that's where we're going next.

Let's Take Control

We all need control. If we go back through evolution, we can see that control is associated with stability and safety, and so wanting control is a fundamental human need – it gives us comfort, which in turn makes us less anxious and stressed. Summarising their paper 'Born to Choose: The Origins and Value of the Need for Control', Lauren Leotti, Sheena Iyengar and Kevin Ochsner say: 'Belief in one's ability to exert control over the environment and to produce desired results is essential for an individual's well-being. It has been repeatedly argued that the perception of control is not only desirable, but it is likely a psychological and biological necessity.'[14]

When we feel in control we are more able to manage difficulties and more able to direct outcomes. When we feel as though we are steering the course of our lives, our world seems stable and we are at the centre of it, deciding on its direction. We can experience a lack of control, therefore, as threatening. It can bring about adrenaline rushes and put us straight into fight, flight, freeze, fawn and flop. When we're not in control we can feel insecure, overwhelmed and powerless. This was the word Paulo used again and again when he started out on his co-parent journey. His break-up was fast and unexpected:

'I just didn't feel like I had any say in anything that was going on. It felt like all my power had been taken away from me. I didn't know how to deal with all the things that were going on. Even the things I couldn't control, like where my ex was choosing to live. Those feelings are awful, they took up all my head space, every last bit of it. It was crazy to focus on the things I couldn't control, but I was fixated on them. It was only when I got called into HR at work to talk about my performance that I realised I needed to get a grip on myself.'

Focusing on things that aren't in our control and that we can't control expends huge amounts of our energy. We need a tool to understand what we can and can't control so we can use our energy and time and resources more efficiently. And guess what? I have a tool for you that does exactly that.

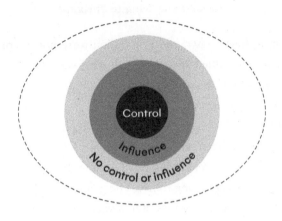

Circles of Control

The only way to feel in control is to understand what is and what isn't in our control – when we understand that we can choose what to focus our time and energy on.

This tool, which is based on the Circles of Influence concept developed by Stephen Covey,[15] can help you recognise which things you can influence and control, and which you can't, even though they may impact you. I want to show you how to use it for your co-parenting.

In your notebook, please draw a circle about the size of the bottom of a can of drink and write 'Control' at the top of it. In this circle I want you to write down everything in your co-parenting that you can control. There won't be lots. It will be things like, what food I put on my children's plates, my behaviour around my co-parent, how I write the handover notes, how I speak to my ex. Everything that stems from you, you can control.

Now I want you to draw a bigger circle around the 'Control' circle and call it 'Influence'. This is the circle of influence. You don't have control here; you have a say in what happens, but you can't *make* it happen. So, for instance: what your kids eat (you might give them broccoli but they might not eat it); how your children feel about your separation (you can influence how they feel by how you behave, but you can't control it); how much influence you have over your co-parent (it's likely that you can influence them by how you are around them, but you can't control them); how you get information from people – you can make yourself open and available, but you can't force people to speak to you. Write as many things here as possible. Some of them you will have more influence over than others and this list will be longer than your 'Control' list.

OK, now draw another circle around the outside. This is your biggest circle, and it's going to be labelled 'No Control or Influence'. This is the circle where most of life happens. These are the things we have no direct impact on at all, but that still concern us and still have an impact on us. In co-parenting it will be things like, 'whether my ex meets someone new', or 'where my ex chooses to live', or 'the type of people your ex hangs out with and the friends they choose to have'. It will be the things they choose to do, the activities they plan, the holidays they go on. These are all things that are happening in your ex-partner's world (remember the Three Worlds?), and you have no control or influence over them. Finish your list and then come back when you're ready.

It can be very hard to accept that we have no influence or control over the things we have written down in the outer circle and even harder to draw the line between what we think we can influence and what we actually can't. Recognising what we don't have influence or control over can be tricky at first, especially if you're just emerging from a relationship where you did have influence over your co-parent. Going back to the Three Worlds tool will help you determine the pieces you can and can't influence, but I do want to acknowledge that sometimes it can just be hard to let go of wanting that influence.

Many of our stresses and anxieties in life come from the concerns in the outer circle of 'No Control or Influence'. If we don't accept that we have no control or influence and we are still trying to change things in the outer circle, then we're putting energy and emotion into things that we have no hope of changing, and it can feel like we are fighting a losing battle. By writing the list, you can see clearly what you can't change.

The fastest way to feeling better (though it's not an easy thing to do) is to let go of these things, let them be and step away from trying to make them different. In fact, reading that you need to let go of those things may have made you panic slightly. If that's the case, don't worry. Use the Finger and Thumb tool (see page 59), take a breath and collect yourself. It's just you and me here and we're looking at ways to help you feel more stable so you can thrive.

Expending energy on trying to change things that are not possible to change will keep you focused in a negative and draining place. It will mean your attention is not on yourself or your children, but on influencing things you can't make a difference to. So stop, and let's focus on the other two points of the circle now to help you feel more anchored.

The middle circle of 'influence' is harder to define. How much energy should you put into influencing something? It can be hard to determine, so here's a method I use to help co-parents do that. Take your 'Influence' list and next to each item I want you to write a number out of ten as to how important it is to you. Next to that number I want you to write, in as brutally honest a way as you can, how much influence you think you have. Score this either one, two or three. Then multiply the two numbers together. It might look something like this:

ITEM	IMPORTANCE	INFLUENCE	TOTAL
How many sweets ex-partner gives Tom	6/10	1/3	6
How Maya experiences handovers	8/10	2/3	16

Using your final scores, put them in order from the highest score to the lowest score. Focus only on the scores that are 12 or higher. The rest try to put aside for now until they either change in importance or how much influence you have over them, or something else about them changes and they move from one circle to another.

There is no point having lots of things that you are trying to influence going on at the same time. Expending your energy like this will detract from your focus of raising happy and resilient children with your co-parent. Focus your energies on the things that are important and that you may be able to change.

And finally, the 'Control' circle. This is you. This is your world, this is your health, your wellbeing, your quality time with your children. This is where you can eat well, go out and have fun and see friends. These are the behaviours you can control that include how you choose to be with your co-parent, such as whether you are polite at handovers, whether you wash the PE kit to be helpful, or what activities you arrange for the children when they're with you. All these behaviours and actions are in your control and this is where your primary focus needs to be. When you focus in on the inner circle, then you will feel happier, more fulfilled and generally satisfied. Much of your time needs to be spent here.

Time for action

I'd like you to commit to three things from your control circle that you'll put into action in the next two weeks. So if that's putting vegetables on your child's plate, speaking politely to your ex at handovers and sending shorter emails to them, then put those into play. Have a go at taking the time to notice that you are in control of these things and how that feels. You may already be doing these things; if so, make sure you pause and notice that. It's important to recognise the positive actions that you take.

I'd also like you to pick two of the topics you wrote down in your outer circle where you have no control or influence and commit to letting go of those for two weeks. See how it feels to give yourself permission to not expend energy on those things for a period of time. Letting go of things in the outer circle can be tricky, so trying it on for two weeks means that you get to practise without completely letting go. By doing it for two weeks, you are much more likely to find it easier to let go in the longer term and prevent yourself from thinking and worrying about the things in here. After two weeks, re-evaluate and see if you even want to go back to engaging with those areas of the outer circle.

Storing your Circles of Control tool

To remember the Circles of Control tool, we will imagine keeping it in our beating heart, because when we feel in control we feel contented and our heart is calm. Imagine your heart is made up of three circles and they are all beating rhythmically together.

Stress Management

We'll move from control to stress now. We need to have control to feel calm and we need less stress to feel calm. We all have stress. Indeed, some stress is important and necessary because it helps move us forward in life. But too much stress over a long period of time can be harmful. Chronic stress can make us ill physically as well as emotionally. And too much stress at once can move us into panic mode. (Remember the Summit tool from page 90 in step three?)

George is 54. He is a co-parent of 15 years and the whole thing has been immensely stressful for him. After a high-conflict breakdown of his marriage to his childhood sweetheart and a subsequent co-parenting arrangement that would get chopped and changed at a moment's notice, parenting with his ex who would make unpredictable changes and seeing the impact on their daughter has led George to hold a lot of stress over a sustained period of time. The anticipation of unpredictability and long, drawn-out arguments meant that, three years into co-parenting, George started to suffer with chronic back pain. He tried everything from injections to swimming to saunas to stretching, but nothing worked. He didn't try working on his mental health as it never occurred to him that his bad back might be linked to the emotional stress of what he was experiencing.

Through his work, George went on a stress management course and quite by chance he started to understand that the emotional strain of his co-parenting was causing him physical pain. Once he understood that, although he couldn't change his ex's behaviour, he found that understanding that he needed to care for his mental health helped him enormously. His back isn't fixed, but he feels emotionally well and resilient.

Managing stress is essential to feel well and healthy. It isn't just about mental health, it's also about physical health. When we find ourselves in a long-term co-parenting situation it can be really stressful for us and so understanding the different types of stress can help us move out of survival mode and into a thriving place.

According to Karl Albrecht, the author of the 1979 book *Stress and the Manager*, there are four categories of stress, and it can be really helpful to understand how each of those categories impact on and relate to our co-parenting.[16] After we've looked at each, I'll give you a tool to help you deal with them. So let's meet the four stress categories. They are time stress, anticipatory stress, situational stress and encounter stress.

Too much stress can move us into panic mode.

Time stress in co-parenting

Time stress is worrying about not having enough time to do something or experience something. In co-parenting, time stress is linked directly to having reduced time with our children and feeling we want to experience a full life with them but in a limited amount of time. The fear of not being with them, the upset at them missing big occasions, the constant adjustments to routines – all place time stresses upon co-parents. Having to fit in homework, after-school clubs and seeing their friends means that as parents we can feel our time with our children slipping away from us. Focusing on quality rather than quantity can be helpful here. Time stress can lead us to feeling overwhelmed and anxious and being snappy and irritable. Ensuring our children have positive and meaningful experiences with us where possible, to increase their sense of belonging and significance, will mean that our relationship with them has depth. A deep and meaningful relationship will be more durable over the test of time.

Shirley is mum to Benji. She had Benji with her every other weekend and a few days each week. Her co-parenting was moving along well, but one of the things Shirley found hard about co-parenting was arranging playdates.

'A lot of our Benji's friends would want to meet him at the weekends and I only had control of whether that happened or not during the weekends that he was with me. In the early years of his schooling, all of the playdate invites would come to *my* phone. People didn't really realise Benji spent every other weekend at his dad's house and even when I'd explained it to them they hadn't really taken it in. Benji would miss out on playdates and parties and I would worry that would impact his friendships. I don't know why I didn't realise it earlier but when I had the lightbulb moment that I could just pass on the playdate invitations to my ex if it was a weekend when my son was there, everything became a lot easier. It didn't always work out, and it always felt a bit weird when my school mum friends were dropping their kids of at my ex's, but holding on to the long-term view was really helpful. Finding ways around the usual is important when you're a co-parent. Being flexible is the biggest thing I have learned and possibly one of the biggest gifts I've given my child.'

Anticipatory stress in co-parenting

Have you ever noticed that you're worrying about something days before it's actually happening? That you're worried about what something is going to be like before you've experienced it? Do you wake up at night dwelling on it, or do you notice that your thoughts keep drifting towards it during the daylight hours? This is anticipatory stress – worrying about the future and being afraid of the unknown or what something could be like. Anticipatory stress is one of the most common types of stress we see in new co-parenting situations. The fear of the unknown, the anticipation of confrontation or difficult conversations with co-parents, knowing you're not going to see your children or that your children are going to be spending time with a new partner who you don't know very well can all contribute greatly to your anticipatory stress. You may not sleep well, you may be grumpy, you may feel drained and exhausted. Revisit your Speed Writing tool (page 68) and go through the exercise again to figure out what is at the heart of what you're worrying about. Practise your Finger and Thumb tool (see page 59) to help keep you calm and relaxed. Have a conversation with your avatar (see page 73) about what's worrying you.

Situational stress in co-parenting

Situational stress usually arises in unexpected situations that you find yourself in where you have no control. Maybe you're walking somewhere and you find yourself lost, it's dark and you're not sure how to get home. Or less extreme, you walk into a party and you realise you only know one person and they're not there and you don't do well in crowds of people you don't know. In co-parenting, you may have a disagreement or perhaps you get an unexpected email or letter from a lawyer. Maybe your child has gone away with your co-parent and you're not exactly sure where they are. Situational stress can cause extreme fight or flight responses and you may respond in a way that you don't recognise in yourself. You might start calling your ex over and over again to try to find out where your child is, or you might send really aggressive emails. You might panic and say things that have a big impact on your co-parenting. Situational stress is very difficult to mitigate and the most important thing is to not take decisions or action that you may later regret. For situational stress, I recommend using your Finger and Thumb tool (see page 59), because it helps you stay in the moment and reduce your adrenaline. It's also helpful to use the Circles of Control tool (page 226) to help you rationalise, if possible, what's happening.

Encounter stress in co-parenting

Being in the same space as people who upset you, you don't like, or who you might be afraid of causes encounter stress. It can also happen in situations that simply make you uncomfortable, such as networking events. In co-parenting, encounter stress is expected. It happens at handovers, it can happen when you're both at your child's birthday party, or you might bump into your co-parent in the high street unexpectedly. Encounter stress can be a part of co-parenting, and until we learn to deal with its impact, it will affect us and how we are. If you get along with your ex, your encounter stress might be with another member of their family, or you may not have any at all. Being aware of how you're responding to being in the same space as someone will be helpful for you in knowing whether you're experiencing encounter stress. When you're aware of when it happens to you, it becomes easier to deal with it. You can make sure you're really familiar with calling up your avatar (page 73) and also thinking things through in advance of how you want to be when you're in the same space as someone you don't want to be near to.

Having an understanding of and recognising the four types of stress can help us prepare in advance for them. The tool that follows gives you strategies to help manage them all.

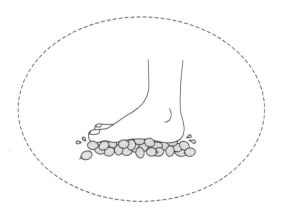

Stress Squasher

In this, the final tool, I'm going to walk you through exactly how to deal with each of the four areas of stress. This tool will take around 30 minutes to complete.

The first thing I want you to do in your notebook is split your page into four quadrants and write one of the four different stress categories in each. You'll need a big space underneath each heading for part two of the tool. Under each thing you write, leave a couple of lines so you can fill in your approaches for dealing with them.

Time Stress	Anticipatory Stress
Situational Stress	Encounter Stress

Re-read the definition of each one again. In each box I want you to brain-dump everything in your co-parenting that is related to each category. So for time stress you might write things about your child having enough time to see all the important people on your side. In anticipatory stress it might be around waiting for a response to a request you've made to your co-parent. In situational stress it will be things like handovers and co-parenting meetings and in encounter stress it will be about the unexpected meetings you have or emails that you get. Be honest with yourself and take your time. Like I've said before, it's not easy to think about these things and writing them down can make them feel very real. But it's only when we know exactly what we're facing, that we can manage it. You can do this.

The next part is all about how we handle each area. Have a read through my suggestions below and then think about how you can apply those to each of your situations that you have written. I want you to write approaches for dealing with the stress next to each one. Below I've suggested tools from the book that might be useful too.

Time stress – practical responses

There are some common themes we see in time stress and they are related to not having enough hours with your child when you're having to share them with your co-parent. So we need to reframe that to find the positive ways we can engage with our kids when it's our time with them. Having one-on-one time with your children can really have a positive impact. Scheduling in just 15 minutes each day with each of your children to do an activity or game of their choosing (ideally not screens) can really deepen your bond with your child. Even if you don't see them very much, this time will become really precious.

Your weeks might also be very busy and it can be easy for children to be overwhelmed by everything and to remember everything that they are supposed to do in each house. One practical approach is to write out weekly schedules that you keep on your fridge so everyone knows what needs to be done and when. This can help anxious kids be calm, which can free up more space for quality time. It's important in those schedules to include your 'parent and child time' so your quality time doesn't get lost in the everyday mush of things that need to be achieved.

Additionally, the Photographs tool (page 49) and the Speed Writing tool (page 68) can be good at helping us keep things in perspective and using the Five Steps of Active Listening (see page 129) with your children can really help deepen your connection with them.

Anticipatory stress – practical responses

Anticipatory stress is best dealt with by making yourself think about scenarios all the way to conclusion. Let me explain. Often when we're worrying about something, we get stuck at a certain point. If you're worrying about your ex coming over in three days to take your children for the weekend, the likelihood is that you'll get stuck imagining that scenario at a certain point. Maybe it's as they ring the doorbell, maybe it's as you close the door behind the children. It can be really helpful to think of the whole scenario so it's complete. Imagine yourself opening the door to your co-parent; you smile and say hello and you hand over your children's bags. You say goodbye to the children and tell them to have a lovely time, and you close the door. Then what? Don't stop there. Imagine yourself taking a moment, noticing how quiet the house is. Maybe you'll cry, maybe you make a drink, maybe you have no plans or are feeling lonely. Whatever it is, think it through to its conclusion and then you can see how likely it is that something difficult will happen, and if so, what it is you need to do to deal with it. When you know what's out in front of you, you know what you need to put in place to help manage it. Perhaps it's having a friend there when you hand over your children so you're not on your own, or calling someone immediately afterwards.

My anticipatory stress was always the worst when I would drop my son off to go on holiday with his dad. Knowing I wouldn't see him for a couple of weeks always put me in a really bad mood in the days leading up to it and I would be super tense. After I dropped him off I would cry at the wheel of my car. After a couple of times I started to message my cousin on the way and tell her I was just about to drop him, and then I would call her straight afterwards. This would be helpful as she would tell me that I was doing the right thing and then she would make me laugh about something stupid. Just knowing there was someone who cared about me and who was available to me was a massive lifejacket. I'd also call my dad. Even though we didn't go into it, I knew he was always there and would just keep me company on the phone for a few minutes while I got myself out of mummy mode and back into Marcie mode.

Much of the content of steps one to five will help you through anticipatory stress, but there are other things that will also help. Writing scripts (see the box below) so you're prepared for a difficult conversation, or waiting until it's a good time to read that email that you're afraid to open are all good coping mechanisms. Put your Self-Management Avatar to work to help remind you that you're doing OK and that it's OK for your kids to spend time with their other parent and use your Circles of Control tool to notice what about your anticipatory stress is and isn't in your control. Remembering that your co-parent might be suffering from anticipatory stress when they're going to see you can also be helpful.

WRITING SCRIPTS

Don't worry, I'm not expecting you to engage your inner Tarantino here, but if you've got a meeting coming up with your co-parent that you're anxious about, then writing out in advance what you want to say can be really helpful. Script writing helps you get your thoughts in order before you need them, it helps you choose the words you want to use (which can prevent conflict) and it helps you remember to say everything you want to say. Have a go at writing things down and then practicing saying them through a couple of times. You don't need to learn it off by heart, but it's helpful to become familiar with it so you can bring the points to mind more easily when you need them. You can use script writing in any of your co-parenting scenarios, not just in relation to anticipatory stress. It can also be a helpful thing to do if your handovers are tricky.

Situational stress – practical responses

Situational stress is all-encompassing and it can be really hard to remember the tools you need when you're in the moment. This is why we've placed all your tools on the body. The more you practise knowing where your tools are, the easier it will be to call them up. As I've said above, for situational stress I recommend using your Finger and Thumb tool a lot, because it helps you stay in the moment and reduces your adrenaline. It will keep you calmer and your responses will be more logical and ordered. I'd also like you to combine Finger and Thumb with the Pause Button; a double whammy like this can really help de-escalate any potential conflict. Active listening, particularly listening without making assumptions, will also help you in situational stress and if you need to bring out the big guns, then please make sure your Self-Management Avatar is on hand to help you. Thinking through situations that might happen and planning for situational stress can also be helpful. You can use the Circles of Control tool to help with some of that, and having your Co-Parenting Plan filled in can also help mitigate unexpected scenarios, as you'll know how to respond and what you've agreed. Understanding your own responses to fear and anxiety and reminding yourself of the five Fs (page 58) can also help you be prepared for situational stress.

Encounter stress – practical responses

Zoe lived really near her ex and his new family. She was five years into her co-parenting journey and one of the things she used to find stressful was that she shared a high street with her ex and his new family. She would worry every time she went to the shops that she would bump into his new girlfriend, and of course from time to time she did. Encounter stress requires you to be able to respond in the moment, usually with how you communicate. Revisiting all the communications tools we learned in step four will help you on your way. In the short term, being prepared for the unexpected can be useful, but having things on your mind all the time can put you on high alert and flood you with adrenaline. The best way to manage encounter stress is to think about it as an outer circle in the Circles of Control. You can't control it, so don't let it overwhelm you. What I would urge you to remember, and what I reminded Zoe about, was that you might not want to see the new girlfriend, but she might not want to see you either. Rather than dreading it, why don't you just smile and say hello as you walk on by. That way, it becomes courteous and calm rather than worrisome. Remember that at the end of the day, we are all human beings. Zoe was able to bring something from the outer circle of no control and no influence into the middle circle of influence, and she became more able to let go of it as a worry.

You now have actions against each of your four stress boxes that you can do to help manage your stress and help prevent it from escalating. I'd like you to pick one from each box that you will think about or start to do straight away to help you step away from stress and towards a happy and thriving place.

Storing your Stress Squasher tool

Let's use our outrageous imagery to remember our Stress Squasher tool! We're going to keep the Stress Squasher in our feet, as we squash those stresses like we are crushing lots of grapes. Imagine them squelching between your toes.

Thriving is all about ensuring that you look after yourself, top up your resilience and have techniques that you can use to manage the challenges. It's so important for your children to see you thriving – by experiencing their parents as happy, fulfilled and resilient, your children can embed this as their blueprint for going through life. Children learn through what they experience and being able to positively experience you dealing with stress and bumps in the road will be hugely beneficial for their happiness and mental wellbeing now and in the future. And you deserve to be happy and to live your life as the adult you want to be, as a flexible and mindful co-parent, and of course as a parent to your child. Let's do our final summary to help you remember everything we've looked at in step six.

If children positively experience you dealing with stress then they will learn how to do that too.

STEP SIX SUMMARY

- We've looked at what we need in order to thrive and have resilience for all the ups and downs in our co-parenting life.
- You've seen that even when you're thriving there will always be stresses and bumps in the road.
- One part of dealing with this is to understand what is causing the stress and which of those bumps you can and can't control.
- It's also very helpful for us to let go of the things we can't control.
- We remembered the importance of staying focused on the bigger picture and we looked at some trip hazards that might get in the way of our co-parenting success.
- We've also talked about why it's actually important to look after our mental health and to not put ourselves at the bottom of the heap in terms of care.
- If we don't, it can impact our health, our happiness and how we show up as parents. Ultimately our children need us to look after ourselves so we can care for them.
- You now have your Resilience Bucket, which is filled to the brim with things that make you thrive and happy. You know what, even if it's not filled to the brim, if you've simply made a start, then that's brilliant right now.
- The Circles of Control tool helps you know which bits of life you can influence and control and which bits you can't.
- And your Stress Squasher tool defined the four types of stress you might feel and some ways to stamp them out.

Storing your tools: The Resilience Bucket we will keep in our right hand carrying our personalised bucket. The Circles of Control we will keep in our heart. The Stress Squasher tool is in our feet. If you're labelling your body outline, then do that now.

Keep taking small steps, keep focusing on thriving. And remember – it's only when you look back to where you were that you'll realise how far you've come.

If we don't change things, how can we expect things to change?

CONCLUSION

You've done it. You've been through all six steps of The Co-Parenting Method! Congratulations. There may have been moments when reading this book that you found challenging. That's understandable – this is a hard topic to tackle – but I'm delighted for you and for your children that you chose to keep going.

The six steps have taken you on a journey that have helped you think hard about the long-term importance of co-parenting effectively, and they've unpacked how to do that. Providing your child with a happy and stable environment through your co-parenting is what will enable them to grow up into resilient adults who can build healthy relationships, something we all want for our children. One of our biggest learning points is that parenting doesn't stop just because you're not with your child's other parent and we still need to think about how to work together so we can do it well.

Parenting doesn't stop just because you're not with your child's other parent.

We know that we'll pass through turbulent times and staying in a long-term mindset while sailing stormy seas can feel as though you're hanging on to a sinking ship by your fingernails. But hang on, and use the tools and stay in your boundaried and respectful mindset, and the storm will pass. Remember in the introduction I said to you, 'It's always fine to start [co-parenting] from now, where you are today, and move forward positively from that place.' Well, it's the same when co-parenting hits those stormy seas. Clamber back on board your boat and keep sailing.

Let me remind you of something else I said right at the beginning of the book. The tools work when you use them and put them into practice. A reminder to you, lovely reader, that you have the agency, the control and the autonomy to make an active choice to use these tools. By choosing to use them you will make a difference to your co-parenting, to your own life and also to your children. We started this book knowing we wanted happy and resilient children – by actioning the tools you'll be able to know you've done everything you can in your co-parenting to achieve that.

By not blaming your circumstances or someone else for how you act, you move towards taking responsibility for your actions, which is essential for showing up as a co-parent for your child. You can take the choice to be collaborative, respectful and forward-thinking with your co-parent. These things are all about your behaviour and are within your circle of control, as is the decision to take action and use the tools you've learned in The Co-Parenting Method.

It's not always going to be easy, you know that already, but by having the strategies in place, by having done the hard thinking, you're much better prepared and able to make this work. By reading this book you've just done an amazing thing for your children. Think about how the improvements you make now will impact them for the rest of their lives.

If you're struggling to begin putting the method into practice, let's see if I can help you take the first step. You've probably written a lot of notes and had a lot of thoughts as you've been through the book. Because you've read the book and you've considered the exercises and you've written or thought about actions you want to take, in the background some of the learning will have already been put into action. So, for instance, you might already be listening better, or being more respectful at handovers. Perhaps your avatar is kicking in without you really being aware of it. Maybe by simply recognising your catastrophic fear you're subconsciously dealing with it. I use coaching language in the book, and in coaching a lot of the change happens between the active thinking, when you're 'at rest'. So the likelihood is, whether you think you have or not, you have already started implementing the method.

You might want to write a weekly action plan to really get going. What is it you will focus on in week one – will it be active listening? And in week two? Maybe you'll spend the week taking your avatar with you everywhere you go. You don't have to use the tools in order. Use them in a way that works for you. And whenever you need a reminder of what to do, just jump back into the book, or revisit the notes that you took to jog your memory of why you're doing this.

If your co-parent hasn't read the book, ask them to consider reading it, and remember, even if they don't, the six steps will give you a structure for yourself, remind you how to communicate well with your co-parent, put better boundaries in place with them and put a good structure in place to help you thrive.

Let's recap each step.

Step one: moving to a long-term mindset

I started by setting out that getting out of a short-term mindset is essential for effective co-parenting. Moving to a longer-term approach where we accept that our actions now, in the present, have a long-term impact on our children's future is so important. Getting out of the win/lose mindset and grasping that winning in the short-term is less important than our children's wellbeing was fundamental in this step, and you learned two tools to help you do that. Your Best Case, Worst Case tool and the Photographs tool helped you build an outline of what you want your co-parenting to be like and how you want your relationship with your adult children to be. Effectively you built a blueprint in step one and the other steps were all about making that blueprint happen.

Step two: managing strong emotions

In step two we focused on big emotions and our primal responses to anxiety and fear. We saw that those big emotions contribute to escalating conflict really quickly and when we're led by our emotions it becomes hard to stay in the long-term mindset. It's so important to get a handle on these emotions because they can derail co-parenting very fast. The three tools we learned in this step were all about helping you feel less overwhelmed in the moment, understand what causes you to become overwhelmed and then, with your avatar, control how much these emotions dictate your communication with your co-parent. By getting a handle on these emotions we can mitigate the negative impact we have on our children when we're in a fight, flight, freeze, fawn or flop response.

Step three: setting boundaries and recognising your co-parent's perspective

Supporting the longer-term view by being able to step into a bigger perspective and having boundaries was the focus of step three. Doing both of those things successfully has a positive impact on your children. Seeing things from your co-parent's perspective and the wider lens of the perspective of the overall relationship is essential for building a collaborative Co-Parental Loop. It means your children have an intrinsic understanding that both of their parents can work together. Doing this within a framework of boundaries makes everything nice and secure and helps us feel comfortable enough to co-parent. By creating your version of all the different worlds, you have a blueprint to remind you what you're aiming for to be happy. It also helps remind you that your co-parent is a person too, and whether you want it for them or not, they are entitled to live a fulfilled life. If you're both making positive choices about your lives as adults, then you'll be able to be more present for your children because you'll be standing firmly in the long-term mindset. Sometimes we need to be brave to make forward progress in co-parenting and you learned the Summit tool to help you do difficult things.

Step four: communicating without conflict

Effective and respectful communication is an essential building block in a good co-parenting relationship. Using communication to reduce conflict and increase collaboration means we are ready to take better decisions together and it creates a secure parenting environment for our children. This impacts positively on your children now and in the future. Inflammatory language can destroy co-parenting and impact significantly on our kids, but it's not just about what we say, it's also about how we listen. In step four we understood that listening well is a key component for de-escalating conflict. We also zoomed in on how our children experience us talking about our co-parent and noted the fact that children often understand things differently to how we mean them. I taught you four tools to help with your communication: the Five Steps of Active Listening; the Pause Button, which helps support good listening; the Reframe tool to move negative or inflammatory phrases to be more neutral or positive; and your What's in a Word tool to help you remember how your children hear what you're saying.

Step five: making good co-parenting decisions

When you have a reliable formula on how to take decisions and a framework with which to do this with your co-parent, then you can keep moving forward together as parents. If you can't make decisions together about your kids, then you're impacting their potential and their experience of you as parents will be left wanting. Using the Meeting Framework to have specific and outcome-led meetings with your co-parent will increase the effectiveness of your co-parental decision-making. Using both the Child-Centred Questions tool and the Pros, Cons, Impact Forumla will help you stay on track with each other and keep focused on what decision is best for your child. Making decisions in advance in your Co-Parenting Plan reduces the need for you to revisit things. Your Charter will help keep you in check about how you're being with each other as co-parents and if you can get to a place where you're using all of those tools your Co-Parental Loop will be nice and secure for your children.

Step six: beyond surviving to thriving

Children who can experience their co-parents as happy and thriving individuals will learn that it is essential to self-care, that happy people are resilient and that even when hard things happen, it's possible to get back to a thriving place. Of course, they'll also experience so much more as a result of you living in a way that brings you happiness and joy; these are just some of the benefits. That's why it's crucial for you to really fill up your Resilience Bucket. You kids will also be watching how you deal with the trickier things that happen in your life, how you handle those bumps in the road, so it's important that you understand what they might be for you and how you respond to them. We looked at control in step six and how there are things we both can and can't control. It's possible to feel overwhelmed by the feelings that can accompany those things that are out of our influence and control and it's important that we have a plan of how to deal with those feelings. It's the same with stress: if we respond badly to stress then our children will witness that, and it will impact them. Having the Stress Squasher tool will really help you identify your triggers in co-parenting and because you're writing down how you're going to counter those triggers or reduce them, you'll be better prepared than just reacting in the moment. You can use your Stress Squasher and Circles of Control tools in other areas of your life too!

The improvements you make now will impact your children for the rest of their lives.

Remembering the Tools

You have 20 tools to help you with your co-parenting. All of these, *when you use them*, will support you on your journey, whether your co-parent is reading this book or not. Here's your final reminder of your 20 tools and where they are stored on your body. Ready? Let's do it.

Best Case, Worst Case: In our left hand we carry our amazing briefcase which contains our best-case scenario.

Photographs: In our eyes, behind our really odd glasses, we have the Photographs tool.

Finger and Thumb: In our bread roll finger and thumb, we have our Finger and Thumb tool.

Speed Writing: In our tummy, or wherever we feel fear, we have our Speed Writing tool, because this way we can remember that our catastrophic fear is what is causing us to react in certain ways. We also keep our fear blasters next to it, to help manage the fear.

Self-Management Avatar: We keep this on our shoulder as we stand next to our avatar.

The Summit: We keep this tool in the very top of our head with our colourful flag sticking out of the top.

Standing in Your Co-Parent's Shoes: We store these in our very memorable shoes.

The Three Worlds: We keep this in our brain, which slowly turns as the world does.

The Five Steps of Active Listening: We keep them in our ear. Maybe you have five steps going into yours.

The Pause Button: We keep it on the inside of our wrist.

The Reframe: We have this crammed into our mouths with our picture frame.

What's in a Word?: We have this tool tied around our throat with our beautiful scarf.

Child-Centred Questions: We keep our Child-Centred Questions attached to our belly button with our question mark.

The Meeting Framework: We keep this tool under our bottom as we sit on our chair.

The Pros, Cons, Impact Formula: We store our formula in our right elbow with our hammer.

The Co-Parent Charter: We don't store the charter on our body but on our fridge.

The Co-Parenting Plan: We don't store the plan on our body but in a visible place in the home.

The Resilience Bucket: We carry our personalised Resilience Bucket in our right hand.

The Circles of Control: We keep our circles in our beating heart.

The Stress Squasher: We store this tool in our feet as we squash those stresses.

Making the future as smooth as possible for your children

Let's just spend a moment looking ahead to the future. The more you think forward, the more you can be prepared for those bumps in the road. Sometimes things crop up that can be destabilising. Thinking them through and planning for them will be helpful. I have some final thoughts for you to take away with you to help future-proof your co-parenting.

Remain flexible

Flexibility is important. Without it we become rigid and set in our ways. It's hard to be collaborative when we're set in stone and it's remaining flexible that will feed your co-parenting relationship and help it thrive. In the early days of my co-parenting, I didn't always find it easy to be flexible. I would really hold on to my time with our son and make sure school holidays were divided almost down to the hour, and of course, that would come back at me. Often what you give out, you get back. Just consider that for a moment.

Flexibility around significant days is also something I want you to think about. In our house, when there are significant days that we want to celebrate and my son is at his dad's house, if a change of schedule isn't possible, we flex. Sometimes we do Mother's Day the weekend before, sometimes we do birthdays a day either side. In many ways it doesn't matter as long as we can let go of the 'shoulds'. It 'should' happen on this day. Well, according to who? You make it work so your child is able to celebrate your special days with you and if it's not exactly on the calendar day it's supposed to be on, then that's completely fine. Asking for a swap is also a great idea as long as you're prepared to swap back in return.

Often what you give out, you get back.

Building in enough time and space for your child

Managing your weekends with your child when you have them every other weekend means it can be easy to want to cram lots of things in, so they see everybody who is important to them. Remember that can be going on in the other house too, so the red flag to watch out for here is that your kids just get no chill time. It might not be perfect and they might not be present for everything you want them to be, but strike a balance and prioritise the things that do seem fundamental and let go of some of the others.

I'll bring summer holidays in here too – if you're both taking them away, remember to look at the four Child-Centred Questions (see page 172) to help yourself understand what they need from their summer holiday. Perhaps they need a break at home between family holidays, perhaps they don't mind. Either way, remember your child is not you and will think differently to you and have different needs. Don't exhaust them.

Blended families

A blended family is the term used for when co-parents have new partners and new children. With that usually comes other people that will be significant in your child's life, uncles and aunts, cousins, grandparents. Blended families can be tricky to navigate and although we don't have time to unpack it all fully here (that's a whole new book!) I do want to spend a moment to give you some tips on how to make a blended family work well.

Being a step-parent or significant adult in a child's life is really hard. Whether you're taking on that role with your new partner's kids, or another adult is taking on that role with your child, it can be a tough hand to play. It's a relationship that needs patience and time and effort. Remember that children have original parents and that a new partner shouldn't try to replace that role. It's about being supportive to the original parents and building your own relationship with the child. It can be massively rewarding for children to have step-parents as they can learn about things they may never have known or experienced. It can be nourishing, nurturing and wonderful.

Making sure all the children in a blended family are treated equally is really essential for helping children know that they are secure and they are loved. One child told me that her biggest fear was to not really be wanted in either of her homes, even though she knew her two families loved her; when things got tricky between the houses she immediately thought that she was getting in the way. Heart-breaking and definitely not true, but this was her feeling and her need was reassurance and love and feeling equal to the other children in her blended family.

I wrote in step four when I told you the example of Amrita and her co-parent about the importance of keeping everybody in the wider family on message. Amrita and her co-parent successfully communicated to their wider family the importance of all of them being consistent in what they were saying about their separation in advance of their daughter's confirmation. Being able to be consistent in what you're saying in a wider blended family is what you're aiming for. So if the co-parents had a difficult ending to their relationship, you can all agree not to discuss the ending because it's not appropriate for the child to know. Make sure everyone is on board with treating all the children equally and telling them that they're loved equally too.

I'll say a hard thing now about grandparents. They may find it difficult to love a step-grandchild as much as a bio grandchild – but they need to not show that. Children, as we've seen, have a different way of taking in information than adults and we need to simplify the messaging and the actions so they are clear that they are loved, they are an equal and that they have unconditional love from their parents and wider family and blended family.

If you find yourself in a blended family I'd like you to consider something called 'all family days' out if you're able to do it without conflict. For the original children of you and your co-parent who seek stability and reassurance, having all members of both of their immediate family get together to take them out can simply be the best days.

Alfie tells us why:

'I have a younger sister in my mum's house and a younger brother and sister at my dad's house. I have a step-mum and a step-dad. One thing that we do a couple of times a year, usually around my birthday and at Christmas, is to all go out together. I'm not sure how it started, but these are my best days each year. We always go and do something, whether it's bowling, cinema, theatre and then eat something altogether afterwards. It's amazing. I have all the people who are important to me around me and I don't have to choose. I don't have to divide myself. These days are my days and they make me feel alive inside.'

Thinking back to step one and all the work we did on the importance of the long term is really crucial for dealing with the idea of blended families. Your children have the potential to have a relationship with their half and step siblings for the rest of their lives. This can offer them a sense of security long after you are no longer here, so nurturing it now will help that to happen. I know that the idea of this can sometimes be hard to get your head around. But accepting your ex's children or indeed your new partner's children as part of your family is probably one of the biggest things you can do for your children. If all you can do right now is to think about it and nothing else, then that's a good start. Keep the door open, don't burn bridges and focus on thriving. The rest will come.

Thank You

I know co-parenting is hard work, I know it's emotional and triggering and I know it's about being around someone who you've chosen not to be in a relationship with anymore. But co-parenting is the most important work of your life. Keeping your children in mind throughout your co-parenting, and the big and small decisions, will help you through.

Co-parenting is the most important work of your life.

Make a commitment to yourself and to your children that you will put into action the tools you've learned in The Co-Parenting Method. Your job as a parent is to make sure your children are safe, happy, resilient and have friends and fun. When you're moving into co-parenting it can be hard to put those things front and centre as there are pressing emotional things that are affecting us. To raise happy kids, we have to put them first. That might mean having a parenting relationship with someone who you don't want to speak to anymore. Use the tools to help you on this journey – you can do it, I know you can.

Thank you for reading all the way to the end. It's been my absolute pleasure to be with you all the way through this journey. Come back to the book anytime – it's here whenever you need it. But don't stop there! For extra resources, tips and support to guide you on your co-parenting journey, head straight to thecoparentingmethod.com and make sure to follow me on Instagram @thecoparentway. I regularly post co-parent tips and insights, and take care as you go onwards from here.

Remember, co-parenting is the hardest thing you may ever do, and it's also one of the most important. I wish you good luck on your co-parenting journey!

RESOURCES

Advice UK
Provides a directory of advice-giving organisations.
adviceuk.org.uk

Association for Family Therapy and Systematic Practice
Information on what's involved in family therapy and a directory of practitioners.
aft.org.uk

CAFCASS
Supports children and young people whose parents have separated and are unable to agree about future arrangements for their children. They have resources for children and adults, including top tips for separated parents written by the Family Justice Young People's Board, a group of young people with direct experience of the family justice system.
0300 456 4000
cafcass.gov.uk

CALM
A free and confidential helpline and webchat for anyone who needs to talk about life's problems.
0800 585858
thecalmzone.net

Childline
Offers a free confidential helpline for children and young people, open 24 hours a day.
0800 1111
childline.org.uk

Families Anonymous
National helpline offers free support to anyone affected by the drug abuse of a family member.
0207 4984 680
famanon.org.uk

Family Lives
Support for parents who are reaching crisis point.
0808 800 2222
familylives.org.uk

Family Rights Group
Provides advice for parents, grandparents, relatives and friends about their rights and options when social workers or courts make decisions about children's welfare. They work with families who are in need, at risk or are in the care system.
0808 801 0366
frg.org.uk

Family Mediation Council
The FMC is a not-for-profit organisation that maintains a professional register of family mediators.
familymediationcouncil.org.uk

Galop (National LGBTQ+ helpline)

Works with and for LGBT+ victims and survivors of abuse and violence.

0800 999 5428

galop.org.uk

Gingerbread

Provides advice, practical support and campaigns for single parents. Offers factsheets and discussion forums.

0808 802 0925

gingerbread.org.uk

Kinship

Provides an independent online information, advice and support hub, just for kinship carers (grandparents, uncles, aunts, older siblings, family friends etc., who take on the care of children). The one place you can go for information, expert advice and support for every stage of your kinship care journey.

0300 123 7015

kinship.org.uk

Mental Health Foundation

Information on all aspects of mental health and emotional issues.

mentalhealth.org.uk

MIND

Mental health charity with a range of online support and information, including an information line and a legal advice service.

0300 123 3393

mind.org.uk

Money Helper Advice Service

Information, tools and advice on money issues.

moneyhelper.org.uk

National Association of Separated Parent Programmes

A one-stop shop to find separated parent programmes in the UK.

naspp.org.uk

National Association of Child Contact Centres

Keeps children in touch with parents following separation within a national framework of child contact centres and services.

naccc.org.uk

National Youth Advocacy Service (NYAS)

Provides specialist information, advice, advocacy and legal representation for children and young people up to the age of 25.

0808 808 1001

nyas.net

NSPCC

Help and advice for adults who are worried about a child or need advice about child protection.

0808 800 5000

nspcc.org.uk

Only Mums and Only Dads

Not-for-profit social enterprise helping parents through separation.

www.onlymums.org or www.onlydads.org

Refuge

Offers a free 24-hour National Domestic Abuse Helpline in partnership with Women's Aid to provide advice and support to anyone experiencing

domestic abuse. Provides safe, emergency accommodation throughout the UK. Website offers a useful 'help for children' section.
0808 2000 247
refuge.org.uk

Respect (Men's advice line)
Support and advice for male victims of domestic violence, information for their families and for men who want to change their violent and abusive behaviour.
0808 801 0327
mensadviceline.org.uk

Reunite International (Child Abduction Centre)
UK charity specialising in international parental child abduction and the movement of children across international borders. They offer a telephone advice line, a mediation service and an information hub.
0116 2556 234
reunite.org

Rights of Women
Provides free, confidential legal advice on a range of issues including domestic abuse, family law, divorce and relationship breakdown.
rightsofwomen.org.uk

Relate
Relationship advice and information for parents who are separating or have separated.
0300 100 1234
relate.org.uk

Resolution

Resolution is a group of family justice professionals committed to taking conflict out of family disputes. Members abide by a code of practice, which encourages solutions based on the needs of the whole family and, particularly, the best interests of children. Includes fact sheets and directories of local solicitors and mediators.

resolution.org.uk

Samaritans

24-hour helpline for confidential emotional support for those experiencing despair or distress.

116123

samaritans.org

Single Parents

Information for single parents

singleparents.org.uk

Shout Crisis Text Line

If you're experiencing a personal crisis, are unable to cope and need support, text 'Shout' to 85258.

giveusashout.org

Support Through Court

A charity that helps people facing the civil and family courts alone, supporting them so they have the fairest hearing possible.

supportthroughcourt.org

ACKNOWLEDGEMENTS

Blake. Your name had to come first as you are the person around whom this methodology was conceptualised. The way you approach life, your honesty, your pragmatism, your love, warmth and generosity make me immensely proud to be your mum. Loving you and keeping you feeling OK and making sure you feel like you fully belong in both your houses is so very important to me.

Ione, for being a proud daughter, being excited about the book, putting up with me writing at weekends and early mornings and exercising incredible patience for someone so young and excitable. Thank you for my cuddles and our dancing.

Woody, my husband, you are undoubtedly my rock. Doing school runs, bringing me cups of tea at mad hours of the morning when I was writing. Quietly championing me in the background, reassuring me that it was an important book to write. Nothing is impossible with you, Woody. I love you so very much and I love our life adventure.

The book would not have happened without the last 16 years of support from my dad, my mum, my brother and my friends and my family. Mum, for feeling everything as much as I did and for your constant love and support. Dad, for me being able to tell you anything and never being shocked and your advice and humour. Alan, for your wise words and counsel and being my bro. Nadine, for the life-long sisterhood.

Jon and James, for stopping doormat tendencies and for late-night tuk-tuk trips and the friendship as our families grow. Ali, for Marylebone nights, the fun and the complete honesty. Sarah, for the trust, the support and the rock-like friendship. Nicki, for impromptu visits and bunches of flowers. And Konrad, for your laughter and counsel. Leora, for being the best neighbour and taking our boys swimming and the honour of seeing our boys get older together. CAPA, all of you, for your quiet unwavering love and the JB.

My Tawil family – you're one of a kind. Nothing exists like you all. A family unit that rallies in tough times and in good times.

And the friends and family who stepped up over and above what I ever expected I was worthy of when times were difficult. And who are still there when times are fun. You know who you are. And I couldn't have done any of it without you.

To all my clients from all over the world and all sides of my work: thank you for jumping in and embracing the change. Change can only happen when you choose to take a different approach to normal and you have all chosen to do that. Thank you for letting me be your guide and your partner on your journey. It is always a privilege.

Writing a book is such an amazing experience. Writing *this* book felt like an honour. Working with the Ebury team at Penguin Random House has been an insightful, professional and warm and safe experience. The wisdom of my editor Leah has been invaluable as she led me through the process and made suggestions on the structure and things to add. She also politely steered me away from anything that sounded ridiculous, and working with her has been both humbling and fun. Thank you, Leah. And thank you to Sam for your steer and your steady hand from start to finish and to everyone at Ebury involved in making this happen.

For Clare, my agent and my guide through this process, thank you for answering my many random and rookie questions and for being sensible, practical and responsive. These are all traits I value highly and I'm so very delighted to be working with you.

For the professionals who I am honoured to share the space with. Family law practitioners who uphold values of respect and integrity in their work and who move mountains to help parents protect their children throughout the separation process, you have only my admiration as you choose the right, but not always the easiest, path.

There are three professionals in particular who have championed me on my journey, who saw the potential for those children of separating parents in my work. Zahra Pabani, you are a formidable, incredible power-house who brings others up the ladder with you. You have opened many doors for me and I can't thank you enough for calling me up that day and establishing our friendship inside and outside of work.

Adele Ballantyne, for your unwavering support of what I do. Side by side we often stand as the non-legal champions of children in a legal environment, and I could not wish for anyone else to walk that road with. The legacy you leave personally and professionally is only positive.

Marc Etherington, a beacon of family justice and of ensuring the welfare of children during separation. Your actions are significant and command the respect of the profession.

To all the kids whose parents are separating. This book is ultimately for you.

NOTES

1. Elisabeth Küber-Ross, *On Death and Dying* (Macmillan, 1969)
2. Eleda Consultancy, https://eledaconsultancy.com
3. 'Top tips for parents who are separated', Family Justice Young People's Board, https://www.cafcass.gov.uk/sites/default/files/migrated/Top-Tips-for-parents-who-are-separated.pdf
4. 'Reducing Parental Conflict: the impact on children', gov.uk, https://www.gov.uk/guidance/reducing-parental-conflict-the-impact-on-children
5. Jon Symonds et al., 'Separating Families: Experiences of Separation and Support', Nuffield Family Justice Observatory (2022), https://www.nuffieldfjo.org.uk/wp-content/uploads/2022/11/nfjo_report_private_law_separating_families_20221128-1.pdf
6. 'Children Come First', Family Solutions Group, https://www.familysolutionsgroup.co.uk/children-come-first/#:~:text=They%20should%20be%20free%20to,can%20endure%20throughout%20their%20lives
7. The President of the Family Division of the UK judicial system in a Family Solutions Group (FSG) webinar in November 2020
8. 'Divorce or separation for parents and carers', The Royal College of Psychiatrists, https://www.rcpsych.ac.uk/mental-health/parents-and-young-people/information-for-parents-and-carers/divorce-or-separation-for-parents
9. These reactions and behaviours by age are taken in part from the Resolution Parenting Through Separation Guide, which I co-wrote with lawyers and therapists. See https://resolution.org.uk/looking-for-help/parents-children-the-law/parenting-through-separation/
10. Positive Intelligence, https://www.positiveintelligence.com
11. John Gottman, *The Seven Principles for Making Marriage Work* (Orion, 2018)
12. Nancy Kline, *Time to Think: Listening to Ignite the Human Mind* (Cassell, 2002)
13. The Gottman Institute, https://www.gottman.com

14. Lauren A. Leotti, Sheena S. Iyengar, Kevin N. Ochsner, 'Born to Choose: The Origins and Value of the Need for Control', *Trends in Cognitive Sciences* 14:10 (2010), pp. 457–63. https://www.ncbi.nlm.nih.gov/pmc/articles/PMC2944661/

15. Steven Covey, *The 7 Habits of Highly Effective People* (Simon & Schuster, 2020)

16. Karl Albrecht, *Stress and the Manager* (Prentice-Hall, 1979)

INDEX

Page numbers in **bold** refer to images.

acceptance 5
accountability 184
action plans 245
action, taking 19, 30, 110–13
active listening 125–31, 132–7, 169
adoption 114–15
adrenaline
    and conflict 120, 157
    and the five Fs response 57, 58, 63
    and lack of control 224–5
    and stress 233, 239, 240
affairs 32–4, 77
aggression 41, 146, 147
Albrecht, Karl 231
ancestors 57
anger
    and badmouthing co-parents 154,
        155–6
    children's 41, 61
    and co-parent perspectives 87–8
    and decision-making 168
    impact on children 78–9
    impact on co-parenting 56
    and inflammatory language 138,
        143, 144
    and the loss cycle 5
    and separation 4, 47
    and the stress response 58
    towards co-parents 44, 56, 63, 156–8
    towards the new partners of
        co-parents 140
    see also rage

anticipatory stress 232–3, 235–6,
    237–8
anxiety 246
    children's 38, 41
    impact on parents 56–7
    and a lack of control 227
    management 59
    separation 38
    and situational stress 239
    and time stress 231–2
    towards co-parents 63
assumptions 129
attention, paying 130

babies 37–8
back pain 230–1
Ballantyne, Adele 11–13, 122, 143
bargaining stage 5
being present, difficulties with 44, 246
Best Case, Worst Case (Practical Tool #1)
    28–31, **28**, 54, 108, 245, 249
bias, confirmation 86
bigger picture 52, 83, 86, 98, 115–16,
    217, 246
blaming approaches 147, 159, 218
blended families 251–4
body language 120, 130, 143, 156
boundary-setting 15, 18, 42, 83–4,
    101–18, 246
brain 58
    development 161
    emotional 70, 97

Index

brain *(cont.)*
  logical/rational 59, 70–1, 97
  and the stress response 56
breathing techniques 145

catastrophic fear 66–71, 77–80, 90, 245
celebrations 23, 43, 72, 143, 170, 251, 253
Chamine, Shirzad 59
change 242
  changing ourselves 81
  and communication skills 123–4
  of separation 1, 5
child development 161–2
Child-Centred Questions (Practical Tool
  #13) 172–5, **172**, 179, 196, 198, 209,
  247, 249, 251
childhood trauma 141–2
children
  acting grown-up/like a carer 40
  adult 42–3, 49–51
  age of 37–43
  and aggressive behaviour 41
  and the arrival of new siblings 223
  behaviour 36, 37–43, 40, 47, 61
  building in enough time and space
    for 251
  and co-partner remarriage 222–3
  communicating with 72, 94, 200–1
  creating a better future for 250
  and the difficulties of living in two
    homes 210
  divided loyalties of 39, 142
  emotional wellbeing 12–13, 21, 36–43, 78
  impact of inflammatory language on
    141–4
  impact of separation on 11, 32–43, 61–3,
    66, 79, 161
  and the importance of maintaining
    positive relationships with both
    parents 12–13
  and insecurity 36
  introducing to new partners 219–21
  keeping in the loop 72, 94
  listening to 12
  and literal language 161–5
  long-term emotional wellbeing 25,
    33–7, 39, 42, 52, 64, 78–9, 121, 142–3,
    240, 243, 247, 248

long-term relationship difficulties in
  33, 39, 42
long-term relationships with 32, 33
minimising damage to 11
and moving home 224
with new partners 218, 222, 223, 251
outcomes 12–13, 25
and overheard conversations 156–8
oversharing with 37, 41, 42, 43, 160
and parental conflict 2, 11–13, 25–6,
  32–43, 47, 52, 61–4, 77–9, 121, 141–4, 247
perspectives of 167, 170–5
putting first 5, 7, 9, 27, 45, 123, 141, 172–5,
  224, 254
resilience of 2, 13, 19–21, 36, 54, 122, 162,
  200, 229, 243–4, 254
and self-blame 40–1, 142
thriving 3, 7, 170
Children Act 1989 x
children's clubs 171, 173–4
children's needs
  and communication skills 124
  and decision-making 171
  failure to attend to 44–5
  health 206
  prioritisation 9–10, 12–13, 23, 45, 194
Christmas 170, 253
Circles of Control (Practical Tool #19)
  226–30, **226**, 233, 238, 239, 240, 242,
  244, 248, 250
clinginess 38
clubs 171, 173–4
Co-Parent Charter (Practical Tool #16)
  167, 183–94, **184**, 194, 208, 209–10,
  247, 250
co-parent meetings 175–80, **177**
'Co-Parent Way, The' (coaching
  methodology) ix, 8–9, 14
Co-Parental Loop 45–8, **45**, 247
  and boundary-setting 104, 246
  and catastrophic fear 67, 68–9, 79
  and the Co-Parent Charter 185, 189, 192
  and co-parent perspectives 83–5, 87,
    246
  and the Co-Parenting Plan 196, 200
  and communication skills 119, 143, 165
  and decision-making 170, 174, 208
  and information-sharing 104

Index

co-parenting
  definition 1–2, 9–10
  reasons to choose 10–21
  as security blanket for children 3,
    10, 34–5
  three worlds of 106–17, **106**
  when it isn't right 3, 21
Co-Parenting Method, The 1–21, 243–54
  aims 15
  and boundary-setting 83–118, 246
  and co-parent perspectives 81, 95–118,
    246
  and communication skills 118, 119–66,
    247
  and decision-making 166, 167–210, 247
  and emotional management 54, 55–81,
    246
  formula 14–15
  getting co-parents to agree to 20–1
  importance of x, 7
  and long-term mindsets 23–54, 245
  six-steps of ix–x, xi, 2, 15, 18, 20
  and thriving 210, 211–42, 248
  see also Practical Tools; Your Body
    Toolkit
Co-Parenting Plan (Practical Tool #17)
  167–8, 193–208, **195**, 208, 239, 247, 250
  and communicating with children
    200–1
  and communicating with each other
    199–200
  and education 203–4
  and expenses 202–3
  and extended families 205
  and health 206
  and logistics 198–9
  participants 197
  rules 201–2
  storage 207, 209–10
co-parents
  badmouthing 32–4, 51, 79, 143, 154–60,
    161–2, 185, 191
  disliking 5, 20, 43–5, 62
  new partners of 139–40, 191, 218–23, 251
  perspectives 81, 95–118, 168, 246
  recognising the contributions of 190–1
  recruiting for The Co-Parenting
    Method 20–1

  respecting the position of x, 20
  toxic 21
  trying to win against 24–6, 37, 47, 52, 79,
    122, 123, 155
  world of 105, 106–17, **106**
coaching 8, 14, 28, 245
collaboration 127–8, 133, 136, 150–2, 224,
    244, 246–7, 250
communication skills 11–12, 34, 118,
    119–66, 247
  and badmouthing co-parents 154–62,
    185, 191
  and the Co-Parent Charter 188–9, 191
  and the Co-Parental Loop 47
  and the Co-Parenting Plan 199–201
  communicating about your new lives
    105
  and decision-making 168–9
  effective 9–10, 13, 15, 165
  and emotional management 55, 62
  Five Steps of Active Listening 129–31,
    134–7, 148, 166
  and 'hot' topics 139, 171
  importance of 120–5
  and inflammatory language 138–54, 247
  and listening skills 125–37, 145
  and literal language 161–5
  negative habits 121, 136
  and not interrupting 125–6, 130, 132–5,
    145, 169
  and pauses 132–40
  and script writing 238
  and small talk 104
  and using the word 'But' ... 152
compartmentalisation 142
competitive parenting 25
compromise 122
concentration difficulties 36
confirmation bias 86
conflict see parental conflict
constructive approaches 146–50
contempt 121
control
  lack of 224–8, 240
  taking 55, 224–30, 244, 248
conversations 104, 156–8, 238
coping 57
cortisol 57, 120

Index

Covey, Stephen 226
critical approaches 121, 146–7
  see also co-parents, badmouthing

decision-making 47, 64, 68, 166, 167–210,
  247
  and Child-Centred Questions 172–5,
    172, 179, 196, 198, 209, 247
  and children's perspectives 167, 170–5
  and the Co-Parent Charter 167, 183–94,
    184, 194, 208–10, 247, 250
  and co-parent meetings 175–80
  and the Co-Parenting Plan 167–8,
    193–208, **195**, 208, 239, 247, 250
  and communication skills 122, 140
  difficulties of 168–70
  and emotional management 55
  failure 68, 79
defensiveness 121
denial 5
depression 5, 41
despair 44
divorce 4–7, 11, 54, 61, 79, 160
  see also separation

education 203–4
emotional brain 70, 97
emotional states, commenting on 152
emotional strain 230–1
emotions, dealing with big ix, 1, 4–6,
    13, 15, 18, 34, 54, 55–81, 118, 144–5,
    179, 246
  and badmouthing co-parents 155, 157
  catastrophic fear 66–71, 77–8, 79
  children and 36, 38, 39, 40, 61, 246
  and the Co-Parent Charter 188, 189
  and co-parent meetings 179
  and co-parent perspectives 85, 87–8
  and co-parenting with someone you
    don't like 44
  and communication skills 9–10, 124,
    144–5, 155, 157
  and Finger and Thumb tool 58–60, **59**,
    80, 91, 96, 108, 124–5, 144–5, 158, 228,
    233, 239, 249
  and the five Fs response 57–66
  impact on parents 56–8
  and inflammatory language 144–5

and long-term mindsets 66, 246
  and the loss cycle 4–5
  and naming emotions 39, 70, 78
  and the Self-Management Avatar 73–80,
    73, 124–5, 140, 143, 145, 151, 156, 179,
    196, 204, 233–4, 238–9, 244–6, 249
  and Speed Writing 68–71, **68**, 80, 90,
    124–5, 233, 237, 249
  and your co-partner's new partner 220
  and your co-partner's remarriage 222
  see also specific emotions
encounter stress 234, 235–6, 239–40
energy levels 228–9
evolutionary theory 56, 224
exams 132
expenses 202–3
extended families 158–60, 205, 252, 253

Family Justice Young People's Board 12
family reference points 43, 94
Family Solutions Group 34–5
favouritism 252
fear 246
  catastrophic 66–71, 77–80, 245
  of co-parenting meetings 176
  impact on parents 56
  naming 70
  physical reaction to 58
  and separation 47
  and situational stress 239
  and The Summit tool 90–3
fight, flight, freeze, fawn or flop (five Fs)
    response 57–66, 246
  and catastrophic fear 66, 67, 79
  and communication skills 124, 144–5, 157
  and decision-making 168
  fight mode 62–3, 64, 144–5, 157
  impact on children 64
  and a lack of control 225
  self-managing 73
  and situational stress 233, 239
financial settlements 162, 203
Finger and Thumb (Practical Tool #3)
    58–60, **59**, 80, 91, 96, 108, 124–5,
    144–5, 158, 228, 233, 239, 249
Five Steps of Active Listening (Practical
    Tool #9) 129–31, 134–7, 148, 166, 169,
    237, 247, 249

flexibility 250–1
future, the, making it as smooth as
    possible 250

'good enough' parents 3, 45
Gottman, John 121, 136
grandparents 158–9, 205, 252, 253
grief 4–5, 23, 43–4

handovers 175
    and boundary-setting 102–4, 105
    and Co-Parenting Plans 193, 198
    and communication skills 141–2
    and encounter stress 234
    and script writing 238
here and now 52, 59–60
holidays 251
hormones 40

imagery, outrageous (memory technique)
    31, 51–3, 71, 77, 93, 131, 152, 175, 180,
    217, 230, 240
imagination 28–30, 49–52, 74–7, 96–100,
    109, 114, 134–5, 180, 217, 230, 240
inflammatory language 138–54, 247
influence 226–7, **226**, 228–9, 240
information-sharing 104, 191–2
interrupting 125–6, 130, 132–5, 145, 169
intimacy issues 11–12
Iyengar, Sheena 224

jealousy 115
joined-up parenting 42, 122, 131, 179, 192

Kline, Nancy 125

language
    aggressive 146, 147
    inflammatory 138–54, 247
    judgemental 146
    literal 161–5
lawyers 24–5, 26, 27
Leotti, Lauren 224
letting go 228, 229–30
life chances 35
life events 23, 94
listening skills 87, 125–37, 169
literal language 161–5

logical/rational brain 59, 70–1, 97
logistics 198–9
long-term mindset 23–54, 118, 245
    and the Best Case, Worst Case tool
        28–31, **28**, 54
    and big emotions 66, 246
    and the Co-Parental Loop 45–8, **45**
    and communication skills 123
    and disliking your co-parent 43–5
    and the long-term impact of
        co-parenting 32–5
    and Photographs 49–54
    and setbacks 217
    and understanding your co-parent's
        perspective 86
loss cycle (five stages of grief model)
    4–5, 23
love 54

MacFarlane, Sir Andrew 35
maintenance agreements 203
marijuana 61, 62
Meeting Framework, The (Practical Tool
    #14) 174, 176–80, **177**, 196, 204, 208,
    209, 247, 250
memory techniques 16, 31, 51–3, 60
    focused repetition 16, 53
    outrageous imagery 31, 51–3, 71,
        77, 93, 131, 152, 175, 180, 217,
        230, 240
    see also Your Body Toolkit
mental health 120, 212, 231
mind-body connection 230–1
mindfulness 59
mindsets
    'winning' 24–6, 37, 42, 47, 61–3, 79,
        122–3, 155
    see also long-term mindset;
        short-term mindset
moving home 223–4

National Institutes of Health 36
National Society for the Prevention of
    Cruelty to Children (NSPCC) 36
needy approaches 147
negativity, reframing 146–7
nervous system 57
nesting arrangements 102

Index

neutral parenting approach 3
  and boundary-setting 107
  and co-parent perspectives 101
  and co-parenting meetings 178
  and communication skills 121, 158,
    203–4
new things, trying 90–3
newborns 37–8
non-verbal cues 130
  see also body language
Nuffield Family Justice Observatory 34

Ochsner, Kevin 224
open minds 130
open questions 14
oversharing 37, 41, 42, 43, 160
overwhelm, parental 1, 44, 68
  and big emotions 55–6, 58, 71, 78, 246
  and the flop response 58
  and stress 231–2, 236, 240

pain 230–1
panic mode 92, 230, 233
parallel parenting 10
parasympathetic nervous system 57
parental conflict
  and Best Case, Worst Case 29
  and big emotions 61–3, 246
  and boundary-setting 111
  and co-parent perspectives 84–5, 96
  and the Co-Parental Loop 47–8
  and communication skills 15, 118,
    119–66, 247
  de-escalation 119
  and decision-making 168
  and disliking your co-parent 43–5
  exhausting nature of 120, 127
  impact on children 2, 11–13, 25–6,
    32–43, 47, 52, 61–3, 64, 77, 78–9, 121,
    141–4, 247
  impact on parents 13–14
  and the Self-Management Avatar 77,
    78–9
  and separation 27
parental resilience 57, 211, 212–17, 219, 220,
  231, 240, 248
parents' evenings 203–4
passive aggression 147

Pause Button, The (Practical Tool #10)
  134–8, **134**, 144–5, 148, 166, 169, 239,
  247, 249
pauses (communication skill) 132–40
people-pleasing 58, 63, 162
perspectives
  children's 167, 170–5
  co-parents' 81, 95–118, 168, 246
Photographs (Practical Tool #2) 49–54,
  79, 108, 143–4, 237, 249
physical health 120, 206, 212, 231
playdates 232
politeness 20, 45, 46, 51, 179
pornography 157
Practical Tools
  Best Case, Worst Case 28–31, **28**, 54,
    108, 245, 249
  Child-Centred Questions 172–5,
    172, 179, 196, 198, 209, 247,
    249, 251
  Circles of Control 226–30, **226**, 233,
    238, 239, 240, 242, 244, 248, 250
  Co-Parent Charter 167, 183–94, **184**,
    194, 208, 209–10, 247, 250
  Co-Parenting Plan 167–8, 193–208,
    195, 208, 239, 247, 250
  Finger and Thumb 58–60, **59**, 80, 91,
    96, 108, 124–5, 144–5, 158, 228, 233,
    239, 249
  Five Steps of Active Listening 129–31,
    134–7, 148, 166, 169, 237, 247, 249
  Photographs 49–54, 79, 108, 143–4, 237,
    249
  Pros, Cons, Impact Formula 180–3,
    181, 209, 247, 250
  Self-Management Avatar 73–80, **73**,
    124–5, 140, 143, 145, 151, 156, 179, 196,
    204, 233–4, 238–9, 244–6, 249
  Speed Writing 68–71, **68**, 80, 90, 124–5,
    233, 237, 249
  Standing in Your Co-Parent's Shoes
    95–101, **95**, 117, 249
  Stress Squasher 235–40, **235**, 242, 248,
    250
  and The Co-Parenting Method 14–15,
    16, 18
  The Meeting Framework 174, 176–80,
    177, 196, 204, 208, 209, 247, 250

The Pause Button 134–8, **134**, 144–5, 148, 166, 169, 239, 247, 249
The Reframe 149–54, 166, 247, 249
The Resilience Bucket 18, 214–17, 220, 242, 248, 250
The Summit 90–3, **90**, 113, 153, 246, 249
The Three Worlds 18, 108–17, **108**, 122, 145, 190, 212, 215, 227, 249
What's in a Word 163–4, 166, 247, 249
pre-schoolers 38–9
present, struggling to be 44, 58, 64, 65
problems, dealing with 212
professional settings, badmouthing co-parents in 157–8
Pros, Cons, Impact Formula (Practical Tool #15) 180–3, **181**, 209, 247, 250
puberty 40

rage, parental 34, 222
record-keeping 18–19
'Reducing Parental Conflict: the impact on children' (guidance) 12–13
reflection 14, 136–8
Reframe, The (Practical Tool #11) 149–54, 166, 247, 249
reframing 145–54, 236
regression 38, 39, 40
relationship difficulties
long-term 33, 39, 42
see also divorce; parental conflict; separation
relocation 223–4
remarriage 222–3
repetition, focused (memory technique) 16, 53
resilience
child 2, 13, 19–21, 36, 54, 122, 162, 200, 229, 243–4, 254
parental 57, 211, 212–17, 219, 220, 231, 240, 248
Resilience Bucket, The (Practical Tool #18) 18, 214–17, 220, 242, 248, 250
Resolution (law association) 27
respectful parenting 3, 13, 46
and boundary-setting 111
and the Co-Parent Charter 185, 190

and co-parenting meetings 179
and communication skills 139, 155, 158–9
responsibility-taking ix, x, 2, 3, 6, 51, 54, 63, 78, 110, 244
risk-taking behaviour 41–2
Royal College of Psychiatrists 36
rules 201–2

sadness 5, 44, 141, 222
scheduling 236
schools 203–4
script writing 238
security/emotional safety/stability 3, 10, 34–5, 74, 243, 254
and blended families 253
and boundary-setting 83–4, 101–2, 104–5, 114, 246
and co-partner remarriage 222
and communication skills 120, 122–3, 125, 141, 143, 154, 165
and decision-making 170–1, 200, 210
lack of a feeling of 65–6
and school 204
self-care 216, 240
self-kindness 81
Self-Management Avatar (Practical Tool #5) 73–80, **73**, 124–5, 140, 143, 145, 151, 156, 179, 196, 204, 233–4, 238–9, 244–5, 246, 249
separation 2, 3, 4–7, 11–13, 27, 54
and boundary-setting 102–3, 105
and catastrophic fear 66–7
and co-parent perspectives 86–7
and the Co-Parental Loop 47–8
and communication skills 159
and decision-making 168
early stages of 1
and expenses 202–3
and extended families 159, 205
impact on children 11, 32–43, 61–3, 66, 79, 141
and lawyers 27
listening to children during 12
and loss of control 225
messy 61–3
and oversharing 37, 41–3, 160
shock of 4, 6–7

Index

separation *(cont.)*
   short-termist approach to 24–6
   see also divorce; parental conflict
separation anxiety 38
shared parenting 10
short-term mindset 23–6, 28, 33, 45, 47,
   52, 245
   and badmouthing co-parents
     55–6, 155
   and big emotions 66
   and communication skills 123
   and understanding the co-parent
     perspectives 86
single parents 46–7
situational stress 233, 235–6, 239
small talk 104
social networks 158–60
social withdrawal 36, 41, 44
special educational needs 157–8, 204
Speed Writing (Practical Tool #4)
   68–71, **68**, 80, 90, 124–5, 233,
   237, 249
Standing in Your Co-Parent's Shoes
   (Practical Tool #7) 95–101, **95**,
   117, 249
step-parents 251–4
stonewalling 121, 131, 135–6, 143
stress 56–8, 63, 248
   anticipatory 232–3, 235–6, 237–8
   chronic 230
   and conflict 120, 133
   encounter 234, 235–6, 239–40
   and a lack of control 227
   situational 233, 235–6, 239
   time 231–2, 235–7
stress management 230–42
stress response 56, 57–8, 63
Stress Squasher (Practical Tool # 20)
   235–40, **235**, 242, 248, 250
Summit, The (Practical Tool #6) 90–3, **90**,
   113, 153, 246, 249
support 6, 191–2
survival mode 25–6
sympathetic nervous system 57

teenagers 36, 40–2, 61–2, 218–19
threat perception 57–8

Three Worlds, The (Practical Tool #8) 18,
   108–17, **108**, 122, 145, 190, 212, 215,
   227, 249
thriving xi, 3, 7, 14–16, 18, 112, 170, 210,
   211–42, 248, 253
   and bumps in the road 217–24
   and control issues 224–30, 233, 238–40,
    242, 244
   and stress management 230–42
   and the Stress Squasher 235–40,
    235, 242
   and The Resilience Bucket 18, 214–17,
    220, 242, 248
time considerations 231–2, 235–7, 251
toddlers 38
tough times 189, 217–24, 250
toxic environments 21, 64
trauma 141–2
trust issues 6, 11–12, 190

'victim' role, taking 160
visualisation 28–30, 49–52, 54, 74–6, 109

What's in a Word (Practical Tool #12)
   163–4, 166, 247, 249
worrying 232–3, 237–8

Your Body Toolkit 16–18, **17**
   Best Case, Worst Case 31, 54
   Child-Centred Questions 175, 209
   Circles of Control 230, 242
   Finger and Thumb 60, 80
   Five Steps of Active Listening
    131, 166
   Meeting Framework 180, 209
   Pause Button 134–5, 137–8, 166
   Photographs 50–1, 54
   Pros, Cons, Impact Formula 183, 209
   Reframe 152, 166
   Resilience Bucket 217, 242
   Speed Writing 71, 80
   Standing in Your Co-Parent's
    Shoes 100, 117
   Stress Squasher 240, 242
   Summit tool 93, 117
   Three Worlds 114, 117
   What's in a Word 164, 166

ABOUT THE AUTHOR

Marcie Shaoul is a renowned expert in co-parenting with years of experience helping families navigate the challenges of parenting together through separation and divorce. In 2016, she brought co-parent coaching to the UK and founded The Co-Parent Way.

She has worked with countless parents to establish healthy, sustainable co-parenting relationships that prioritise the wellbeing of children. Her innovative and award-winning methodologies are grounded in empathy, clear communication and practical strategies that empower parents to collaborate effectively, even in the most difficult circumstances.

A co-parent herself since 2009, Marcie brings both personal and professional experience to her work, developing tools that enable parents to raise thriving children despite separation. Her work has transformed the lives of families worldwide, and she is deeply committed to guiding parents toward a brighter, more harmonious future for their children.

She lives in London with her husband, two children and dog Coco.